Backcountry Press Presents

Wildflower!   **Alps**

Including the M   s,
Russian Wilde

Ken DeCamp

Editing and scientific review by
Julie Knorr and Julie Kierstead Nelson

In association with
THE CALIFORNIA NATIVE PLANT SOCIETY

Alpine spicy wintergreen (*Gaultheria humifusa*)

Find this book online at www.backcountrypress.com and www.store.cnps.org
© Copyright 2017 by Backcountry Press - First Edition

Book layout by Kenneth DeCamp and Backcountry Press
All photos by Kenneth DeCamp
Back cover map by Jason Barnes

Front cover, clockwise from top: Waterfall in Canyon Creek, California bog asphodel (*Narthecium californicum*), false Solomon's seal (*Maianthemum racemosum*), firecracker flower (*Dichelostemma ida-maia*)

Published by Backcountry Press • Kneeland, California
Technical editing and proofing by Michael Kauffmann

ISBN 978-1-941624-11-1
Library of Congress Control Number: 2017960640

Kenneth DeCamp, 1943- .
Wildflowers of the Trinity Alps
Including the Marble Mountain Wilderness, Russian Wilderness, & Trinity Divide

Looking west from the Stony Ridge Trail in the Trinity Alps Wilderness.

Table of Contents

Introduction

As a professional botanical photographer I have spent almost 50 years tracking down wildflowers throughout the Pacific Northwest, the Blue Ridge Mountains, and Switzerland. In that time, I have hiked hundreds of miles and taken thousands of photographs. I have also invested in a library of botanical manuals and field guides because I've discovered that taking pictures of wildflowers is one thing, knowing what they are is another entirely. I determined early on that large technical botanical manuals were hardly what an amateur wanted to stuff into a pack and why smaller, regional field guides were so popular with backpackers and dayhikers. As an amateur, I have not been immune to this sentiment and is precisely why I settled on this format. I believe most people, in order to identify a wildflower, want to make a simple comparison between the flower they have found and a good representational photograph.

While spending time in the Blue Ridge Mountains and the Swiss Alps shooting wildflowers and waterfalls I came across two beautifully produced wildflower guides. The first was a delightful little publication titled *Great Smoky Mountains Wildflowers* which ultimately became the prototype for this guide, and the second a *Flora des Kantons Bern* gifted me by my Swiss family. While vastly different in size and scope, they both held two valuable attributes: beautiful photographs adjacent to descriptive text. The guide to the Bernese Alps is over 1200 pages and weighs almost 3 pounds—hardly conducive to use in the field, however the lightweight Smoky Mountains guide is a hiker's dream.

I read somewhere that mountains are here to frame the beauty of wildflowers. I would go a few steps farther and say that mushrooms, lichens, crab spiders, rainbow trout, juncos, and bears (among other things) are also framed by the mountains and that mountains would only be piles of rock without them. Too often people ignore the complexities of the landscape and are simply awed by the grand vistas. It is my contention that the grand vistas would be far less "grand" without all the little things that give them the qualities we seek when we visit. Not that the peaks and valleys, rivers and streams aren't commanding or breathtaking—that's not my point. My point is that what should take your breath away is the wholeness and complexity of it all—from the massive rocky monoliths right down to the little organisms.

A few years ago while I was lying in the leaf litter shooting photographs of a tiny orchid at a popular recreation site, a man came up and asked what I was taking pictures of. As it turned out he was a local Native American with deep cultural ties to this particular place and when I showed him the orchid (hard to spot under the best of circumstances) he was amazed. "I've been coming here for over 40 years," he said "and I have never seen this." Soon he was down on his hands and knees alongside me while I worked the shutter. His wife and two boys went on to play in the creek while he and I talked plants. This became an outstanding and educational afternoon for both of us. He learned something about tiny things most people walk over and I learned a bit about local history—a fair trade.

One last thought: In the words of my Grandmother—who was a very wise woman—"keep yer eyes peeled, lest you miss something important.'"

You will find photographs and descriptions of 505 species, subspecies, and varieties in this guide, enough to keep you reading around the campfire for many seasons. Enjoy!

Ken DeCamp
September 1st, 2017

Acknowledgements

When I asked my professional botanist friends and co-authors, Julie Knorr and Julie Kierstead Nelson, to review a wildflower guide I had assembled, review they did, quickly bringing to my attention that the world of California botany had been turned upside down with the publication of the 2012 *Jepson Manual*. They graciously offered to set this guide on the right path. What we have, due to their efforts, is an up-to-date guide to wildflowers for this botanically unique region.

Our collective hope is that you find this guide irresistible, indispensable, and beautiful, and that it comes to occupy valuable space in your pack or on your bookshelf. We also hope it fills the gaps in your knowledge about wildflowers in this geologically and biologically diverse area. We would like to see its pages become dog-eared, water stained, dirt encrusted, wrinkled, torn, and in eventual need of duct tape to hold it all together through years of use and abuse. There could be no better testament to a person's curiosity about the natural world than to find them in possession of a field guide worn beyond recognition.

I want to extend my heart-felt thanks to my wife Pam, who has exhibited endless patience throughout the process of producing this guide, so much so that, at times, the well has come close to running dry. It's been her good eye that has led to some wildflower discoveries on hundreds of trips into the back country. The same can be said for my son and daughter and several of my grand kids who have accompanied me into the hills and have found themselves unwitting botanical explorers.

Thanks are also due to my friend of almost half a century and Forest Service co-worker Clyde Hill who shared his interest in plants with me back in the late 60s and who introduced me to the more scientific side of botany with Vesta Holt's *Keys for Identification of Wildflowers, Ferns, Trees, Shrubs, Woody Vines of Northern California*, which became a persistent denizen in my pack.

I want to thank Marsha Fickert—retired civil engineer—for the tremendous amount of organizational work that she did in the background. She created spreadsheets, converted files, and provided an additional set of eyes in the proofing process. Her assistance in managing the large amount of information in this book was invaluable. Marla Knight, retired Forest Botanist on the Klamath National Forest, helped with identifications and tips on where to look for certain wildflower populations.

Alice Jones, a long time Trinity County resident and acquaintance whose book *Flowers and Trees of the Trinity Alps* was, for over 25 years, at home in my pack. Her eagerness to share knowledge about local botany was an inspiration to me beginning when I was just 10 years old. I met her for the first time at the old Minersville Ranger Station where her husband was the District Ranger. Alice has passed, but her memory and contributions will live on. Her book, recently updated, is still available and a good addition to anyone interested in local flora.

My daughter, Heather Vanhorn, took valuable time away from her horses, pack mule, husband, and kids to help edit the introductory pages and common names index.

When organizing the wildflowers in our guide we found it wise to follow the example set by Mark Turner and Phyllis Gustafson in their excellent book *Wildflowers of the Pacific Northwest* published in 2006.

Region covered by this guide

My original intent was to cover only the Trinity Alps Wilderness. But because the Alps are so closely tied to the Russian Wilderness, Marble Mountain Wilderness, Trinity Divide (also known as the Trinity Mountains), and the Scott Mountains I decided to include them as well. So, I am delineating the chunk of land encircled by Interstate 5 and Shasta Lake on the east, Highway 96 on the north and west, and Highway 299 on the south. Highway 3 bisects the area north to south and the Gazelle-Callahan-Salmon River Highway bisects it East to west. The Pacific Crest Trail also bisects the area. Generally speaking all of these mountains are considered to be part and parcel to the larger geologic area known as the Klamath Mountains (see back cover).

Wildflower names—common versus scientific

I grew up knowing wildflowers, trees, and shrubs by their common names. Wild ginger was wild ginger regardless of the fact that there were different varieties. If the roots smelled like ginger then that's what it was. Traveller's Delight was just that—I'd never heard of western clematis. Originally, that was the focus of this book—wildflowers sorted by color and alphabetically by common name because I assumed that was what people would be most comfortable with. I quickly learned that it became more efficient to sort wildflowers by family, species, color, and habit.

Common names, as I've come to learn, are a dime a dozen. The same wildflower can have several common names that are often shared with other flowers, but each has only one scientific name. In order to keep a focus on the amateur observer, we decided to not abandon the common name concept all together and to that end we introduce each flower by its common name or names, listing them in relative order—most accepted or widely used first, followed by its scientific name.

Blooming seasons

The mountains referred to in this book are vast and it would be foolish to think that I have photographed every wildflower there is to find. There are just too many physical variables in the natural world to allow for that kind of wishful thinking. Geology, ranges in altitude, and variable weather conditions make it almost impossible to nail down a definitive date for a particular bloom which, for some shrubs and plants, can begin as early as mid-December in the lower elevations, and continue into late October or even November in the high country. Extreme snow years can delay blooms by a month or more. Drought years can have the opposite effect and bring the bloom on very early.

No matter how familiar you think you are with an area, there is always something new and unexpected that can be found. The broad landscape here may not change much throughout a lifetime but the little things that make up that big picture do. These are often hard to define and almost impossible to quantify. True familiarity with an area only comes with frequent visits. It helps to have a second or third set of eyes along because what is obvious to one person is less so to another. As a help of limited nature, I have included the approximate locations and dates of when I found and photographed the wildflowers included in this book.

Serpentine

The northern half of the Trinity Divide and the easternmost one-third of the Trinity Alps, generally known as the "Red" Trinities, are comprised of this highly mineralized rock. When first exposed to the elements (say in a roadside cut) it is a pale green to almost black but, because of its high iron content, it rusts when exposed to air and water resulting in soils and rock outcrops that are a distinctive red to ocher. Because of its highly mineralized nature, it gives rise to some unique plant communities like cobra lily fens and western azalea thickets. A great place to introduce yourself to the serpentine plant community is along the Fen Interpretive Trail at Kangaroo Lake located on the north end of the Trinity Divide.

Orchids

Several varieties of orchids and heterotrophs occur in this area and they are all beautiful, relatively inconspicuous, or hard to find. All orchids require an association with specific soil fungi and should **NEVER** be disturbed. Digging them up and transplanting them to your garden is a surefire way to kill them. Enjoy them where you find them, take lots of photographs, but whatever you do—leave them alone!

Heterotrophic plants: parasites and mycotrophs

Green plants are considered autotrophs because they photosynthesize—making sugar from water and carbon dioxide. The world of heterotrophic plants is complicated but all have moved away from total energy production from photosynthesis toward obtaining organic carbon either from other living beings or through a symbiotic relationship with a fungus. Heterotrophic plants include parasitic and mycotrophic forms.

Parasitic plants include ground-cones and broomrapes. These species contain no chlorophyll and obtain all nutrients by directly tapping the root system of host plants. Dwarf mistletoes (*Arceuthobium* spp.) are also parasitic. The oak mistletoes (*Phoradendron* spp.) are hemiparasites. These species obtain water and some nutrients from its host tree, but also photosynthesize.

Mycotrophic plants are represented in our area by species in the heath (Ericaceae), orchid (Orchidaceae), and broomrape (Orobanchaceae) families. These plants all obtain nutrients through an intermediary mycorrhizal fungi. Mycorrhizal relationships between fungi and plant are symbiotic, in that the fungi expands the root surface area and increases nutrient and water absorption for the plant while the fungi gets nutrients in return. Mychotrophs exploit this symbiosis by parasitizing the hyphae and the fungi unwittingly feeds the mycotroph. Some species in the heath family have both leafless (heterotrophic) and leaf-bearing (autotrophic) forms.

Insectivorous plants photosynthesize but need an energy boost. They obtain this by trapping insects and digesting their nutrients. Species like *Darlingtonia californica* survive on nutrient poor serpentine soils buy supplementing nutrients in this way.

Because of their unique standing in the plant community, I have set aside a section for regional heterotrophic plants.

Introduced, naturalized, and invasive plants

Naturalized plants are non-natives that do not need human help to reproduce and maintain themselves over time. Even though their offspring reproduce and spread naturally (without human help), naturalized plants do not, over time, become native members of the local plant community. Many naturalized plants are found primarily near human-dominated areas. Sometimes, naturalized is used (confusingly) to refer specifically to naturally reproducing, non-native plants that do not invade areas dominated by native vegetation.

An invasive plant has the ability to thrive and spread aggressively outside its native range. A naturally aggressive plant may be especially invasive when it is introduced to a new habitat. However, since invasive plants also reproduce and spread without human help, they also are naturalized—invasives are a small, but troublesome, sub-category of naturalized plants. Klamath weed is an invasive that you will encounter along roads and trails and in meadows throughout the high country and seems to be spread in the feed and feces of stock animals.

Wildflower photography

A simple rule applies here—use a tripod. Hand-holding your camera is fine for snapshot photographers, but if you want great, in-focus shots, and good depth of field there is nothing like a platform to steady your camera. You might also consider using a remote shutter release if your camera supports it. I prefer to shoot on cloudy days or in early morning or early evening when the sun is off the flower. If that isn't possible, I shade the flower with whatever I have at hand—my pack, a shirt, jacket, or myself. Shooting out of the sun brings out the best possible color saturation and reduces glare caused by direct sunlight. Glare can be reduced further by using a polarizing filter which also helps bring out more color. Shoot at the highest f-stop possible for best depth of field but experiment with your settings to produce backgrounds of varying intensity. Having a blurred background can lend a nice effect to your photograph by reducing clutter that might interfere with small details in the plant. Always remember to cover the viewfinder during each exposure to prevent light entering from the back of the camera.

My tripod is one of the most versatile, least expensive and lightest on the market today—the Sunpak Fieldmaster. Because each leg works independently it offers amazing adaptability in different terrain situations. It can center your camera lens from 9" above ground level (perfect for shooting low growing subjects) to about 6' (great for people or landscapes). I also carry a small but sturdy table-top tripod that weighs just a few ounces but which has proven invaluable when shooting tiny subjects only a couple of inches tall like mushrooms.

If you are a digital photographer I recommend shooting RAW files for the simple fact that you can literally "re-shoot" the photograph later on your computer, refining things like exposure, white balance, and shadow and/or highlight intensity. I prefer to do my initial RAW processing in the current versions of Nikon Capture NX-D, Luminar or Aurora HDR and then, occasionally, Photoshop to polish everything off. A little time spent adjusting for light and shadow, color saturation and contrast can turn an ordinary photograph into one worthy of keeping and showing off. If using Aurora HDR 2017, bracket your shots and coalesce the images to bring out the best in highlights and shadows. One of the beauties of digital photography is that you can shoot as much as you want, whenever you want and instantly discard what you don't like.

Personally, I prefer Nikon products and currently shoot with two—the D810 and the D600. My macro lens is the Nikon 85mm. When backpacking I carry the 85mm and a 28-300 zoom which allows me versatility for most applications with the exception of long distance wildlife shots. I also have Nikon GPS units that attach to both cameras. It takes a bit more battery power to GPS each shot but the advantages of using them far outweigh the disadvantages especially when recording the exact locations of wildflowers, mushrooms, and lichens for future reference.

History of place names

Anyone familiar with the Forest Service map of the Trinity Alps Wilderness knows that I must have gotten it wrong when I chose to use "Stewart's Fork" instead of "Stuart's Fork." Well, here's the skinny—I'm a map buff and collector. In my collection of area maps dating from the late 1800s and early 1900s this stream is referred to as Stewart's Fork, not Stuart's Fork. It wasn't until much later that the spelling was changed and I'm thinking it might have been a simple clerical error that stuck and became accepted. Historical accuracy is important and I have always used Stewart's over Stuart's and will continue to do so. Also, Stewart's Fork is not a creek as many people suppose. It should be accurately referred to as The Stewart's Fork of the Trinity River.

I've always been fascinated with the history of this area and, fortunately, I grew up here at a time when a few of the Trinity and Shasta County old timers were still around—characters like Bill Foster, Russel Bassham, Ed Scott and Emilio Cromaz. They were ranchers, wagon drivers and miners and entertained me for hours with stories about the "good-old days" in these mountains. Through them I gained some interesting insights into the past including the history surrounding what is now known as Lady Gulch. Many years ago the ladies occupying the house at the entrance to this gulch were engaged in illicit boudoir maneuverings with miners working along upper Coffee Creek. One has to remember that these were rough and tumble times and very few, if any, women lived in the mining camps. At any rate, as a nod to its colorful past and to historical accuracy (as noted on early maps of the area) I still refer to this site as Whorehouse Gulch but if you, prefer its new nom d'plume, Lady Gulch, have at it!

Similar Wildflowers

Several groups of wildflowers look so much alike and share so many common traits that telling them apart can be almost impossible for the amateur and even professional botanists. Those problematic species include arnicas, asters, stonecrops, and the small to medium sized blue lupines among others. Stonecrops are of special interest because the Klamath Mountains are the center of distribution and diversity for a group challenging to tell apart. These beautiful succulents all have basal clusters of thick, fleshy leaves and stems topped with clusters of many five-petaled flowers. The species differ in the shape, size, and attachment of stem and basal leaves, in the colors of petals and anthers, and the degree to which the petals spread. Flower color ranges from white to cream, yellow and pink. Common species in the book area are cream stonecrop, *Sedum oregonense*, abundant on the divide around Mt. Ashland and ranging south to the Russians and the Trinity Alps; The Eddys stonecrop, *Sedum kiersteadiae*, prevalent in the Eddys and Scott Mountain, west to Canyon Creek in the Alps; and Heckner's stonecrop, *Sedum laxum* subsp. *heckneri* (not pictured), in a band from the Trinity/Humboldt County boundary north through eastern Del Norte and western Siskiyou Counties. Canyon Creek stonecrop, *S. paradisum* subsp. *paradisum* (not pictured), is a rare species known from far eastern Humboldt County, east and north through Trinity County to the mountains north of Shasta Lake in Shasta County. Hybrids occur in the Trinity Alps.

I would also like to note that certain plants hold a special fascination for me, especially in terms of their cultural and historical significance. Throughout this guide you will find expanded descriptions of these plants which can lead to problems with maintaining the alphabetic order of some species. I've tried to minimize this problem but have found it to be unavoidable in some instances.

Parts of a flower:

petals
(corolla)

flower stalk
(pedicel)

filament
anther } stamen

pistil {
ovary
style
stigma

sepals
(calyx)

Salmon Mountains wake robin

bell catchfly

showy phlox

If the petals of a flower radiate uniformly away from the center, as is the case with the bell catchfly and showy phlox shown above, the flower is considered radially symmetrical or regular. Among other regular wildflowers are roses and buttercups.

blue or gay penstemon

upper lobe

lower lobe

mountain violet

If a flower can be divided equally down the center presenting a mirror image as in the case of the blue penstemon and mountain violet shown above then the flower is considered bilaterally symmetrical or irregular. Among other wildflowers considered irregular are monkeyflowers, skullcaps and monkshoods.

wood anemone, Columbia windflower

petaloid (petal-like) sepals

numerous stamens and pistils

Parts of an anemone flower.

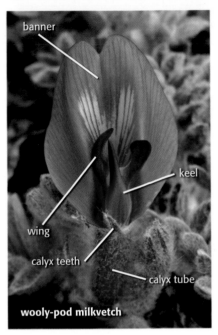

banner

keel

wing

calyx teeth

calyx tube

wooly-pod milkvetch

Parts of a pea flower.

disc flowers

ray flowers

bracts (phyllaries)

showy railardella

Parts of a composite (radiate) head.

Siskiyou fireweed

four-parted stigma

petals in fours

calyx

inferior ovary

Parts of an evening-primrose flower.

Parts of an iris.

Parts of an orchid.

Reflections on
Upper Albert Lake

Bear grass
Xerophyllum tenax)

INSIDE-OUT FLOWER, REDWOOD IVY
Vancouveria planipetala
Barberry family

3 or 6 petals

Plants range to 2' tall and are loosely branched. The leaves are compound, with angular heart-shaped leaflets, each about 1 to 1½" across. Flowers grow in loose panicles, with six petals, and are ¼" across or smaller. Each petal has two small yellow anthers near the base. It prefers dry, shaded areas at lower elevations. The leaves of the inside-out-flower are beautiful in autumn when they turn bright red and yellow. The flowers on this plant are so tiny and delicate that people often pass by without ever seeing them, and that's a shame. I photographed the flowers along the Canyon Creek Trail in late May and the leaves at the Stewart's Fork Trailhead in November.

WHITE TRITELEIA, WHITE BRODIAEA, FOOL'S ONION
Triteleia hyacinthina
Brodiaea family

3 or 6 petals

This is a flower of wet meadows, vernal pools, and seeps which grows from low to mid-elevations. It is a tall plant, often reaching 24" in height, topped with a dense cluster of white, bowl shaped flowers with prominent green mid-veins. Occasionally, the flowers are tinged with light purple. The leaves are long and narrow with a prominent ridge extending the length of the back. I photographed these on Musser Hill just off Highway 3 west of Weaverville in June.

WESTERN BISTORT, AMERICAN BISTORT
Bistorta bistortoides
Buckwheat family

3 or 6 petals

Western bistort is a tall plant found in subalpine meadows throughout the area covered by this guide. The white to pinkish flowers grow in dense clusters at the tops of tall stems and, perhaps, the most noticeable things about them are the protruding anthers which give the flowers a decidedly hairy look. I photographed this one on Scott Mountain in July. I've also found it around Lower Albert Lake in the Russians.

INSIDE-OUT FLOWER
Vancouvaria planipetala
Barberry family

WHITE TRITELEIA
Triteleia hyacinthina
Brodiaea family

WESTERN BISTORT
AMERICAN BISTORT
Bistorta bistortoides
Buckwheat family

NAKED-STEM BUCKWHEAT
Eriogonum nudum
Buckwheat family

3 or 6 petals

Here is a buckwheat you don't have to get out of your car to see. The white and yellow versions are common alongside roads and highways everywhere. It is tall (2' or more), loosely branched, with small rounded flowering heads. It prefers dry, open and exposed sites. Stems often turn red in the fall. I photographed the white ones along Highway 3 near Lewiston in early October and the yellow ones near Buckeye Ridge in June.

GREENE'S BUCKWHEAT
Eriogonum strictum var. *greenei*
Buckwheat family

3 or 6 petals

It was the clusters of ball shaped, creamy white flowers that first caught my eye while driving the Salmon River Highway just west of Callahan. They appeared to float above the low rounded mats of small, fuzzy, egg shaped, and fleshy leaves in typical buckwheat fashion. This species favors dry, open, rocky sites. For the amateur, buckwheats can be maddeningly difficult to identify but this one is a relatively easy—look for a mat-forming buckwheat with cream to pink colored flowers and densely white-woolly leaves in the mid to high elevations.

Note: Another small, white woolly-leaved mat forming buckwheat, *E. ovalifolium*, is also present in the Klamath Mountains.

BEAR VALLEY BUCKWHEAT, BEAR BUCKWHEAT
Eriogonuim ursinum
Buckwheat family

3 or 6 petals

The creamy—sometimes yellow—flowers of this pretty buckwheat bloom in a compact head atop long stalks and some may be lightly tinged with pink. The leaf stems I photographed were predominantly red and the slightly hairy leaves were green tinged with red. It grows on a wide range of substrates in exposed dry rocky or gravelly sites. I photographed this population below Hirz Mountain Lookout near Shasta Lake in late May.

Note: *Eriogonum ursinum* var. *erubescens,* or blushing wild buckwheat, also occurs in this area. The plant structure is the same but the flowers are tinged pink or maroon. It is a Klamath Mountain endemic which was discovered and described by Julie Knorr (co-author) and James Reveal both of whom are buckwheat experts. It is confined to an area west of I-5 from the Scott Bar Mountains north of Yreka south along the Trinity divide to Bully Choop—a peak just south of Shasta Bally.

NAKED-STEM BUCKWHEAT
Eriogonum nudum
Buckwheat family

GREENE'S BUCKWHEAT
Eriogonum strictum var. *greenei*
Buckwheat family

BEAR VALLEY BUCKWHEAT, BEAR BUCKWHEAT
Eriogonum ursinum
Buckwheat family

WESTERN SOLOMON'S SEAL
Maianthemum racemosum
Butcher's-broom family

3 or 6 petals

I have included two different photographs of this wildflower found commonly across North America. One image is from the higher elevations and another from lower elevations found in the foothills to the coast.

The flowering stalks in higher elevations are 8" to 10", leaves are more compact, shorter, thicker, and leathery. The flowers are larger and bloom in thick bunches on the end of the shorter, often upright stalk. I photographed this above Upper Albert Lake in the Russian Wilderness in September.

In lower elevations the species prefers shaded areas where it blooms in early spring. The elegant long stems and large, alternate, parallel veined leaves are diagnostic. Some plants reach 3' or more in length and become droopy the longer they are. The loosely clustered flowers bloom at the ends of long stalks. In the fall the leaves turn a beautiful gold accentuated by satin red berries. I photographed these along the Dog Creek Road (the old Delta Toll Road) near Clear Creek Campground on the Trinity Divide.

STARRY FALSE LILY OF THE VALLEY, STARRY SOLOMON'S SEAL
STARRY SOLOMON'S PLUME
Maianthemum stellatum
Butcher's-broom family

3 or 6 petals

This species enjoys stream sides, swampy meadows, and springs but can also be found under a shaded forest canopy. The flowers are white with lance shaped petals that usually curve slightly downward from the calyx along an unbranched stem. Bright green leaves up to 6" long clasp the stem and are folded along the mid-rib. The plant can be up to 2' tall. This one was photographed along the Bowerman Meadows Trail.

WHITE HASTINGSIA, RUSH LILY
Hastingsia alba
Century plant family

3 or 6 petals

White hastingsia is a flower common in damp open spaces like meadows where it stands head and shoulders above the rest. On the grassy slopes around Papoose Lake I've actually seen flowering stalks approaching 5'. Its leaves are elongated and basal and 1' to 3' in length. The flowers grow along a slender axis up to 18" long that can be branched or not. They are a beautiful translucent white with purplish central vein that lends them a silvery look. I photographed this one in Van Matre Meadows but you will find them in mid to high elevation meadows throughout the Trinities.

Note: *Hastingsia* was named for Serranus Clinton Hastings (1814–1893) first Chief Justice of the Supreme Court of California.

WESTERN SOLOMON'S SEAL - low elevation
Maianthemum racemosum
Butcher's-broom family

WESTERN SOLOMON'S SEAL - high elevation
Maianthemum racemosum
Butcher's-broom family

STARRY FALSE LILY OF THE VALLEY
Maianthemum stellatum
Butcher's-broom family

WHITE HASTINGSIA, RUSH LILY
Hastingsia alba
Century plant family

23

SAND LILY
Leucocrinum montanum   3 or 6 petals
Century plant family

Sand lily is more at home in the dry, volcanic soils of eastern Siskiyou and Shasta counties but, while it may not be common in this neck of the woods, it occurs on similar substrates in the Klamath Mountains. The flowers are stark white and grow to 3" or 4". I photographed this in Morris Meadows in the drier areas near the upper end of the meadows.

WESTERN FALSE-ASPHODEL
Triantha occidentalis subsp. *occidentalis*   3 or 6 petals
False asphodel family

This is a wildflower of mid to high elevation wet meadows and marshy areas. A dense cluster of white flowers with six broad, prominent stamens appear almost tiered at the tops of 1' to 1½' rust colored stems with sticky hairs. The slender, grass-like leaves are basal, long, and narrow. I photographed this in a small meadow at Upper Albert Lake in the Russian Wilderness in September.

FOOTHILL DEATH CAMAS, PANICLED ZIGADENE
Toxicoscordion paniculatum   3 or 6 petals
False-hellebore family

Foothill death camas is not as common as meadow death camas and enjoys drier sites at mid-elevations. The flowers bloom in a loose, multi-branched cluster called a panicle along the upper part of the stem as opposed to meadow death camas which has a tighter, unbranched flower formation near the top of the stems. Other-wise, the flower color and shape and overall structure of the two species are much the same. I photographed these on Scott Mountain in late July.

MEADOW DEATH CAMAS, BLACK SNAKEROOT, STAR LILY
Toxicoscordion venenosum var. *venenosum*   3 or 6 petals
False-hellebore family

Meadow death camas is common in or around wet meadows from the coast to low and mid elevations in the Trinity Alps. The plants can reach to 10" with small white flowers blooming in a tight formation along the upper third of the stem with prominent stamens. These plants are known to be poisonous to livestock, especially sheep. As an interesting side note, Amy Stewart writes in her book *Wicked Plants: The Weed That Killed Lincoln's Mother & Other Botanical Atrocities* that members of the Lewis and Clark expedition became violently ill after possibly eating the roots of this plant, mistaking it for a similar, non-poisonous variety known as blue camas. If you find it necessary to follow in their footsteps, do so without eating things you can't identify! I photographed these in an open meadow alongside the road to the Stoney Ridge Trailhead in mid-June.

SAND LILY
Leucocrinum montanum
Century plant family

WESTERN FALSE-ASPHODEL
Triantha occidentalis subsp. *occidentalis*
False asphodel family

FOOTHILL DEATH CAMAS, PANICLED ZIGADENE
Toxicoscordion paniculatum
False-hellebore family

MEADOW DEATH CAMAS
Toxicoscordion venenosum var. *venenosum*
False-hellebore family

GIANT WHITE WAKEROBIN, SWEET TRILLIUM
Trillium albidum
False-hellebore family

3 or 6 petals

Trilliums are perennial favorites of mine. I have photographed them all over the world and they never lose their magic. They surprise you in deeply shaded and wet areas, popping up with their showy displays when you least expect it. This is the largest of the trilliums in this area, with erect flowers sitting directly atop the leaves. I've seen these over 16" across with flower petals standing up 4" high. Flowers are magnificent and cannot be confused with any of the other trilliums. I photographed these at Natural Bridge near Hayfork but they occur throughout these mountains

SALMON MOUNTAINS WAKEROBIN, TRILLIUM
Trillium ovatum subsp. *oettingeri*
False-hellebore family

3 or 6 petals

This gregarious little trillium likes to hide in stream side thickets, in the shaded edges of wet meadows, and mesic forest understory at mid to high elevations throughout the area. The snow white flowers stand out in the shadows like little stars. The plants themselves are about 7" tall with three deep green leaves near the top of a naked stalk. A single, three-petaled flower nods just above the leaves. I photographed this little beauty where Buck Creek enters the North Fork of Coffee Creek in late May.

CALIFORNIA CORN LILY, FALSE HELLEBORE
Veratrum californicum var. *californicum*
False-hellebore family

3 or 6 petals

Corn lilies grow commonly throughout the Klamath Mountains, often by the hundreds, in damp to wet meadows and on slopes following the melting snow. They are beautiful plants and the leaves, in particular, are very photogenic. By early summer plants can sometimes reach heights of 7' and are topped with clusters of white flowers. These were photographed in a meadow below Russian Lake in the Russian Wilderness but I've also photographed them in the meadows below Parker Divide in the Trinity Alps.

BEAR-GRASS
Xerophyllum tenax
False-hellebore family

3 or 6 petals

Bear-grass deserves special attention in this guide for two reasons: first, bear-grass is dependent on fire for regeneration and second, because it has cultural significance to western Native Americans. Native Americans use the tough, fibrous leaves (which turn white when dried and are easily dyed) when weaving intricate designs into baskets. Because the plant responds well to fire, and thrives in burned areas, tribes tend large patches with periodic burning, which encourages vigorous new growth. The snow-white flowers emerge in compact club-shaped racemes at the tops of stems that can reach 6' in height. The tough leaves are grass-like, forming mounded bunches at ground level. Shorter leaves emerge along the flowering stalk. I took these photographs in July in Horse Creek Meadows in the Trinity Alps but it is common throughout these mountains.

GIANT WHITE WAKEROBIN, SWEET TRILLIUM
Trillium albidum
False-hellebore family

SALMON MOUNTAINS WAKEROBIN, TRILLIUM
Trillium ovatum ssp. *oettingeri*
False-hellebore family

CALIFORNIA CORN LILY; FALSE HELLEBORE
Veratrum californicum var. *californicum*
False-hellebore family

BEAR-GRASS
Xerophyllum tenax
False-hellebore family

27

LONG-TUBED IRIS, SLENDER IRIS

Iris tenuissima subsp. *tenuissima*   3 or 6 petals
Iris family

Members of this group of wild iris are highly variable in petal structure and color-ation, but all have a long corolla tube of 1″ to 2½″. In some, the petals are wide and streaked with deep reddish-purple and yellow. In others, the petals are long, narrow, and sparsely colored with blue to purplish-red veins without the yellow. All of them are fairly tall, growing to 10″. The top photograph was taken along Swift Creek and the lower one was taken along Stewart's Fork, both in the Trinity Alps.

QUEEN'S CUPS, BRIDE'S BONNET, BEAD LILY, CLINTONIA

Clintonia uniflora   3 or 6 petals
Lily family

This beautiful little member of the lily family is a gregarious one. It can be found in large groups at mid to high elevations in shaded and damp sites. The flowers are white and the entire plant rarely gets taller than 6″. There is only one flower per plant, hence the name *uniflora*. Late in the season the flowers are replaced by shiny blue berries from which it derives one of its common names, bead lily. The name "queen's cups" was derived in 1903 by Julia W. Henshaw in her book *Mountain Wildflowers of Canada*. Referencing the Queen of England she says "It certainly is the queen of all the lovely flower-cups found blooming in the mountain valleys of Western Canada, its white petals making a chalice well worthy of the First Lady of the land." I photographed the flowers and fruit on the trail to Granite Lake in the Trinities but look for them throughout the Klamath Mountains.

**LONG-TUBED IRIS
SLENDER IRIS**
Iris tenuissima subsp. *tenuissima*
Iris family

Shown are two variations

**QUEEN'S CUPS
BRIDE'S BONNET
BEAD LILY**
Clintonia uniflora
Lily family

White flowering fawn lilies in this area: Julie Nelson notes that the fawn lilies are a confusing group. They hybridize, there are intermediates, and sometimes we see evidence of past hybrid events when one of the parents is no longer anywhere in the neighborhood. Common traits for *Erythronium* include a preference for shaded sites where they bloom in large colonies. The flowers are nodding and usually solitary, though they can have as many as 3 per stem on var. *citrinum* and var. *roderickii*. The petals are recurved in all three species. The elongated leaves of all three are varying shades of green with white or brown mottling. Plant height ranges from 6" to 9."

CALIFORNIA FAWN LILY
Erythronium californicum   3 or 6 petals
Lily family

This Northern California endemic has flowers that range in color from snow-white to cream, are yellow at the throat, and sometimes with a band of orange or reddish brown striations. Unlike *E. citrinum var. roderickii*, the anthers are white or cream colored. I photographed these above French Gulch but I've also seen them along the Ditch Grade between Igo and Platina (SW of Redding) and along Slate Creek on the east side of the Trinity Divide.

CREAM FAWN LILY, LEMON FAWN LILY
Erythronium citrinum var. *citrinum*   3 or 6 petals
Lily family

Cream fawn lily has a broader distribution than Scott Mountain fawn lily and occurs occasionally in this area. The two are similar in appearance with the exception of the anthers which are white or cream colored in var. *citrinum*. Flowers are white with a lemon yellow throat surrounded by a slight band of yellow to orange striations fading to light pink or purple as they mature. Despite the similarity in the color of flowers and anthers, cream fawn lily's short style (½" or less) distinguishes it from California fawn lily, which has a longer style. I took this photograph near Lowden Ranch above the Trinity River in April.

SCOTT MOUNTAIN FAWN LILY, RODERICK'S FAWN LILY
Erythronium citrinum var. *roderickii*   3 or 6 petals
Lily family

Scott Mountain fawn lily is endemic to the Trinity River Basin from Scott Mountain to the area around Lewiston and Weaverville. What sets var. *roderickii* apart from var. *citrinum* are the anthers which vary from lilac to brick red. As the flowers age, the petal tips turn a delicate lilac color. A deep reddish-brown band of striations encircle the base of the petals at the throat. I photographed these along Scorpion Creek in March, but they are well represented throughout the indicated area.

CALIFORNIA FAWN LILY
Erythronium californicum
Lily family

CREAM FAWN LILY
LEMON FAWN LILY
Erythronium citrinum var. *citrinum*
Lily family

SCOTT MOUNTAIN FAWN LILY
Erythronium citrinum var. *roderickii*
Lily family

SHASTA FAWN LILY
Erythronium shastense   3 to 6 petals
Lily family

This newly described species is endemic to limestones surrounding the McCloud and Squaw Creek Arms of Shasta Lake where they prefer deep shade on north facing slopes. The snow white flowers have deep orange centers, are striated, and age to a light purple. The stamens are prominent and topped with deep orange anthers. They bloom at the tops of naked stalks up to 8" in height. The matching pairs of basal leaves are mottled, some with dark reddish-green and others with faint silvery-white. I photographed these in the limestone below Hirz Mountain Lookout. **Note**: there is abundant limestone throughout parts of the Klamath Mountains, a lot of it highly inaccessible, so it is reasonable to believe that there could be as-yet-undiscovered populations of this species elsewhere.

REDWOOD LILY
Lilium rubescens   3 or 6 petals
Lily family

Drive up any of the roads leading to trailheads on the east side of the Trinity Alps from May to early July and you will find beautiful displays of this amazing lily. The flowers, in large clusters at the tops of tall stems, start out a beautiful white with cinnamon spots, turning a deep wine-purple with age. The petals are glossy, like they have been waxed to a high sheen. The smell is delicious and intoxicating, making anyone want to stretch out in a patch of them and take a nap! I photographed this group along the road to the Granite Peak Trailhead but the road to the Swift Creek Trailhead is a sure bet as well.

PURPLE-FLOWERED WASHINGTON LILY
Lilium washingtonianum subsp. *purpurascens*   3 or 6 petals
Lily family

The purple-flowered Washington lily's flowers sport fewer cinnamon spots than subsp. *washingtonianum* and turn a beautiful wine-purple in the throats and petal tips with age. Flowers also lack the yellow mid-rib of subsp. *washingtonianum*. It occurs at mid to high elevations in the Trinity Alps and associates with huckleberry oak thickets where the long flower stems poke out into sunlight. I photographed this bunch along the North Fork of Coffee Creek but another good place to see them in the Trinity Alps is along the Long Canyon Trail before you enter the meadows and just above the Bowerman Meadow cutoff.

WASHINGTON LILY
Lilium washingtonianum subsp. *washingtonianum*   3 or 6 petals
Lily family

Named for Martha Washington, this lily is, indeed, the first lady of the large lilies. The white flowers are decorated with small cinnamon spots and bloom in large clusters at the tops of tall stems, sometimes poking out through road and trail side brush. There is a yellow mid-rib in the lower half of each petal, and the flowers age white or rarely pale pink. I photographed this group just below Hirz Mountain Lookout above Lake Shasta. This is not a common lily but occurs over a large geographic area. **Note**: The two subspecies can be difficult to distinguish. Geography helps as subsp. *purpurascens* tends to occur to the northwest of Mt. Shasta and toward the Klamath Mountains, and subsp. *washingtonianum* tends to occur to the southeast of Mt. Shasta and into the Cascades and Sierras.

SHASTA FAWN LILY
Erythronium shastense
Lily family

REDWOOD LILY
Lillium rubescens
Lily family

PURPLE-FLOWERED WASHINGTON LILY
Lillium washingtonianum subsp. *purpurascens*
Lily family

WASHINGTON LILY
Lillium washingtonianum subsp. *washingtonianum*
Lily family

FAIRY BELLS, HOOKER'S FAIRY BELLS
Prosartes hookeri   3 or 6 petals
Lily family

The way the little clusters of creamy, bell shaped blossoms hang beneath their canopy of large deep green leaves is the most enchanting part about this cute wildflower. The species is common along shaded sites at lower elevations but keep a watchful eye because the flowers are easy to miss. The stems and leaves spread horizontally from the main stem, which can be up to 24" long. I photographed these along the Stewart's Fork Trail in early May.

PURDY'S FRITILLARY
Fritillaria purdyi   3 or 6 petals
Lily family

Finding this little fritillary reaffirmed my long held belief that, when searching for wildflowers, you can never visit the same area too often. To my surprise, I found it blooming in a large colony where I've walked dozens of times at various seasons, just not March. A field of what I thought were small white stars caught my attention through the trees and at the edges of an old road. The "stars" turned out to be the snow white edges of the fleshy flower petals. Plants are erect with stems from 4" to 10" tall. Ovate leaves crowd the bottom of the stem with a single, small, lance shaped leaf midway. A raceme of one or more bell shaped flowers nod at the tops of the stems. The snow white petals have yellowish-green centers, streaked with deep maroon spots. Sometimes the flowers are tinged with a light pink. *Fritillaria purdyi* is a rare plant, restricted to northern California, and is endemic to serpentine soils.

TWISTED-STALK
Streptopus amplexifolius var. *americanus*   3 or 6 petals
Lily family

Twisted-stalk resembles the fairy bells illustrated above and could be confused with them but for the interesting twist in the thin stalks. Each flower stalk emerges below the leaves and supports one or two blooms which, as I've discovered, can be variable in color—from white to purple. Perhaps most noticeable are the bright red to orange berries that form in late summer. Twisted stalk is common across the region, from the high country to the coast. This photograph was taken along Big French Creek in late May. I photographed the berries at the outlet stream below Sugar Pine Lake in September.

SLIMLEAF ONION, PAPER ONION
Allium amplectens   3 or 6 petals
Onion family

I've only found this onion once, and that was around the edges of a serpentine wetland alongside the road to the Stoney Ridge Trailhead in the Trinity Alps. All of the plants were about 12" tall with large clusters of beautiful white to deep pink flowers. It prefers vernally wet areas in clay or serpentine, which is common habitat in the eastern Trinity Alps. I photographed these on Stoney Ridge in June.

FAIRY BELLS
HOOKER'S FAIRY BELLS
Prosartes hookeri
Lily family

PURDY'S FRITILLARY
Fritillaria purdyi
Lily family

TWISTED-STALK
Streptopus amplexifolius var. *americanus*
Lily family

SLIMLEAF ONION, PAPER ONION
Allium amplectens
Onion family

CALIFORNIA LADY'S SLIPPER
Cypripedium californicum   3 or 6 petals
Orchid family

This beautiful little orchid prefers serpentine soils and is fairly common at lower elevations in the eastern portion of the Trinity Alps and the northernmost portions of the Trinity Divide. It likes water and grows in abundance in marshy areas and next to springs and streams. The inflated lower petal forms the slipper, which is white with light pink markings and about ¼" broad. The upper sepal and the lateral petals are greenish yellow, extending to the sides like wings, while the other two sepals are joined and located behind the slipper. The over arching hood is the same color as the sepals and holds the stigma and anthers. Three to ten flowers grow in the axils of leaf-like bracts along stems that can reach 2'. These photographs were taken next to a spring along the Swift Creek Trail. Along Highway 3, as it winds over Scott Mountain, is another sure bet for finding them.

MOUNTAIN LADY'S SLIPPER
Cypripedium montanum   3 or 6 petals
Orchid family

In my experience, this orchid is reclusive and difficult to find. It grows in small, scattered groups often hidden in deeply shaded, dry mixed conifer and hardwood stands. Its stems are erect and can be 24" or more in height with one to three slippers on the upper stem. The alternate leaves are lance shaped. The "slipper" is white with beautiful light purple streaks along the edges of the opening and inside. The elongated lateral petals are a deep purplish brown and twisted. The top sepal, which looks like an upright petal, is purplish brown and lightly streaked with yellow. The two lateral sepals are partly fused and hang behind the slipper. A large, bright yellow column hangs over and extends into the opening of the slipper and has several reddish brown spots arrayed around the edge. I am not one to toss around the word "lovely" often but this orchid really is lovely.

RATTLESNAKE-PLANTAIN
Goodyera oblongifolia   3 or 6 petals
Orchid family

Rattlesnake plantain is a common, early summer bloomer. The flowers are small, white, tubular, and alternately attached near the tops of tall, leafless stems. Each leaf of the basal rosette has a distinctive netted white stripe down its center. The upper petals form a hood over the lower petals and the opening created looks suspiciously like a fish with its mouth open. They like dry, open places in older mixed forests at elevations up to 7,000 feet. I photographed this plant on Bolt's Hill above Lewiston Lake in May.

CALIFORNIA LADY'S SLIPPER
Cypripedium californicum
Orchid family

MOUNTAIN LADY'S SLIPPER
Cypripedium montanum
Orchid familyy

RATTLESNAKE PLANTAIN
Goodyera oblongifolia
Orchid family

FLAT SPURRED PIPERIA, ROYAL REIN-ORCHID
Piperia transversa   3 or 6 petals
Orchid family

Until just recently I'd only found this beautiful, inconspicuous little orchid blooming above Keswick Lake in the Sacramento River Canyon. However, while scrambling around in a patch of manzanita and young pines on the Trinity Divide in late May I encountered it again. The population above Keswick consisted of two plants. The one on the Divide was solitary and though I spent some time looking I only found the one. The species is 8" tall with tiny ¼" white flowers which open alternately along the stem. There are two deep green, small, oval, basal leaves. It is found in a broad range of habitats including conifer and mixed evergreen forests, oak woodlands, and chaparral. I photographed these along Trinity Mountain Road near Jackass Peak in late May.

ALASKA REIN-ORCHID, ALASKA PIPERIA, SLENDER-SPIRE ORCHID
Piperia unalascensis   3 or 6 petals
Orchid family

Though not small by any means, this member of the orchid family is none-the-less inconspicuous. The flowering stems grow to 25" holding slender ¼" greenish-white flowers arrayed alternately along the upper half. Large, deep green basal leaves lay flat to the ground. The species prefers coniferous and mixed evergreen forests, generally on dry sites. I photographed these alongside the old and little used Horse Creek trail in the Trinity Alps in August.

WHITE-FLOWERED BOG-ORCHID, BOG CANDLE
Platanthera dilatata var. *leucostachys*   3 or 6 petals
Orchid family

This orchid is a common inhabitant of wet, sub-alpine meadows throughout the area. It is a stand-up plant from 7" to 40" tall with tapered leaves and showy snow-white to creamy flowers that are scattered or thickly clustered along the stalk. Even though the flowers are white and abundant, the shorter plants (which are most common in this area) can often be lost in taller grasses. The tall ones, while not as common, are easily spotted. This is one wildflower that you should get up close and personal with because they are beautiful and delicate. I photographed the one on the left one in Van Matre Meadows and the gigantic version on the right in Bower-man Meadows, both in late July in the Trinity Alps.

FLAT SPURRED PIPERIA, ROYAL REIN-ORCHID
Piperia transversa
Orchid family

ALASKA REIN-ORCHID, ALASKA PIPERIA
Piperia unalascensis
Orchid family

WHITE-FLOWERED BOG ORCHID, BOG CANDLE
Platanthera dilatata var. *leucostachys*
Orchid family

WESTERN LADY'S TRESSES, CREAMY LADY'S TRESSES
Spiranthes porrifolia   3 or 6 petals
Orchid family

There is no mistaking this beautiful and elegant member of the orchid family. The creamy white, elongated tube shaped flowers bloom in a dense, spiral spike up to 24" in height. They prefer vernally damp, open, sunny places where they grow in large colonies. I photographed these on Stoney Ridge in the Trinity Alps in late May.

HOODED LADY'S TRESSES
Spiranthes romanzoffiana   3 or 6 petals
Orchid family

The creamy white flowers bloom from July through September arranged in three rows that spiral along a tall, erect stem. The basal leaves are up to 5" long becoming undeveloped bracts further up the stem. While lady's tresses are consider uncommon in some areas, the opposite is true in the wet meadows of the Trinity Alps. I have also found them growing in dry, gravelly sites along the coast just inland from the beaches. I photographed this one in the meadows above Big Caribou Lake in the Trinity Alps in late August.

MILK MAIDS, TOOTHWORT
Cardamine californica   4 petals
Mustard family

This species in one of the earliest bloomers in the region. I've found fully developed flowers in the middle of December with blooming continuing into April. While leaves are variable, the common name is derived from a leaf shape which can resemble a dog's canine. Delicate flowers are ½" diameter with four white petals, white to pinkish, close at sun down, and open again at sunrise. Plants grow to 12" tall. Look for them in a variety of habitats including shady slopes, open woods, and moist hillsides at lower elevations. I photographed these on a hillside near Lowden Ranch above the Trinity River in early April.

NUTTALL'S TOOTHWORT
Cardamine nuttallii   4 petals
Mustard family

This small, low-growing toothwort loves wet, open, mid-elevation meadows. The flowers occur in loose clusters at the tops of 5" to 8" stems. They are small and mostly white, with just a hint of pink before they fully open. I shot this one in Union Meadows in late May near receding snowbanks along the stream pouring down from the Parker Divide in the Trinity Alps.
Note: Other *Cardamine* species occur in this area including *Cardamine angulata* and *Cardamine cordifolia* but distinguishing between them is difficult.

WESTERN LADY'S TRESSES
Spiranthes porrifolia
Orchid family

HOODED LADY'S TRESSES
Spiranthes romanzoffiana
Orchid family

MILKMAIDS, TOOTHWORT
Cardamine californica
Mustard family

NUTTALL'S TOOTHWORT, NUTTALL'S CARDAMINE
Cardamine nuttallii
Mustard family

41

SPRING DRABA, WHITLOW GRASS
Draba verna   4 petals
Mustard family

This teeny wildflower grows in huge masses on relatively dry, exposed hillsides early in the spring. Branched flower stalks rise from a tiny rosette of lance or spoon shaped leaves. Each stalk sports one single white flower with a reddish calyx and four deeply lobed petals—so deeply lobed that a casual observer might count 8 petals. Take your time and watch for this beautiful but clandestine species. I photographed these in the Bolt's Hill area above Lewiston Lake.

WATER CRESS
Nasturtium officinale   4 petals
Mustard family

Water cress is common in wet, mid-elevation meadows throughout the Trinity Alps. Look for it early in the spring where it grows with marsh yellow cress and Nuttall's toothwort. The flowers cluster in dense heads at the tops of 6" to 7" stalks and decorate large areas alongside stream banks. I photographed these in Union Meadows in late May but have also found them in the meadows around Big Carmen Lake in the Scott Mountains.

WHITNEY'S MILK VETCH, BALLOON POD MILK VETCH, WHITNEY'S LOCOWEED
Astragalus whitneyi   5 irregular petals
Pea family

The most memorable characteristic of this plant are the inflated white and red seed pods that look suspiciously like little balloons. The compact plants have stiff stems decorated by narrow, lance shaped, alternate, pinnately compound leaves which are folded at the margins into cup shapes. The pea-shaped flowers are creamy white and tinged with pink. It likes open, exposed, rocky sites—so watch for them near ridge tops. While considered uncommon in some regions, it is found throughout the Klamath Mountains. I have found it in several areas including Upper Stoddard Lake and East Boulder Lake in the Trinity Alps, and along the Pacific Crest Trail in the Scott Mountains. I photographed these above Gumboot Lake on the Trinity Divide in early June. The inset photograph of the "balloon" seed pod is provided courtesy of Meredith Parks and was taken at the ABCD Lakes in the Marble Mountain Wilderness Area in August.

SICKLE-KEELED LUPINE
Lupinus albicaulis   5 irregular petals
Pea family

This locally common plant grows to 18" and are multi-branched with several stalks of flowers on each plant. The keel parts of the flowers are creamy white to purple, while the flags are a light brownish-tan. Leaves are covered with silky hairs. It prefers open dry slopes in foothills and mountains, especially along the shoulders and cutbanks of Highway 3 from the Stewart's Fork Bridge all the way to Trinity Center. A good place to safely check them out is in the vicinity of the intersection of Highway 3 and Bowerman Ridge Road between Covington's Mill and Trinity Center.

SPRING DRABA, WHITLOW GRASS
Draba verna
Mustard family

WATER CRESS
Nasturtium officinale
Mustard family

WHITNEY'S MILK VETCH
Astragalus whitneyi
Pea family

SICKLE-KEELED LUPINE
Lupinus albicaulis
Pea family

LONG-STALKED CLOVER
Trifolium longipes   5 irregular petals
Pea family

This locally common clover blooms all summer in meadows and along stream banks in the mid to higher elevations. Multiple white to purple-pink flowers grow on 2"-15" stalks. I have found them growing in some unlikely places. Once, while climbing the serpentine rock face at the head of Upper Bowerman Meadows below Lake Anna in the Trinity Alps, I came face to face with several blooming in the crevices and small rock shelves a few yards below the lake. I photographed this bunch in the meadow below the outlet of Doe Lake in the Trinity Alps.

RUSTY SAXIFRAGE
Micranthes ferruginea   5 irregular petals
Saxifrage family

This delicate little saxifrage grows at higher elevations in the Trinity Alps where it prefers wet ledges, seepage slopes, stream banks. Flowering occurs in summer-early autumn. Small white flowers are often camouflaged by the granite and sandy gravel in which it grows. The masses of loosely branched red stems will probably catch your eye before the flowers do. I photographed this bunch in August in rocks at the edges of melting snow banks near the top of the pass between Alpine and Smith Lakes. I have also seen it on the ridge between Salmon and Ward Lakes.

NORTHERN TWO-EYED VIOLET, WEDGE-LEAVED VIOLET
Viola cuneata   5 irregular petals
Violet family

This violet favors open pine and oak forests, often on serpentine soil in the mid to high elevations. Like most violets, it is an early bloomer and can be found, often in abundance, blooming March to August. Most of the plants I've found have been less than 6" with basal leaves that are heart-shaped, leathery, and toothed on the margins. The flowers are white, tinged with faint purple with deep purple spots on all but the lower petal, which has a orange-yellow spot and purple veins extending from the throat. The two top petals have light yellow in the throat while lateral petals have a yellow beard. I took the large photograph along the road to the Lake Eleanor Trailhead and the smaller photograph along the Swift Creek Trail, both in late May.

OREGON VIOLET, HALL'S VIOLET
Viola hallii   5 irregular petals
Violet family

This is a violet of open, rocky, and serpentine slopes and flats. The plants cluster in small, sprawling mounds with many flowering stems 2" to 9" in height. The leaves are deeply dissected and the leaflets lance-shaped. The lower petal and two flanking petals are creamy white with a yellow beard and deep yellow spots accented with dark purple veins extend from the throat. The two upper petals are smaller than the others and are a deep burgundy-purple. I photographed these on Scott Mountain in late July where I found large colonies decorating roadside slopes.

LONG-STALKED CLOVER
Trifolium longipes
Pea family

RUSTY SAXIFRAGE
Micranthes ferruginea
Saxifrage family

NORTHERN TWO-EYED VIOLET
Viola cuneata
Violet family

OREGON VIOLET, HALL'S VIOLET
Viola hallii
Violet family

MACLOSKEY'S VIOLET
Viola macloskeyi   5 irregular petals
Violet family

MaCloskey's violet is a meadow violet that favors wet or damp expanses where it often blooms in large colonies in grass that obscure it from view. It is 2" or 3" in height and the tiny, white flowers are the size of a small fingernail. Basal leaves are round and cupped. The lower petal has deep purple veins extending from the throat with a few less obvious veins on the two lateral petals. The lateral petals and the two upper petals have yellow-green spots extending outward from the throat with a sparse, translucent beard. I took this photograph in Bullard's Meadow along Union Creek in late May.

WESTERN HEART'S EASE, TWO-EYED VIOLET
Viola ocellata   5 irregular petals
Violet family

This is a low elevation species blooms in March-July in rocky areas often on serpentine soil. It is characterized by elongated, heart-shaped leaves and flowering stalks up to 8". The flowers are stark white with deep purple veins and a yellow-orange spot at the throat on the lower petal and purple spots and yellow beards just above the throat on the two flanking petals. The backs of the petals are purple. I took this photograph near Potem Creek above Shasta Lake in mid-May and while I've never seen it in Trinity or Siskiyou Counties there are records of it from New River and South Fork of the Trinity River as well as from Gray's Falls on the Trinity River.

WOOD ANEMONE, COLUMBIA WINDFLOWER
Anemone deltoidea   5 symmetrical petals - ovary superior
Buttercup family

As with all *Anemones*, the large, white "petals" aren't petals but sepals holding fine yellowish, star-like stamens rising out of the center. This is a delicate plant that grows to 8" tall with a whorl of three, wavy edged leaves just above the mid-point of the stem. It loves shaded, moist areas and is one of those wildflowers that make the hike into the Duck Lakes so delightful. I photographed these along the trail to Big Duck Lake in the Russian Wilderness but they are also common along the trail to Granite Lake in the Trinity Alps.

WESTERN BANEBERRY, RED BANEBERRY, CHINABERRY, DOLL'S EYE
Actaea rubra   5 symmetrical petals - ovary superior
Buttercup family

The creamy-white flowers of this plant are absolutely gorgeous but beware its beauty. All parts of the plant are poisonous and an adult could experience serious problems after eating as few as six of the berries while two berries could be fatal to a child. The bright red berries are so bitter that it is doubtful anyone would be foolish enough to swallow them. Better safe than sorry though—keep curious little hands away from the enticing fruit. The deep green compound leaves occur in threes, are coarsely toothed with deeply lobed margins, and hairy on the undersides. The flowers bloom in panicles with 3 to 5 petal-like sepals and several prominent stamens. It is hard to confuse this wildflower with any other in this area. I photographed the flowers along Stewart's Fork in mid-June and the berries along the shoreline of Sugar Pine Lake in early September, both in the Trinity Alps.

MACLOSKEY'S VIOLET
Viola macloskeyi
Violet family

WESTERN HEART'S EASE, TWO-EYED VIOLET
Viola ocellata
Violet family

WOOD ANEMONE, COLUMBIA WINDFLOWER
Anemone deltoidea
Buttercup family

WESTERN BANEBERRY
Actaea rubra
Buttercup family

SISKIYOU RUE-ANEMONE
Enemion stipitatum   5 symmetrical petals - ovary superior
Buttercup family

This is an uncommon and elusive little flower. The delicate white to pale blue flowers, with petals that are actually sepals, are small and bloom March-May at the tops of long, thread-like stalks which often nod toward the ground. The diminutive size, scattered nature, and the fact that they prefer moist, shaded areas make them hard to find. There is a single basal leaf divided into three lobes and then divided into three again. I photographed these near a waterfall in late April in the southern-most portion of the Trinity Divide at about 2000' in May.

GRASS-OF-PARNASSUS
Parnassia palustris   5 symmetrical petals - ovary superior
Grass-of-Parnassus family

This beautiful little wildflower likes its feet in the water and, like little stars, decorates meadows, stream banks, and lake shores. The late-blooming flowers are prominently veined with a crown of deep yellow stamens and pistils which are solitary atop tall stems. They can catch your attention from yards away. I photographed this group in late September on the shoreline of L Lake in the Trinity Alps when almost every other annual plant had succumbed to frost and ice.

Note: *P. cirrata* var. *intermedia*, and *P. fimbriata also* occur in the region . They differ from palustris in these ways: *P. palustris* has entire petals and fan shaped staminodes - a seemingly sterile stamen often without an anther - ending in globe-tipped slender projections. *P. cirrata* has fringed petals with staminodes similar to *P. palustris*. *P. fimbriata* has fringed petals and stubby yellow green staminodes, without the long slender projections of the other two species. They all grow in similar habitats.

LITTLE PRINCE'S PINE
Chimaphila menziesii   5 symmetrical petals - ovary superior
Heath family

This little wintergreen grows to 6" in height on stout, reddish stems. Leaves are oval to elliptic, often with white central vein, pointed tips, and usually toothed. Flowers are white or white lightly tinged with pink, are solitary, or number up to three per stem. The petals curve back slightly, exposing a blunt green stigma in the center. Stamens are prominent. Look for it in shaded woods. It is more solitary than its larger cousin, *Chimaphila umbellata*. I photographed this little bunch above Seven-up Lake in the Trinity Alps Wilderness in September.

ONE-SIDED WINTERGREEN, SIDEBELLS WINTERGREEN
Orthilia secunda   5 symmetrical petals - ovary superior
Heath family

The stems of this wintergreen are unbranched, 6" to 8" tall, and woody at the base. Leaves are egg shaped, entire or finely toothed, and are basal—they are not stiff like *Chimaphila* species. The flowering stalk is curved at the top with a cluster of small, greenish white flowers hanging down one side of the flower stalk. The flowers resemble small closed bells with upward-curving protruding styles. Like the other wintergreens described here, this one likes deep shade and moist soils at mid to higher elevations. I photographed these along the Boulder Creek Trail just above Boulder Creek in August.

SISKIYOU RUE-ANEMONE
Enemion stipatum
Buttercup family

GRASS-OF-PARNASSUS
Parnassia palustris
Grass-of-Parnassus family

LITTLE PRINCE'S PINE
Chimaphila menziesii
Heath family

ONE-SIDED WINTERGREEN
Orthilia secunda
Heath family

WHITE-VEINED SHINLEAF, WHITE-VEINED PYROLA, WHITE-VEINED WINTERGREEN
Pyrola picta   5 symmetrical petals - ovary superior
Heath family

This pretty little wintergreen has—true to its name—white-veined, bright-green, egg-shaped leaves arranged in a basal rosette. The flowering stalk is leafless and 4"-8" in height with alternate, nodding, white flowers with deep yellow stamens and a prominent, elongated style. As with the other wintergreens, this one likes damp, shaded sites. I photographed these in the rocky area above Lower Russian Lake in September.

WESTERN SPRING BEAUTY, CANDY FLOWER
Claytonia obovata   5 symmetrical petals - ovary superior
Miner's lettuce family

The flowers of *Claytonia obovata* are similar to those of *C. serpenticola*, but the leaves are oval shaped, have strong parallel veining, and grow in opposite pairs. Flowers are either snow white or light magenta pink with prominent pink anthers. Look for it as snow banks recede in the mid-high elevations of the Trinities. I photographed the pink version on Scott Mountain in early July and the white version at Kangaroo Lake in areas still wet from melting snow.
Note: Research by Tommy Stoughton has resurrected an older species name, *Claytonia obovata*, for plants that grow in northern California and southern Oregon.

MINER'S LETTUCE
Claytonia perfoliata   5 symmetrical petals - ovary superior
Miner's lettuce family

Miner's lettuce is common and grows at low to mid-elevation throughout Northern California. It prefers moist, shaded areas and often occurs in large and lush colonies. A cluster of small white to pinkish flowers sprout from what appears to be a single, large, round leaf which is, in fact, two opposite leaves that have fused. Other leaves are more basal. This miner's lettuce has elliptic to diamond or kidney shaped basal leaves, while the similar *C. parviflora* has linear basal leaves. Miner's lettuce got its name from early miners who learned that, if eaten, it would ward off scurvy in a diet dominated by meat and beans. It has a pleasant taste and is high in vitamin C.

FROSTED MINER'S LETTUCE
Claytonia perfoliata forma *glauca*   5 symmetrical petals - ovary superior
Miner's lettuce family

Another version of miner's lettuce found in the area is known locally as frosted miner's lettuce. Alice Jones refers to it in her book as *Claytonia perfoliata* forma *glauca*. It is typically small with leaves that are mottled with a whitish bloom giving them a silvery look. The white to pink flowers of are similar as are the leaves. Look for this version along the road to the Stewart's Fork Trailhead and again along the lower reaches of the trail where it typically blooms in May and early June.

WHITE-VEINED SHINLEAF
Pyrola picta
Heath family

WESTERN SPRING BEAUTY, CANDYFLOWER
Claytonia obovata
Miner's lettuce family

MINER'S LETTUCE
Claytonia perfoliata
Miner's lettuce family

FROSTED MINER'S LETTUCE
Claytonia perfoliata forma *glauca*
Miner's lettuce family

SERPENTINE SPRING BEAUTY
Claytonia serpenticola   5 symmetrical petals - ovary superior
Miner's lettuce family

If you've ever walked in to Union Meadows or up the Stony Ridge Trail in late spring or early summer you have undoubtedly seen this gorgeous little wildflower—by the thousands. They literally carpet the ground as snow banks recede. The predominant colors are pink or white striped with pink. Along the Parker Divide and the trail to the Battle Creek Divide the flowers are snow white, sometimes with a faint pink striation to the petals. The anthers can either be deep rose magenta or faintly pink. The leaves are lance shaped. This species is restricted to serpentine soils of the Klamath Mountains.

CANDYFLOWER
Claytonia sibirica   5 symmetrical petals - ovary superior
Miner's lettuce family

This is a tiny *Claytonia* that frequents damp places like the edges of springs and seeps from the coast to the mid-elevations. The flowering stems rise from a basal rosette of fleshy, oval leaves, are unbranched and topped with loose clusters of white to pale lavender flowers. Petals are deeply veined and stamens a deeper lavender color. Heart-shaped leaves vary from green to bronze. I photographed these along Little Deep Creek in the Trinity Alps.

SHOWY ROCK MONTIA
Montia parvifolia   5 symmetrical petals - ovary superior
Miner's lettuce family

Like *Claytonia sibirica*, this common *Montia* prefers moist locations. I've found it in several places but wet scree slopes or edges of springs, seeps, and creeks are preferred. The stems are red or reddish green and topped with a loose cluster of pale pink flowers, the tips of which can be either notched or entire. The basal leaves are fleshy, mostly oval and green to olive-green, tinged with red, and sometimes decorated with deep red spots. I photographed these on the open slopes above Little Duck Lake in August and the small photograph on the slopes above Upper Albert Lake in early September, both in the Russian Wilderness.

SERPENTINE SPRING BEAUTY
Claytonia serpenticola
Miner's lettuce family

CANDYFLOWER
Claytonia sibirica
Miner's lettuce family

SHOWY ROCK MONTIA
Montia parvifolia
Miner's lettuce family

FIELD MOUSE-EAR CHICKWEED
Cerastium arvense
Pink family
5 symmetrical petals - ovary superior

This is a low, matted wildflower grows to 8" to 10" in height. Stems are hairy and sticky nurturing lance-shaped opposite leaves. White flowers are borne in loose clusters and have five deeply cleft petals. It prefers open, shaded sites and is common throughout the area. I photographed this one above Kangaroo Lake along the Pacific Crest Trail in July.

BALLHEAD SANDWORT
Eremogone congesta
Pink family
5 symmetrical petals - ovary superior

Ballhead sandwort forms a small cushion of bright green needle-like leaves. The flowers grow in heads at the tops of stems up to 12" tall. The flower heads can be dense or loose. I've found it growing in dry, sandy, or rocky soils—usually in crevices at higher elevations. The main photograph was taken at Emerald Lake and the small inset at Log Lake, both in the Trinity Alps.

BIG-LEAF SANDWORT
Moehringia macrophylla
Pink family
5 symmetrical petals - ovary superior

Even though this wildflower grows in profusion in certain areas you really need to get down in the dirt to appreciate it. The plants are typically only 1" to 1¼" tall. Leaves are 1" to 2" long, opposite, and lance shaped. The tiny flowers (¼" across) grow in groups of 2 to 5 in loose, terminal clusters. I shot these growing along the Stewart's Fork Trail near Little Deep Creek in mid-May.

FIELD MOUSE-EAR CHICKWEED
Cerastium arvense
Pink family

BALLHEAD SANDWORT
Eremogone congesta
Pink family

BIG-LEAF SANDWORT
Moehringia macrophylla
Pink family

DOUGLAS' STITCHWORT, DOUGLAS' SANDWORT
Sabulina douglasii
Pink family

5 symmetrical petals - ovary superior

The tiny white flowers are 1/4" in diameter and arranged in a loosely branched formation on thin, hair-like stalks. They are so light that photographing them presented a real challenge—just breathing set them off. The petals are striped lengthwise, gathering around a deep-green center, prominent yellowish ovary, and gently curved stamens. Leaves are almost non-existent. The plants I found were widely scattered and sometimes growing in close association with Nuttall's sandwort. Because of the scattered nature of the populations this is an easy one to pass by so pay close attention to the ground and watch your step! This was another find on the serpentines of Scott Mountain in late May.

NUTTALL'S SANDWORT
Sabulina nuttallii var. *gregaria*
Pink family

5 symmetrical petals - ovary superior

Look for this tiny wildflower on dry hillsides at higher elevations—mainly on the serpentine soils of the Red Trinities and the Trinity Divide. It forms loose mats ranging from 3" to 5" in height. The stems and awl shaped leaves are a rusty-olive green, hairy, and sticky-glandular. The tiny white flowers are five-petaled with five stamens and five sepals, growing in loose clusters. I photographed this bunch near the top of the pass between Deer and Summit Lakes in the Trinity Alps.

BOUNCING BET, SOAPWORT
Saponaria officinalis
Pink family

5 symmetrical petals ovary superior

This is a naturalized invasive found along the Trinity River where it intermingles with stands of willow at waters edge. It does well along roadsides and in oak woodlands where the ground has been disturbed. The plants I've photographed have been 24" to 36" tall, leggy, loosely branched, with loose clusters of white flowers that age to pink. The flower petals are slightly reflexed, narrow at the center, flaring outward, and terminating in both rounded and notched tips. It's hard to miss this one if you spend any time at all on the Trinity River. I photographed these at waters edge near Junction City in August.

DOUGLAS'STITCHWORT
DOUGLAS' SANDWORT
Sabulina douglasii
Pink family

NUTTALL'S SANDWORT
Sabulina nuttallii var. *gregaria*
Pink family

BOUNCING BET, SOAPWORT
Saponaria officinalis
Pink family

BELL CATCHFLY
Silene campanulata
Pink family

5 symmetrical petals - ovary superior

This wildflower is common throughout the Trinities at lower elevations. It likes shaded forest openings where they often grow in large groups. Stems are erect with nodding flowers. Leaves are lance shaped. The flowers are white to greenish and have five petals, each of which is deeply divided into four to eight linear segments. The reflexed petals sit deep into the bell shaped calyx, which gives rise to its common name. I have photographed this along the lower sections of the Canyon Creek, the North Fork of the Trinity River Trails and around Trinity Lake.

DOUGLAS' CATCHFLY, DOUGLAS' CAMPION, MOUNTAIN CAMPION
Silene douglasii var. *douglasii*
Pink family

5 symmetrical petals - ovary superior

This pretty little catchfly blooms in large troops in open, rocky, meadows at mid to high elevations. Look for the green and deep purple striped "bell" with deeply two-lobed, white petals folding back from the opening. Plants are typically 12" to 14" tall. It is fond of steep and almost inaccessible ridgetops like the one where I shot this photograph above Big Blue Lake in the Russians in September.

LEMMON'S CATCHFLY
Silene lemmonii
Pink family

5 symmetrical petals - ovary superior

The alternating light and dark green striped bell is very pronounced and pinches sharply down to where the very thin, curly white to delicate lilac four-lobed petals flare outward. I found this little catchfly blooming on the open, rocky slopes above Lower Caribou Lake in the Trinity Alps in late August, but it is fairly common at mid to high elevations throughout the area covered by this book. The photograph was taken alongside the outlet to Middle Caribou Lake in early September.

BELL CATCHFLY
Silene campanulata
Pink family

DOUGLAS' CATCHFLY
Silene douglasii var. *douglasii*
Pink family

LEMMON'S CATCHFLY
Silene lemmonii
Pink family

STRINGFLOWER, INDIAN CARTWHEELS
Silene nelsonii, sp. nov. ined.   5 symmetrical petals - ovary superior
Pink family

This is a most gorgeous showy and large wildflower that grows to 3" in diameter. Its five snow-white petals are cleft into four long narrow lobes, the central two being wider and longer than the outer two. The entire plant grows to about 5" in height. Leaves are small, grayish-green, basal, and covered with fine hairs. Alice Jones reported finding it in Norwegian Meadows (private property) near Trinity Center. Julie Nelson indicates that she has seen it at Burnt Ranch, on Underwood Mountain and on the Yolla Bolla Ranger District Compound. I photographed these at Natural Bridge near Hayfork.

GOAT'S BEARD, BRIDE'S FEATHERS, SPAGHETTI FLOWER
Aruncus dioicus var. *acuminatus*   5 symmetrical petals - ovary superior
Rose family

This tall plant with gorgeous, feathery tufts of flowers frequents shaded, wet sites at mid-elevations. I've stood with 6' tall plants, so this one gets tall. Leaf margins are toothed and the leaflets lance shaped. The flowers are white to cream, numerous, minute, blooming on long stalks giving it the appearance of feathers. My preferred common name is bride's feathers. This species is common in wet areas from 1,000' to 6,000'. I photographed this one along Trinity Mountain Road on the Trinity Divide in mid-June.

WOOD STRAWBERRY
Fragaria vesca (*Wald-Erdbeere* in Swiss-German)   5 symmetrical petals - ovary superior
Rose family

If you can find the tasty fruits on this plant consider yourself lucky, because critters usually beat us to them. You might confuse this one with the mountain strawberry but there are definite differences. For one, the leaves on the wood strawberry are deeply dissected, deeply veined, and not hairy on the edges. The terminal tooth of the central leaflet is equal to the teeth on either side of it. Petals of the wood strawberry usually overlap and the sepals are narrower than in mountain strawberry. I photographed the flowers along the Swift Creek Trail in the Trinity Alps. The berry I photographed along the trail to Chrindi Station below the Stockhorn in Switzerland. I know this is supposed to be a local wildflower guide, however, even though they don't speak the same language, they are identical and my tastebuds couldn't tell the difference. Eaten with a bar of Swiss chocolate I'd say they taste even better in Switzerland!

MOUNTAIN STRAWBERRY
Fragaria virginiana   5 symmetrical petals - ovary superior
Rose family

The leaves of this strawberry are blue-green, hairless on the upper surface, but hairy along the toothed edges. Typical of all strawberries, the leaves are divided into three leaflets. In this species, the terminal tooth of the central leaflet is much smaller than the two teeth on either side of it. Leaf veins are present but not prominent. The white flowers nestle into the leaves and the petals are almost round. It grows in meadows and open woods along stream banks. The small berries are delicious—if you can beat the birds, chipmunks, and mice to them! This photograph was taken along the Union Creek Trail in late May.

STRINGFLOWER, INDIAN CARTWHEELS
Silene nelsonii, sp. nov. ined.
Pink family

GOAT'S BEARD, BRIDE'S FEATHERS,
Aruncus dioicus var. *acuminatus*
Rose family

WOOD STRAWBERRY
Fragaria vesca
Rose family

MOUNTAIN STRAWBERRY
Fragaria virginiana
Rose family

CARROT-LEAVED HORKELIA
Horkelia daucifolia   5 symmetrical petals - ovary superior
Rose family

Horkelia daucifolia closely resembles its cousin, threetooth horkelia. It blooms in large colonies in open, sunny sites and prefers serpentine soils. The flowering stalks, which can stand upright or lie flat on the ground, are a bright maroon-red and hairy. The 11-21 narrowly oval leaflets are so hairy that they appear silvery. Flowers bloom in compact clusters, but unlike *H. tridentata*, the snow-white petals of *H. daucifolia* emerge narrowly from the center, flare into a spatulate shape, and are notched at the tips. I photographed this one on Scott Mountain in July.

THREETOOTH HORKELIA
Horkelia tridentata   5 symmetrical petals - ovary superior
Rose family

This gregarious little wildflower sprawls across the ground. While some of the flowering stalks stand upright, most hug the ground. Hairy red stems hold deep-green leaves with 5-11 oval leaflets which are hairy and sharply notched at the tips. The flowers are small, about ½" to ½" across with five widely spaced, narrowly oval petals that surround and flare away from a central ring of stout stamens. They are common everywhere in open sunny places but I've found them to be especially abundant on serpentine soils. I photographed these along the Stoney Ridge Trail in May.

PICKERING'S IVESIA, SILKY MOUSETAILS
Ivesia pickeringii   5 symmetrical petals - ovary superior
Rose family

The common name silky mousetails is quite fitting for this species because the leaves are soft and flexible to the touch. The conspicuous, narrowly tapered leaves grow in compact, erect bunches 8" to 10" long. The flowers are inconspicuous and borne in loose clusters at the tops of 10" to 15", thin, reddish stems and are about ½" in diameter. The white or pink tinged petals are narrow at the base then curve away becoming almost round with slightly wavy tips and surround 20 large, soft yellow stamens. The sepals are deep maroon tinged. The entire plant—including leaves, stalks and sepals—is covered with fuzzy white to gray hairs. This is an uncommon wildflower endemic to the Klamath Mountains and serpentine soils in particular. It favors sunny, dry mountain meadows where I've found it blooming alongside skullcaps and carrot-leaved horkelia. I photographed these on Scott Mountain in late June.

PARTRIDGE FOOT
Luetkea pectinata   5 symmetrical petals - ovary superior
Rose family

This beautiful little wildflower is particularly fond of rocky cliff faces and scree slopes at high elevations where it forms dense, verdant green mats that hug and encircle the rocks. Its fan shaped, deeply dissected leaves are crowded at the base of the plant. The white, alternate flowers occur on 8" to 10" flowering stalks that are nearly leafless. In the fall, the flowering stalks, seeds still attached, turn a beautiful rusty brown, which is quite beautiful in contrast with the deep green of the leaves and the surrounding rocks. I photographed this one above Log Lake in the Trinity Alps.

CARROT-LEAVED HORKELIA
Horkelia daucifolia
Rose family

THREETOOTH HORKELIA
Horkelia tridentata
Rose family

PICKERING'S IVESIA, SILKY MOUSETAILS
Ivesia pickeringii
Rose family

PARTRIDGE FOOT
Luetkea pectinata
Rose family

63

ELEPHANT EARS, INDIAN-RHUBARB, UMBRELLA PLANT
Darmera peltata   5 symmetrical petals - ovary superior
Saxifrage family

Along every river and the smallest tributary streams you will find elephant ears. They are beautiful and graceful plants that decorate and shade stream banks throughout the area covered by this book. The leaves are large, often more than 24" across, nodding at the end of a long stem, and bright green. They have their feet in the water and the thick rootstocks climb over and around submerged rocks. The first indications of their presence in the spring are the naked flowering stalks that push their way up and out of the water in dense flat sprays of small white flowers, each of which has a central cluster of pink pistils. At flowering time, the leaves are just beginning to emerge from the water.

BROOK SAXIFRAGE
Micranthes odontoloma   5 symmetrical petals - ovary superior
Saxifrage family

This is a relatively common saxifrage found alongside streams, the shorelines of lakes, and wet-meadows at higher elevations throughout the area. It is easily recognized by its evenly toothed and rounded leaves that can be up to 3" across. The tiny flowers are loosely clustered near the top of a tall stalk and each petal has two tiny greenish-yellow dots near the base. I photographed these in the meadow below Mirror Lake in the Trinity Alps.

COW PARSNIP, GIANT HOGWEED
Heracleum maximum   5 symmetrical petals - ovary inferior
Carrot family

The most noticeable thing about cow parsnip is its size—I've seen plants over 7' tall. It towers over all the other herbaceous plants while hanging over trails and dusting passers-by with loose petals and pollen all summer long. In my opinion, broken stems emit a surprisingly pleasant odor. Look for them in any mid-to-high elevation meadow and alongside trails where you will, no doubt, do battle with it while carrying a heavy pack. I've photographed this from the coast to the upper elevations including Siligo Meadows in the Trinity Alps. This photograph was taken along the East Fork of Stewart's Fork Trail below Bee Tree Gap.

WHIPPLEVINE, YERBA DE SELVA
Whipplea modesta   5 symmetrical petals - ovary inferior
Hydrangea family

This trailing vine-like wildflower blooms at the ends of decumbent stems with brownish bark that peels away in small, narrow strips. Four to six white flowers form a dense raceme, with four to six petals, and prominent stamens. Preferring lower elevations, it grows in large, spreading populations which are not particular about habitat. I have having found this species in chaparral, open forest, and along stream banks. I photographed this in Prairie Creek State Park on the coast in late April but it can also be found along Swift Creek in the Trinity Alps, near Whiskeytown Lake in the Whiskeytown N.R.A., and near Sawyer's Bar in Siskiyou County. It appears to be widespread throughout the coast range.

ELEPHANT EARS, INDIAN-RHUBARB
Darmera peltata
Rose family

BROOK SAXIFRAGE
Micranthes odontoloma
Saxifrage family

COW PARSNIP, GIANT HOGWEED
Heracleum maximum
Carrot family

WHIPPLEVINE, YERBA DE SELVA
Whipplea modesta
Hydrangea family

GRAY'S LOVAGE
Ligusticum grayi   5 symmetrical petals - ovary inferior
Carrot family

This common wildflower grows in the low to mid elevations where it prefers drier, open meadows and slopes. Tall, leafless stems rise out of a large basal clump of deep green, feathery leaves. The inflorescence is called an umbel, in which smaller branches radiate from the same point at the top of the main stem. Each umbel branch is topped with another umbel—terminating in tiny, elegant snow-white flowers. Small but prominent stamens radiate from the center of each flower. I photographed these along the Boulder Creek Trail in August.

BIGSEED BISCUITROOT, LARGE-FRUITED LOMATIUM
Lomatium macrocarpum   5 symmetrical petals - ovary inferior
Carrot family

When I've encountered this wildflower it has almost always been at higher elevations on rocky ridgetops and open slopes. The leaves are a gray-green and finely dissected. Chipmunks are especially attracted to the flower heads in late summer—much as they are to the dry flower heads of various buckwheats—harvesting the seeds and storing them away for the long winter ahead. I photographed this example on the ridge between Foster and Lion Lakes in the Trinity Alps. In this shot the flowers have yet to open but when they do they are a soft, purplish white and gathered in dense compound umbels at the tops of short stems.

Note: Tracy's lomatium (*Lomatium tracyi*) also occurs in this area but has flowers that are deep reddish-purple

SWEET-CICELY
Osmorhiza species   5 symmetrical petals - ovary inferior
Carrot family

This is a mid-elevation wildflower of deeply shaded, damp sites. The long-stalked, deep-green leaves are mostly basal, heart shaped, and deeply divided with toothed margins. Flowers are small, white, and bloom in a loose cluster at the tops of long stems. Plants are tall—up to 2' and sometimes more. I photographed these along Stewart's Fork Trail above Morris Meadows in mid-June.

RANGER'S BUTTONS, SWAMP WHITEHEADS, WOOLY-HEADED PARSNIP
Sphenosciadium capitellatum   5 symmetrical petals - ovary inferior
Carrot family

This gorgeous wildflower prefers wet places such as the shorelines of lakes, streams, or marshy meadows. It grows to 5' or more on stout, branched stems. The leaves are oblong, 4" to 15", and divided three or four times. Lance-shaped leaflets are irregularly toothed or lobed and ½" to 5" long. The distinctive white flowers, aging to light brown, grow in large clusters of tight, round heads at the tops of the stems. I photographed these in a wet meadow below Mt. Ashland. I retired from the Forest Service after 35 years and have to admit—my spiffiest uniforms never had buttons like these!

GRAY'S LOVAGE
Ligusticum grayi
Carrot family

BIGSEED BISCUITROOT
Lomatium macrocarpum
Carrot family

SWEET-CICELY
Osmorhiza species
Carrot family

RANGER'S BUTTONS, SWAMP WHITEHEADS
Sphenosciadium capitellatum
Carrot family

67

ELK CLOVER
Aralia californica
Ginseng family

5 symmetrical petals - ovary inferior

While not a true clover, elk clover is found throughout the lower elevations of the Klamath Mountains where it is the only member of the ginseng family native to California. Plants grow 4'-8' tall on thick, non-woody, stems. Pinnately compound, leaves can be up to 6' long with leaflets to 1'. Striking greenish-white flowers decorate the end of the leaf stalks with white globes from June-August and produce dark purple or black fruit in the fall. Elk clover is associated with damp, shaded sites alongside streams, near seeps, springs, and shorelines. I photographed the flowers along Canyon Creek in mid-July, and the fruit at the Stewart's Fork Trailhead in early November.

MOUNTAIN BOYKINIA
Boykinia major
Saxifrage family

5 symmetrical petals - ovary inferior

Boykina prefers streambanks, springs, and other damp, shaded areas. Some people mistakenly call it elephant ears because of slight similarities in leaf structure. Elephant ears are much larger, however. Overall height of the plants can range from 2' to 3', with deeply cleft and toothed leaves ranging from 4" to 8" across. The small white flowers grow in dense clusters with petals about ¼" long. Bright yellow nectar glands in the centers of the flowers attract a variety of insects. In the fall *Boykinia* leaves often turn a gorgeous red and orange as illustrated in the small inset. I photographed this one at a spring along the trail to Stonewall Pass in the Trinity Alps in May.

CREVICE ALUMROOT, SMALL-FLOWERED ALUMROOT
Heuchera micrantha
Saxifrage family

5 symmetrical petals - ovary inferior

This is a beautiful, graceful plant that loves moisture and shade. It is most often found growing in rocky outcrops in the proximity of streams or deep, shaded canyons. It is a gregarious plant, often occurring in large colonies. Look for it on rocky outcrops along the Stewart's Fork Trail at lower elevations. I photographed this bunch at the Little Deep Creek crossing along Stewart's Fork Trail in May.

SIERRA SAXIFRAGE
Micranthes aprica
Saxifrage family

5 symmetrical petals - ovary inferior

The first things you notice about this small saxifrage are the bright white flowers, deep orange anthers, and the bright green pistils and ovaries. The entire flowering cluster are 1"-2" wide and the stems about 4" - 5" tall. It favors rocky and wet alpine meadows next to receding snowbanks or meltwater streams. I photographed these in a small meadow below Kangaroo Lake and the inset in Union Meadows in the Trinity Alps in early June.

ELK CLOVER
Aralia californica
Ginseng family

MOUNTAIN BOYKINIA
Boykinia major
Saxifrage family

CREVICE ALUMROOT, SMALL-FLOWERED ALUMROOT
Heuchera micrantha
Saxifrage family

SIERRA SAXIFRAGE
Micranthes aprica
Saxifrage family

BRITTLE-LEAVED SAXIFRAGE, FLESHY-LEAVED SAXIFRAGE

Micranthes fragosa
Saxifrage family

5 symmetrical petals - ovary inferior

This is a saxifrage that likes open, damp, grassy meadows. It grows to 7" tall with slightly hairy stems that are loosely branched with flowering clusters at the tops of each. The white petals flare away from the center of the flower and several stamens topped with buttery yellow anthers surround the central pistil. I photographed these in the meadow just below Doe Lake in mid-August.

OREGON SAXIFRAGE, EARLY SAXIFRAGE

Micranthes oregana
Saxifrage family

5 symmetrical petals - ovary inferior

This saxifrage has a basal rosette of egg-shaped leaves toothed along the margins. The tall (to 14"), erect, branched stems have a cluster of small white flowers crowded near the tops. Flower petals are round to egg-shaped and white. The anthers are orange to purplish. It favors wet meadows and the shaded edges of lakes and streams. I photographed these around a spring just above the shoreline of Sugar Pine Lake in September.

THREE-PARTED MITERWORT, THREE TOOTHED MITERWORT, THREE-CORNERED BISHOP'S CAP

Ozomelis trifida
Saxifrage family

5 symmetrical petals - ovary inferior

I found this beautiful saxifrage blooming along the lower reaches of Stewart's Fork Trail in late May. I can't tell you how many times I've walked that trail but in the course of 54+ years this was the first time I had ever seen it—though I may have noticed the leaves and thought they were those of crevice alum root or Mertens' saxifrage. All this proves my assertion that, with careful observation, new discoveries can always be made. The tiny, beautiful, snow white (sometimes purple) flowers are striking. Flowering stalks are over 12" tall, rising out of widely oval, shallow, palmately lobed leaves. The flowers bloom along the stem and are cup shaped with deep, 3-cleft petals flaring outward. They prefer moist, shaded places.

JOINT-LEAVED SAXIFRAGE

Saxifragopsis fragarioides
Saxifrage family

5 symmetrical petals - ovary inferior

The flowers of this gorgeous saxifrage are multi-colored, with white petals and stamens accented with bright yellow and red ovaries. They bloom on upright stalks (some approaching 6") above a bunch of deeply toothed, oval and dark green leaves. This photograph was taken on the rocky clefts and shelves below Upper Albert Lake in the Russians.

BRITTLE-LEAVED SAXIFRAGE
Micranthes fragosa
Saxifrage family

OREGON SAXIFRAGE, EARLY SAXIFRAGE
Micranthes oregana
Saxifrage family

THREE-PARTED MITERWORT
Ozomelis trifida
Saxifrage family

JOINT-LEAVED SAXIFRAGE
Saxifragopsis fragarioides
Saxifrage family

COILED-BEAK LOUSEWORT
Pedicularis contorta   5 irregular petals forming a tube
Broomrape family

This odd little wildflower is fairly common and readily identifiable because of the small, drooping white flowers with pale yellow accents behind deep maroon spots. Flowers resemble little louse critters, hence the name. Basal and lower stem leaves are 2" to 8" long and highly divided into linear segments. Flowers occur along a tall 10" to 12" spike. The upper lip curves sharply downward to meet the three lower lobes. I've found it in the drier meadows surrounding Carter's Little Mud Lake and Caribou Lake in the Trinity Alps, below the outlet of Big Blue in the Russian Wilderness, and around Wolverine and Upper Wright Lakes in the Marbles. I photographed this one in mid-August in the meadows at the back of Upper Caribou Lake.

TRINITY MONKEYFLOWER
Erythranthe trinitiensis   5 irregular petals forming a tube
Lopseed family

This small and showy monkeyflower was described in 2013 and, except for this guide, won't be found in any of the current botanical manuals as of 2017. I'll wager odds that even seasoned botanists have been walking over this one for years. It is diminutive with most plants less than 2" tall and the flowers are pea-sized. It is endemic to the regional serpentine soils where it likes wet meadows and open ground beneath a canopy of mixed conifers. The floral tube is a deep buttery-yellow, becoming white as the petals open, and limned with rose red at the petal tips. It is indeed, striking. I found a particularly nice population interspersed with Siskiyou phacelia in a high elevation area on the west side of the Trinity Divide in late June.

CALIFORNIA SKULLCAP
Scutellaria californica   5 irregular petals forming a tube
Mint family

I found and photographed this beautiful skullcap along the trail to Canyon Creek Lakes in late June. It was blooming in the pockets of an exposed granite outcrop where I've photographed several other wildflowers through the years. This was my first sighting of this particular skullcap and I can't tell you how many times I've been up this trail. *The Jepson Manual* indicates that the flowers are mainly white to light yellow, sometimes tinged with pink or blue and that it sometimes hybridizes with the blue species *Scutellaria antirrhinoides*. This was very interesting to me because it was in this same area that I found a healthy population of *S. antirrhinoides* as well as the hybrid *S. californica* X *antirrhinoides* illustrated in the small photograph.

HOT ROCK PENSTEMON
Penstemon deustus   5 irregular petals forming a tube
Plantain family

As its name implies, this species likes dry, open, rocky outcrops and hillsides. The flowers bloom in multiple whorls along a stem that are 10" to 20" tall. The petals are shallowly recurved and white (sometimes tinted with faded magenta) and streaked with deep purple. The buttery yellow flower tubes are small and about ½" long. I have found it at lower elevations along the Trinity River near Reading Creek and at the tops of ridges in mid-summer and early fall throughout the Trinity Alps and Russian Wilderness areas. The yellowish-green leaves are opposite and raggedly toothed. I photographed these near Middle Falls along Canyon Creek in mid-May.

COILED-BEAK LOUSEWORT
Pedicularis contorta
Broomrape family

TRINITY MONKEYFLOWER
Erythranthe trinitiensis
Lopseed family

californica X antirrhoides

CALIFORNIA SKULLCAP
Scutellaria californica
Mint family

HOT ROCK PENSTEMON
Penstemon deustus
Plantain family

TRINITY PENSTEMON, TRACY'S BEARDTONGUE
Penstemon tracyi　　　　　　　　　　5 symmetrical petals forming a tube
Plantain family

This beautiful *Penstemon* is a rare Klamath Mountain endemic confined to meta-morphic rock crevices and cliff faces in the Trinity Alps. The white to pink flowers form elongated tubes arranged in drooping clusters and are hairy on the lower lip. Stems are woody. The leaves are mostly basal, oval to rounded, thick, and leathery. Smaller leaves are arranged in opposite pairs up the flowering stalk. It took two years and several trips up Packer's Peak to find them in bloom but I finally lucked out in the rocky outcrops halfway up the trail from Big Flat. Though difficult to get to, it was worth the effort. I photographed these in early June.

BEAUTIFUL STICKSEED
Hackelia bella　　　　　　　　　　5 symmetrical petals forming a tube

This is, perhaps, the showiest of the stickseeds blooming in this area and one that few hikers could possibly miss. It is widespread throughout the mid-elevations in these mountains and tends to grow in large colonies at the edges of meadows where soils are relatively dry. The plants are loosely branched, often reaching heights of 2' or more, with open clusters of snow-white flowers. I photographed these in Union Meadows along the trail to Foster Lake in late May.

DWARF HESPEROCHIRON
Hesperochiron pumilus　　　　　　5 symmetrical petals joined into a tube
Borage family

After a few of years of searching, I finally found this tiny *Hesperochirion* in full bloom. Documented observations put the bloom time in mid-June but that never worked for me. Recently I started my search beginning in May and was rewarded by finding a small population—right place at the right time! The beautiful little flowers dotted a wet, grassy meadow near where Alice Jones and Bill Ferlatte recorded their finds in the 1950s and 60s. As my friend Max Creasy likes to say—these are "belly flowers." To fully appreciate them you need to get down in the dirt for a close-up look. They are thumbnail size, with a corolla that is disc to slightly cupped in shape standing on a short stalk about 1½" tall above a rosette of oval to lance shaped leaves. The petals are bright white with deep purple veins emanating from an orange-yellow center arrayed with prominent yellow stamens and dark purple anthers. The center of the flower is hairy. I photographed these in Big Flat in early May.

POPCORN FLOWER, CRYPTANTHA
Plagiobothrys species and *Cryptantha* species　　5 symmetrical petals forming a tube
Borage family

This is one group of wildflowers that can cause even seasoned botanists unending heartburn. There are over 100 species in California alone. I've chosen to simplify matters for those of us who suffer heartburn for a variety of other reasons and lump these little beauties together. If, upon close inspection, they resemble the photo-graphs shown on the opposite page you can be relatively certain that you have, what we commonly refer to as, "popcorn flowers." Generally speaking the flowers of *Plagiobothrys* and *Cryptantha* bloom in dense clusters, are small, snowy-white with somewhat ruffled edges. *Cryptanthas* are bristly-hairy while *Plagiobothrys* are soft hairy. As a general rule, *Cryptantha* prefers dry, exposed flats, and grassy hillsides while *Plagiobothrys* prefers damp to wet meadows, vernal pools and stream banks.

TRINITY PENSTEMON, TRACY'S BEARDTONGUE
Penstemon tracyi
Plantain family

BEAUTIFUL STICKSEED
Hackelia bella
Borage family

Cryptantha spp

Plagiobothrys spp

DWARF HESPEROCHIRION
Hesperochirion pumilus
Borage family

CRYPTANTHA and POPCORN FLOWER
Plagiobothrys species and *Cryptantha* species
Borage family

WESTERN MORNING GLORY
Calystegia occidentalis   5 symmetrical petals forming a tube
Morning glory family

The whole aspect of this plant is "stiff" to the touch. The light olive-green leaves, are more-or-less arrow shaped, small, and covered with a dense mat of stiff hairs. The stems, likewise, are stiff and so covered with those same stiff hairs that they appear whitish. Their growth habit is not luxuriant like other morning glorys. It is sparser in appearance and hugs the ground in a sprawling habit—preferring open, sunny and rocky locations. The flowers are typical of other morning glorys—about 2" across but sometimes a larger. I photographed this one along the trail to Marshy Lakes from Tangle Blue but it is quite common along Highway 3 growing on the cutbanks between the Bowerman Ridge intersection and Trinity Center. A similarly hairy, trailing native morning glory, *Calystegia malacophylla*, is also common in our area.

NUTTALL'S LINANTHUS
Leptosiphon nuttallii subsp. *nuttallii*   5 symmetrical petals forming a tube
Phlox family

The showy five-petaled flowers are a creamy white with deep yellow anthers. The leaflets are tough, deeply palmately divided, and spiny. The plants are 7" to 10" tall but grow in large mats. I found this attractive linanthus growing in large colonies all along the trail from Boulder Creek to Conway Lake and over the slopes surrounding Conway Lake. I shot these along Boulder Creek before starting the climb to Lion and Conway Lakes in August.

MOUNTAIN NAVARRETIA, NEEDLE-LEAVED NAVARRETIA
Navarretia divaricata   5 symmetrical petals forming a tube
Phlox family

This tiny *Navarretia* is 2" to 4" tall with needle-like leaves and tubular shaped flowers massed in a ball at the tops of the stems. The flowers range from white to pale blue. Petals fan outward exposing yellow anthers and long stamens. I photographed this in Big Flat in the Trinity Alps but have also seen it on Musser Hill near Weaverville.

WESTERN MORNING GLORY
Calystegia occidentalis
Morning glory family

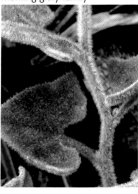

NUTTALL'S LINANTHUS
Leptosiphon nuttallii
  subsp. *nuttallii*
Phlox family

MOUNTAIN NAVARRETIA
Navarretia divaricata
Phlox family

CREAM STONECROP
Sedum oregonense   5 symmetrical petals forming a tube
Stonecrop family

Like several other species noted in this book, telling the difference between those that are closely related can be confusing. Cream stonecrop and the other similar white- to yellow-flowered *Sedum* are no exception. Cream stonecrop is a Klamath Mountain endemic which prefers rock outcrops from 3,000'-7,000'. Botanist Nick Otting confirmed that stonecrops found along the ridge above Little Duck Lake in the Russian Wilderness are, indeed, cream stonecrop. I photographed these in early June but the species flowers from June-August depending on elevation and exposure. .

MOUNTAIN HELIOTROPE, SITKA VALERIAN
Valeriana sitchensis   5 symmetrical petals forming a tube
Valerian family

Valerian sitchensis is distinguished by large clusters of snow white flowers tinged with light pink in the buds bloom atop 2' - 4' tall stems. Stamens and pistils are prominent. Prefered habitats include moist, shaded sites at the edges of meadows, near springs, and running water. Coarsely toothed leaves grow the length of the stout stems. I photographed this at the edge of the meadow at Lower Albert Lake in the Russian Wilderness in September.

DRAPERIA, WEIRD FLOWER
Draperia systyla   5 symmetrical petals forming a tube
Waterleaf family

Weird flower is a California endemic that grows from the Trinity Alps south through the Sierra Nevada. It is low-growing and has several stems about 5" long. Its hairy leaves are simple, opposite, and 1" to 2" long. The flowers range from white to pale violet, are funnel shaped, about ½" long, and clustered at the ends of short, branched stems. Preferred habitat includes woodlands, talus, and rock crevices from low- to mid-elevations. This photograph was taken along the Stewart's Fork Trail.

SCOTT MOUNTAIN PHACELIA
Howellanthus dalesianus   5 symmetrical petals forming a tube
Waterleaf family

This diminutive phacelia is a rare ground hugger that can be difficult to find. It is endemic to serpentine soils where it prefers disturbed areas alongside trails and roads. The flowers grow at the ends of short pedicels, are ¼" across, creamy white, with deep purple spots near the base of each petal. Inspect the flowers closely and you will see that the petals are united at their bases and form a broadly bowl-shaped tube. The deeply veined leaves vary from 1" to 2" in length, have smooth edges, and are hairy. I photographed these on Scott Mountain in a year when they were abundant, but most years it takes some looking to find them. A good place to see them is along the Fen Trail at Kangaroo Lake.

CREAM STONECROP
Sedum oregonense
Stonecrop family

MOUNTAIN HELIOTROPE, SITKA VALERIAN
Valeriana sitchensis
Valerian family

DRAPERIA, WEIRD FLOWER
Draperia systyla
Waterleaf family

SCOTT MOUNTAIN PHACELIA
Howellanthus dalesianus
Waterleaf family

WHITE WATERLEAF, FENDLER'S WATERLEAF
Hydrophyllum fendleri var. *albifrons*   5 symmetrical petals forming a tube
Waterleaf family

Fendler's waterleaf is a secretive plant—hiding in deep shade amongst other wet meadow plants. Finding it can be an accidental affair unless, of course, you are spending a lot of time on your hands and knees crawling through dense undergrowth. On the advice of Julie Knorr, I found a nice population growing along the trail to South Fork Lakes in mid-June. California waterleaf (page 276) is also in the area and could be confused with white waterleaf. The plants I found were 12" in height, with leaves 6" to 8", bright green, and deeply cleft. The snow-white flowers were blooming in a compact head—all but hidden beneath the canopy of leaves.

CANYON NEMOPHILA, WHITE NEMOPHILA
Nemophila heterophylla   5 symmetrical petals forming a tube
Waterleaf family

This little *Nemophila* (5" to 8" tall) favors deeply shaded canyons and ravines where it associates with an oak or mixed hardwood canopy. The delicate, white, five-petaled flowers, fuzzy oak shaped leaves, and habitat are diagnostic. The anthers are white with a tiny purple stripe running the length which extend well beyond the cup surrounding the ovary. I shot the large photograph on Bowerman Ridge and the small inset above French Gulch on the Trinity Divide both in June.

BABY BLUE EYES
Nemophila menziesii var. *atomaria*   5 symmetrical petals forming a tube
Waterleaf family

This is, by far, the largest and showiest of local *Nemophila*s. The plants are 4" to 6" in height, olive green, with hairy, opposite, pinnately lobed leaves. Flowers are 3/4" to 1" in diameter, snow white, faintly tinged with blue at the margins of the petals, with lines of small black dots extending from the tube to the tips. I found colonies blooming with cream cups and heron's bill on open, dry, rocky slopes along Canyon Creek Road in mid-April. The drive up Canyon Creek is beautiful at any time but doubly so with *Nemophila* in bloom.

WHITE WATERLEAF
FENDLER'S WATERLEAF
Hydrophyllum fendleri var. *albifrons*
Waterleaf family

CANYON NEMOPHILA,
WHITE NEMOPHILA
Nemophila heterophylla
Waterleaf family

BABY BLUE EYES
Nemophila menziesii var.
atomaria
Waterleaf family

MEADOW NEMOPHILA
Nemophila pedunculata
Waterleaf family

5 symmetrical petals forming a tube

Several varieties of nemophila bloom throughout the lower elevations of the area covered by this book. All of them seek out the same kind of habitat... shaded and moist forested or grassy areas. The flowers of this one are small, stark white with deep bluish-purple veins running the length of the petals. The leaves are deeply cleft and fuzzy. I photographed these along Deadwood Road near Lewiston in May.

SIERRA BABY BLUE EYES, SIERRA NEMOPHILA
Nemophila spatulata
Waterleaf family

5 symmetrical petals forming a tube

Except for the purple spots at the tips of each petal, this delicate nemophila closely resembles its cousin the meadow nemophila and their habitat requirements are very similar. Both like shaded and damp grassy areas. Both are low growing. The flowers are relatively short lived... disappearing quickly as daily temperatures build in the spring. It is common around the north end of the Sacramento Valley in the foothills between Redding and Shasta Lake but I've not encountered them anywhere else on the Trinity side of the Divide other than Hay Gulch. I photographed these in Hay Gulch on the east side of Trinity Lake in May.

VIRGATE PHACELIA
Phacelia heterophylla var. *virgata*
Waterleaf family

5 symmetrical petals forming a tube

This *Phacelia* stands mostly erect and the stems and leaves are a pale silver-green covered with stiff hairs, which in a certain light, makes the plant look even more silvery. Leaves are oblong, mostly basal with smaller ones up the stem, 1/2" to 5" long and deeply veined. Flowers are bell shaped with petals fused for 2/3 their length and grow in dense, tightly coiled clusters. Stamens extend well beyond the petals. It is common throughout this area in higher elevation forests, talus slopes and open rocky areas. I photographed these along the road to the Stoney Ridge Trailhead.

MEADOW NEMOPHILA
Nemophila pedunculata
Waterleaf family

**SIERRA BABY BLUE EYES,
SIERRA NEMOPHILA**
Nemophila spatulata
Waterleaf family

VIRGATE PHACELIA
Phacelia heterophylla
var. *virgata*
Waterleaf family

CATERPILLAR PLANT
Phacelia mutabilis
Borage family   5 symmetrical petals forming a tube

This *Phacelia* is common throughout sub-alpine areas of these mountains and loves the dry, sandy, disturbed soil along trails. As is typical of many *Phacelia* species the deeply veined, egg shaped, stiffly-haired leaves are diagnostic. The white flowers with long stamens occur in thick, coiled clusters that unfurl as the flower matures. I photographed on the trail above Doe Lake in the Trinity Alps.

CALIFORNIA MISTMAIDEN, CALIFORNIA ROMANZOFFIA
Romanzoffia californica
Borage family   5 symmetrical petals forming a tube

There are steep, wet cliff faces along Canyon Creek Road where blooms of California mistmaiden are so thick they look like elegant, white waterfalls cascading over the rocks. It's one of the best places in this area to see them. The tiny, delicate, funnel or bell shaped, white flowers bloom upright on loosely branched, slender stems. They are lightly veined with a deep yellow throat. The small, deep green leaves are basal, hug the ground, and are round but deeply cleft. The plants like running water or other wet, marshy places. I photographed these along Canyon Creek Road in mid-April.

CALIFORNIA HESPEROCHIRON
Hesperochiron californicus
Borage family   5 symmetrical petals joined into a bell

This is a wildflower of open, wet, boggy meadows. It blooms as the snow melts at mid to high elevations, often in large colonies. A single, bell-shaped, white to pink flower blooms on a 2" to 3" stalk rising from a basal rosette of six to eight leaves, 1" in diameter. The leaves are hairy and olive green. I photographed these on Scott Mountain in July but have also photographed them in Morris Meadows in late May. They occur commonly throughout the area.

CATERPILLAR PLANT
Phacelia mutabilis
Waterleaf family

CALIFORNIA MISTMAIDEN,
CALIFORNIA ROMANZOFFIA
Romanzoffia californica
Waterleaf family

CALIFORNIA HESPEROCHIRON
Hesperochiron californicus
Waterleaf family

WHITE PLECTRIS, WHITE SEABLUSH
Plectris macrocera   5 petals joined into a bell
Valerian family

This little member of the Valerian family grows straight as a post and, in the populations I've found, around 4" to 14" tall. The opposite leaves are somewhat elliptical with short petioles, and are widely spaced along the stems. The beautiful little tubular shaped flowers flare away at the tips, are mostly white and tinged with light pink. As in the other valerians, stamens are prominent. The colonies I've found seem to prefer open, sunny sites and are common along certain stretches of the road to the Canyon Creek Trailhead in the Trinity Alps. I photographed these in early April.

SHORT SPURRED PLECTRIS
Plectritis congesta subsp. *brachystemon*   5 petals joined into a bell
Valerian family

There is not much that differentiates *Plectris congesta* from *P. macrocera* but on your hands and knees with a magnifying glass differences can be found. Upon close inspection, a tiny spur can be seen extending outward below the lower lip of the lower petal, just outside the corolla tube. The corolla tube itself is behind the spur and descends down into the calyx. Other than the spur the two are the same with respect to flower color, the structure of the leaves, and stems height. I found and photographed these in a meadow above Lewiston Lake in mid-May.

WESTERN YARROW
Achillea millefolium   Flowers in composite heads
Sunflower family

This is a common wildflower of open, damp to dry meadows and slopes. It can be found in bloom from May into late October. The fern-like leaves are pleasantly aromatic, pinnately divided, hairy, and becoming smaller as they ascend the flowering stalks. The ray flowers are white and surround a small group of tiny yellow disc flowers in a flat-topped cluster. I photographed these along the Paynes Lake Trail in the Russians in mid-August.

PEARLY EVERLASTING
Anaphalis margaritacea   Flowers in composite heads
Sunflower family

Pearly everlasting comes by its name honestly. It blooms early and the flowers persist well into the fall season—often the last bloom you will see before snow arrives. I have no doubt that beneath the first snows of winter, you could still find flowers looking as fresh as if they bloomed in early July. The white involucral bracts of the heads remain pristine for a long time. Plants are fairly tall but loosely branched and the weight of the flowering heads often bends the stalks to the ground. I photographed these along the Canyon Creek Trail near the Sinks in late September, but you will find it along backcountry trails from the coast to the mountains.

WHITE PLECTRIS, WHITE SEABLUSH
Plectris macrocera
Valerian family

SHORT SPURRED PLECTRIS
Plectritis congesta subsp. *brachystemon*
Valerian family

WESTERN YARROW
Achillea millefolium
Sunflower family

PEARLY EVERLASTING
Anaphalis margaritacea
Sunflower family

ALPINE PUSSYTOES
Antennaria media
Sunflower family   Flowers in composite heads

This little pussytoe is easily recognized—even without a bloom—by its small, low growing rosettes of fuzzy, pale gray-green leaves. It likes open rocky areas in the high country where often there is nothing else growing in the vicinity. The fuzzy flowers bloom atop a 6" stalk and indeed look like cat's toes. I photographed these in the rocks above Big Blue Lake in the Russian Wilderness in September.

SAWYER'S PUSSYTOES
Antennaria sawyeri
Sunflower family   Flowers in composite heads

As if there weren't enough cats in the high country here's one more—a brand new one! I found Pete Figura, a biologist with the California Department of Fish and Wildlife, crawling around in the dirt near Stonewall Pass studying this little pussytoe and in 2014 he described *Antennaria sawyeri* as a "new" species. The plants are mat forming, 7" tall, with gray-green leaves, and stems covered with fine whitish fuzz. Lance to egg shaped leaves alternate along the entire length of the flowering stalk. Individual plants are either male or female. In this photograph, the flowers are beginning to turn brown with age but early in development they are creamy white. This photograph was taken near Stonewall Pass in early August.

GREENE'S BRICKELLBUSH
Brickellia greenei
Sunflower family   Flowers in composite heads

You will probably smell this wildflower long before you ever see the blooms. To me the odor is distinct, sharp, and somewhat obnoxious. It is fairly common at lower elevations in the Trinity Alps growing in large colonies in rocky, open sites where it favors serpentine soils. The 6" to 24" stems are covered with sticky hairs and topped with creamy to yellow-white rayless flowers. The photograph was taken along the lower reaches of the Bear Creek Trail in the Trinity Alps in August.

FREMONT'S CALYCADENIA, FREMONT'S WESTERN ROSINWEED, KLAMATH CALYCADENIA
Calycadenia fremontii
Sunflower family   Flowers in composite heads

This wildflower can be found blooming at lower elevations throughout the summer and fall, often retaining its blooms well into November. I've found it to be widespread in open and sometimes disturbed areas along roads throughout Trinity County. The plant can reach to 40" but 12" to 16" is more the norm. The stems are brown, strongly erect, with alternate, linear leaves which are bunched along the stems. The leaves and stems are hairy. The slightly reflexed ray flowers are generally white (sometimes aging to pink) but can also be cream or yellow. The leaves are sticky and smell slightly of varnish. I photographed these along the Rush Creek Road near Lewiston in September but trails above Shasta Lake are another good place to spot it.

ALPINE PUSSYTOES
Antennaria media
Sunflower family

SAWYER'S PUSSYTOES
Antennaria sawyeri
Sunflower family

GREENE'S BRICKELLBUSH
Brickellia greenei
Sunflower family

FREMONT'S CALYCADENIA
Calycadenia fremontii
Sunflower family

DUSTY MAIDENS, HOARY PINCUSHION, HOARY FALSE YARROW
Chaenactis douglasii   flowers in composite heads
Sunflower family

This little *Chaenactis*, but for flower color and leaf structure, resembles its relative Shasta pincushion (*C. suffrutescens*) but *Chaenactis douglasii* is an herb and *C. suffrutescens* is a woody subshrub. It grows in low, spreading mats with small, compact leaves that are fleshy and dark green. The greenish-red flowering stems are erect, tall (around 7" or so), and leggy. The compact heads of deep magenta flowers gradually turn snow white as they fully open. Individual flowers have 5 recurved, sharply pointed petals surrounding a group of prominent stamens. The population I found and photographed in mid-June was blooming in a disturbed area along the east side of the Parks Creek Road—near the summit with the Pacific Crest Trail.

SHASTA PINCUSHION, SHASTA CHAENACTIS
Chaenactis suffrutescens   Flowers in composite heads
Sunflower family

In *Selected Rare Plants of Northern California*, Julie Nelson and Gary Nakamura list Shasta pincushion as a rare Klamath Mountain endemic. The deeply cleft, fern-like leaves are silvery green, somewhat fuzzy, and sticky to the touch—as are the flowering stalks and flower heads. The small, ½" to ¾" in diameter, cream-colored flowers are discoid (without ray flowers) and thus lacking obvious petals on the flowers head. Each solitary flower sits on a 3" to 6" stalk above the leafy mound. It favors serpentine soils where, though regionally rare, can be locally abundant on rocky, steep, exposed serpentine road-cuts. I photographed these at the North end of Trinity Lake along Trinity Mountain Road in late May.

PEREGRINE THISTLE
Cirsium cymosum   Flowers in composite heads
Sunflower family

Peregrine thistle grows to 5' in height, has slender stems, with white-hairy leaves that clasp the stalks. What really gives it away are the loose bunches of creamy white flower heads. It prefers moist environments at mid to high elevations, often on serpentine or other rocky areas. I took this photograph alongside the road to Kangaroo Lake on the Trinity Divide in July.

OX-EYE DAISY
Leucanthemum vulgare   Flowers in composite heads
Sunflower family

This naturalized European immigrant is a common road-side flower throughout Northern California—from the foothills of the Central Valley to the Coast. I've not found it inside the Trinity Alps, Russian or Marble Mountain Wilderness areas but I do see it along the roads to the trailheads. The large white ray flowers, bright orange-yellow "eye" of disc flowers in the center, and its unpleasantly pungent odor make it readily identifiable. Stems can be up to 2' tall. Leaves are toothed and wider at the tip with lower leaves tapered to a long petiole. Leaves on the stem are mostly sessile. Look for it along Highway 3 in the Trinities and the road to the Duck Lakes Trailhead on the east side of the Russians.

DUSTY MAIDENS, HOARY PINCUSHION
Chaenactis douglasii
Sunflower family

SHASTA PINCUSHION, SHASTA CHAENACTIS
Chaenactis suffrutescens
Sunflower family

PEREGRINE THISTLE
Cirsium cymosum
Sunflower family

OX-EYE DAISY
Leucanthemum vulgare
Sunflower family

91

LITTLE-LEAF SILVERBACK LUINA, LITTLE-LEAF LUINA
Luina hypoleuca   Flowers in composite heads
Sunflower family

In mid-May, as I was driving along Trinity Mountain Road/East Shore Drive (one becomes the other at the East Fork of the Trinity River) I spotted this attractive plant growing in a steep, rocky crevice on a road cut. At that time the leaves were fully formed into a beautiful silvery green mound about 30" across but the flowers were just tiny white buds. On several subsequent trips watched attentively in order to catch it in full bloom. Exactly one month later, in mid-June, I was rewarded with fully developed flowers. The leaves are egg shaped, green above, densely white-woolly below, mostly entire or slightly toothed, and alternate along erect stems. Clusters of disc flowers emerge at the ends of the stems and are creamy white with deep, buttery yellow to orange anthers. The thing that sticks out of each disc flower is a tube made of the 5 anthers fused together, and at the end of the tube the 2-branched style emerges. There are no ray flowers.

WESTERN SWEET COLTSFOOT
Petasites frigidus var. *palmatus*   Flowers in composite heads
Sunflower family

Coltsfoot is fairly common throughout this region at lower to mid-elevations. It likes its feet in running, fresh water and finds shade beneficial. In the spring, usually in early April, thick flower stalks emerge and grow to 24" or more. The large, palmately lobed leaves emerge after the stalks but before the large heads of white to lavender flowers begin to open. As with most wildflowers, the closer you get to these the more beautiful they appear. The Julies insist that the vanilla fragrance of the flowers isn't bad either! The individual tubular flowers have five petals that flare away at the tips and surround the pistils that are sheathed in the deep purple anthers. Because of its habitat requirements, leaf structure, habit, and tendency to grow in large populations coltsfoot could be mistaken—prior to blooming—for mountain boykinia. Once in flower there should be no confusion. A good place to see them is along Canyon Creek Road, which is where I photographed these in mid-April.

DRUMMOND'S ANEMONE
Anemone drummondii var. *drummondii*   Many petals
Buttercup family

Often covering entire hillsides of open subalpine slopes, this is a common high country companion throughout the entire area covered by this guide. It is one of the earliest bloomers, often peeking out from beneath receding spring snowbanks. Each plant has several stems up to 12" tall which sport solitary white flowers. The leaves are finely dissected and hairy. White "petals" are actually sepals that surround a mass of tiny yellow stamens clustered around multiple greenish pistils in the flower's center. Drummond's anemone is easily recognized by the soft blue tinge on the underside of the sepals. This photograph was taken on Parker Divide in the Trinity Alps in late May.

LITTLE-LEAF SILVERBACK LUINA, LITTLE-LEAF LUINA
Luina hypoleuca
Sunflower family

WESTERN SWEET COLTSFOOT
Petasites frigidus var. *palmatus*
Sunflower family

DRUMMOND'S ANEMONE
Anemone drummondii
var. *drummondii*
Buttercup family

WESTERN PASQUEFLOWER, EINSTEIN HEADS
Anemone occidentalis   Many petals
Buttercup family

Because, once seeds mature, the flowers of this anemone give way to big rounded, shaggy masses of plumose-tailed achenes they've come to be referred to fondly as Einstein heads. The resemblance between the scientist and the seed head is pretty amazing. The flowers often push their way through receding snowbanks and are some of the earliest bloomers in the high country. Like the other anemones, the white petals are not petals at all, but petal-like sepals about 1 1/4" long, surrounding masses of yellow-orange stamens and greenish pistils. One of the best places to see western pasqueflower is at the upper end of Long Canyon on the mountain-sides near the chute leading to Lake Anna. I photographed the flowers in Long Canyon in the Trinity Alps and the seed heads on Mt. Ashland in southern Oregon.

MARSH MARIGOLD
Caltha leptosepala   Many petals
Buttercup family

This absolutely gorgeous wildflower is one of the earliest species to emerge in the high country, often peeking from beneath snow banks as they recede in early May. Huge colonies grow in wet, marshy places like Upper Union Meadows just below Parker Divide. Most people are surprised to learn that marsh marigolds have no petals. The white "petals" are actually sepals and each about 3/4" long. The flowers bloom at the ends of stout stalks and are topped with numerous yellow stamens. The dark green basal leaves are oblong to round and are folded along the central axis. It is common to find them blooming alongside alpine buttercups (page 168). I photographed these in the meadows between West Boulder and Telephone Lakes in July.

NEVADA LEWISIA
Lewisia nevadensis   Many petals
Miner's lettuce family

Nevada lewisia can be found at mid-elevation in damp meadows throughout the Trinity Alps. The plants and flowers are tiny, 1"-2" tall, and hide, for the most part, in newly emerging meadow grass—making them difficult to spot. The small, deep green leaves are linear and fleshy. Flowers are white with olive green throats and streaks of green running from the throat to the petal tips. Careful, attentive obser-vaton is the best way to find them. I photographed these in Union Meadows but they also occur in Morris Meadows, pocket meadows along the North Fork of Coffee Creek, and on Scott Mountain.

WESTERN PASQUEFLOWER
Anemone occidentalis
Buttercup family

MARSH MARIGOLD
Caltha leptosepala
Buttercup family

NEVADA LEWISIA
Lewisia nevadensis
Miner's lettuce family

BITTERROOT
Lewisia rediviva   Many petals
Miner's lettuce family

All *Lewisia* species are gorgeous, but for sheer size and beauty this one takes the proverbial cake. The large, showy flowers crown what—at first glance seems to be "barren" serpentine—like a carpet in late spring and early summer. The translucent snow-white flowers emerge from a fleshy taproot and are tinged from beneath by pink to magenta sepals. Numerous white filaments topped with bright pink anthers comprise an array of stamens. I photographed these on the slopes of Scott Mountain in a year when the bloom was quite extensive. There were so many of them it was hard to walk in some places without stepping on them. It is well worth the drive and relatively short walk just to see these and the myriad other species that grace this wildflower hot spot.

Historical note: I love this traditional Shoshone and Flathead Indian story about bitterroot told to me by my grandmother... "One day an elderly woman couldn't find food for her family and started crying. The sun sent a red bird to comfort her. The bird told her that every place her bitter tears fell, a root, nourished by her love, would grow. The root and flower would be colored by the woman's white hair. The taste would be flavored by her bitter tears and the flower would be tinted by the bird's red feathers... and she would always have food for her tribe."

Bitterroot, or "spetlum" as the Flathead call it, is an important part of their diet, but is considered a luxury or delicacy as opposed to a staple. Subsequently, a basket of bitterroots is equal in value to that of a horse. The Flathead and neighboring tribes time spring migrations with the blooming of the bitterroot—May is known as "bitterroot month." The Shoshone believe the small red core found in the upper taproot had special powers, notably being able to stop a bear attack. The roots also have medicinal uses.

The 19th century botanist Frederick Pursh named the plant in honor of Meriwether Lewis, who collected it during the Lewis and Clark Expedition and brought it back for study. Bitterroot is the state flower of Montana, where Lewis made his discovery.

THREE-LEAVED LEWISIA
Lewisia triphylla   Many petals
Miner's lettuce family

This tiny lewisia hides in plain sight. The flowers are typically less than ¼" across and the entire plant will hardly grow beyond 2" in height. I once discovered them while walking to Little Granite Lake from Doe Lake in the Trinities—finding that I had been walking over large populations of them while searching for the storm damaged trail. They grow in shaded, wet, grassy meadows and conifer forests from 4,000'-7,500'. It can be found between Upper Albert Lake and the ridge above Big Blue in the Russians and the upper slopes above Little Granite Lake in the Alps.

COTTON GRASS
Calliscirpus criniger   no obvious petals
Sedge family

This easily recognized member of the sedge family frequents wet meadows, seeps, and fens throughout the high country. The flowers bloom in loose tufts at the tops of stems that are 10" to 14" tall. This photograph was taken in a wet meadow alongside Highway 3 where it passes over the summit of Scott Mountain. I have also found it in the meadow around Taylor Lake in the Russians and in Van Matre Meadows in the Trinity Alps.

BITTERROOT
Lewisia rediviva
Miner's lettuce family

THREE-LEAVED LEWISIA
Lewisia triphylla
Miner's lettuce family

COTTON GRASS
Calliscirpus criniger
Sedge family

CREAMBUSH, ROCK SPIRAEA, OCEANSPRAY
Holodiscus discolor   Alternate leaves - 5 symmetrical petals ovary superior
Rose family

Creambush is a common shrub that grows on steep hillsides, ridgetops, rocky slopes, in the crevices of rocky outcrops, and cliff faces at mid to high elevations throughout the area covered by this book. The beautiful displays of white flowers hang in thick terminal clusters at the end of the branches. They have a decidedly fuzzy look because of the numerous prominent stamens. The deep green leaves are ovate in shape, toothed or lobed at the margins, and serrate with prominent pinnate veins. Native Americans use the straighter stems for arrow stock—which gives rise to the common name arrowwood. I photographed these on Mt. Ashland in Southern Oregon but look for it everywhere.

OSO BERRY, INDIAN PLUM, INDIAN PEACH
Oemleria cerasiformis   Alternate leaves - 5 symmetrical petals ovary superior
Rose family

This loosely branched shrub grows in moist, shaded areas at lower elevations in the Trinities. The flowers open in late winter to early spring and grow in pendulous racemes. Petals are white and emerge from between elongated sepals. Male and female flowers grow on separate plants. The leaves are narrowly oval with the edges slightly rolled under. The fruits, green at first, turn apricot-colored and then a deep blue when ripe and are usually covered with a whitish waxy coating. I photographed this bunch along Clikapudi Trail above Shasta Lake, and the adolescent fruit along the Upper Trinity River. It is found throughout the area.

NINEBARK
Physocarpus capitatus   Alternate leaves - 5 symmetrical petals ovary superior
Rose family

In the early 70s, when I first began to record the plants of the Trinity Alps with pencil and paper, this was the subject of my first drawing. I still have it hanging on my wall and every time I look at it floods of pleasant memories surrounding that day return. The rounded clusters of small snow-white flowers bloom at the ends of reddish stems. The palmately lobed leaves resemble those of a maple. The bark is loose and flaky which, as Alice Jones indicates, gives rise to its name—supposedly, if you run your hand down the branch nine pieces of bark will be captured. Look for it along streams and by springs throughout the area covered by this book. I've found it around Shasta and Trinity Lakes as well as low- to mid-elevations in the surrounding mountains. I photographed these along a stream below Kangaroo Lake in the Trinity Divide.

PACIFIC PLUM, SIERRA PLUM, KLAMATH PLUM
Prunus subcordata   Alternate leaves - 5 symmetrical petals ovary superior
Rose family

This small tree can reach heights of 20′ but more often it forms thickets of shrubby bushes 8′ to 10′ tall. It is a lower elevation tree of streams and shaded hillsides below 5000′. The branches are rough, crooked, and occasionally spiny. Leaves are ovate to round and up to 2″ long. Flowers grow in a loose cluster. The crabapple-sized reddish fruits mature in late summer—good luck finding any though, as they are favored by wildlife. I photographed these near Shasta Lake but look for them throughout the foothill country of the Trinities.

CREAMBUSH, ROCK SPIRAEA, OCEANSPRAY
Holodiscus discolor
Rose family

OSO BERRY, INDIAN PLUM, INDIAN PEACH
Oemleria cerasiformis
Rose family

NINEBARK
Physocarpus capitatus
Rose family

PACIFIC PLUM, SIERRA PLUM, KLAMATH PLUM
Prunus subcordata
Rose family

WESTERN CHOKECHERRY
Prunus virginiana var. *demissa*   5 symmetrical petals - ovary superior
Rose family

When I was a kid growing up in Lewiston I spent many late summer afternoons picking chokecherries for my mom and grandmother, who made big batches of jelly and syrup from the mouth puckering fruit. Chokecherries grow in thickets to 30' tall. Branches hold long racemes decorated with white flowers and crowns of deep yellow stamens. In late summer long bunches of deep purple cherries develop and are scarfed up by birds, squirrels, chipmunks, and bears. Look for them along streams where they can get their feet in water or on damp hillsides. I photographed the flowers in early June along Deadwood Creek, and the fruit at Lowden Ranch in early September—both near Lewiston.

BITTER CHERRY
Prunus emarginata   5 symetrical petals ovary superior
Rose family

Bitter cherry grows throughout the Klamath Mountains, often in impenetrable thickets on rocky, well drained hillsides. The branches are reddish. The leaves are oval, finely toothed, and 1" to 2" long. The small, white flowers are grouped in little round-topped bunches at the ends of short branchlets. The fruit is a bright, almost translucent red, each about ¼" in diameter and favored by birds. If you want a memorable experience, pop a handful into your mouth and chew 'em up! They are mouth puckering bitter. The photograph of the flowers was taken in Union Meadows and the fruit on the slopes above Stoddard Lake, both in the Trinity Alps.

THIMBLEBERRY
Rubus parviflorus   5 symetrical petals ovary superior
Rose family

One of my great joys when backpacking in the high country is finding ripe thimbleberries along the trail. If you are lucky enough to get to them before the birds and chipmunks, they can bring any hike to a complete halt. When ripe, the berries lift off like little reddish-purple beanie caps and the taste is outstanding. They are easily recognized with their large dark green, palmately divided leaves and white, wrinkly-petaled flowers. I shot these blooms near Enni Camp on the trail to Papoose Lake in August and the fruit along the Deacon Lee Trail in the Russians in September.

WESTERN POISON-OAK
Toxicodendron diversilobum   5 symetrical petals ovary superior
Sumac family

If you do not know this species yet, learn to identify it before hiking along low to mid-elevation trails. Remember the old maxim: "Leaves of three, let it be!" It is usually a shrub but it can climb trees as a vine to a height exceeding 40'. In late summer the deep green, oily leaves turn a beautiful deep red which makes it an attractive plant—I know a woman who unknowingly picked some for the centerpiece of her Thanksgiving table! I'll leave the rest to your imagination. Leaves are deciduous, leaving bare twigs with telltale white berries attached when they fall. It grows in deep shaded woods and open, dry hillsides from 1,000'-4,000'. Look for it along low elevation trails like Canyon Creek and the North Fork of the Trinity River. If you find that you have been exposed, wash the affected area with hard soap and cold water. Hot water only encourages the spread of the oil that causes itching.

WESTERN CHOKECHERRY
Prunus virginiana var. *demissa*
Rose family

BITTER CHERRY
Prunus emarginata
Rose family

THIMBLEBERRY
Rubus parviflorus
Rose family

WESTERN POISON-OAK
Toxicodendron diversilobum
Sumac family

MOUNTAIN WHITETHORN
Ceanothus cordulatus
Buckthorn family
5 symetrical petals - ovary inferior

This *Ceanothus* is a stout, thorny shrub that grows in dense thickets in dry, exposed places. Cross country travel through thickets of mountain whitethorn can be a painful experience as well as good places to pick up oodles of deer ticks. The leaves are mostly oval and, like many other *Ceanothus* species, have three prominent veins. The small, white flowers bloom in small, dense clusters up to 2" across. Like other members of the buckthorn family the massed flowers impart a sickly sweet smell. I photographed these along the road to the Stony Ridge Trailhead.

BUCKBRUSH, WEDGELEAF CEANOTHUS
Ceanothus cuneatus
Buckthorn family
5 symmetrical petals - ovary inferior

This is a common *Ceanothus* throughout the foothills of the area covered by this guide, and the earliest *Ceanothus* to bloom in spring. The oppositely arranged branches are stiff and light gray to white. The gray-green leaves are leathery, evergreen, ¾" long, and obovate. Small white flowers bloom in loose clusters along the stems and, like most of the *Ceanothus* shrubs, have an overpoweringly sweet smell that triggers allergic reactions in some people. I photographed these on Bowerman Ridge above Trinity Lake.

SNOWBRUSH, TOBACCO BRUSH, VARNISH LEAF
Ceanothus velutinus
Buckthorn family
5 symetrical petals - ovary inferior

Snowbrush is a high country favorite of mine. The large, elliptic to ovate, leathery, shiny green leaves, emit a wonderful spicy aromatic smell when warmed by the sun. My dad would occasionally pick leaves and put them beneath his pack straps where the constant rubbing accentuated the smell. As the sun warms the slopes where it grows, the "sap" they exude clings like varnish to the tops of the leaves, giving it the other common name, varnish leaf. I photographed these near the top of the ridge on the Old Caribou Trail in the Trinity Alps in August.

CALIFORNIA COFFEEBERRY
Frangula californica subsp. *occidentalis*
Buckthorn family
5 symetrical petals - ovary inferior

There are several subspecies of coffeeberry found throughout this area, but commonly it is a woody shrub or small tree that grows to around 15' in height in dry areas from the floor of the Central Valley to the foothills of the Trinity Alps and Trinity Divide. The leaves are elliptical, 2" to 3" long, with prominent pinnate veins, smooth leaf margins, that are deep green above and yellowish beneath. The greenish-white flowers are small, star shaped and grow in inconspicuous clusters. The fleshy fruit is small, ½" in diameter, and a deep purple black in late summer. It has a surprisingly pleasant coffee flavor and was used by early settlers in lieu of coffee. I photographed the flowers along the Trinity River in mid-June and the fruit in the same location in early September.

MOUNTAIN WHITETHORN
Ceanothus cordulatus
Buckthorn family

BUCKBRUSH, WEDGELEAF, CEANOTHUS
Ceanothus cuneatus
Buckthorn family

SNOWBRUSH, TOBACCO BRUSH, VARNISH LEAF
Ceanothus velutinus
Buckthorn family

CALIFORNIA COFFEEBERRY
Frangula californica subsp. *occidentalis*
Buckthorn family

TRAILING GOOSEBERRY, GROUND GOOSEBERRY
Ribes binominatum   5 symetrical petals - ovary inferior
Gooseberry family

This is a small, trailing gooseberry, that forms low mats that spill over and hug rocks and downed woody debris in dry, open meadows. The woody stems are thorny and no fun to wade through unless you're wearing boots. Leaves are small, 2" to 3" across, dark green, lobed, toothed, and slightly fuzzy. The small white to greenish-white flowers are sticky and bloom in small clusters which, later on in the season, produce spiny, sweet fruits. Gloves are absolutely required if you want to sample one! I photographed this one in Union Meadows in early June where they grow in abundance.

STICKY CURRANT
Ribes viscosissimum   Alternate leaves - 5 symmetrical petals - ovary inferior
Gooseberry family

This is a common, loosely branched shrub, growing 4' to 5' in height at the edges of meadows and other mixed conifer openings in the mid- to high elevations. The leaves are stiff, dark green, deeply veined, and shaped like a maple. Flowers are white lightly tinged with pink, tubular in shape, with the petals flaring at the tips. Julie Knorr says the plant's fragrance is her favorite part of the plant. I photographed the flowers near the trail to Eaton Lake in the Russians in August and the inset of the fruit in Grizzly Meadows in the Trinity Alps in September.

WESTERN SERVICEBERRY
Amelanchier alnifolia   Alternate leaves - 5 symmetrical petals ovary superior
Rose family

This is a stiffly branched shrub that forms dense thickets on rocky hillsides throughout the Trinities. The white flowers have long petals, are ruffled, and bloom in tight clusters along the branches. In the fall they yield a dry, blue apple shaped fruit. The leaves are oval and toothed above the middle. The berry clusters are sometimes covered with orange rust. I photographed these along the trail to Lilypad Lake in the Trinity Alps in July.

TOYON, CHRISTMAS BERRY, HOLLYWOOD
Heteromeles arbutifolia   Alternate leaves - 5 symmetrical petals ovary superior
Rose family

I prefer the name Christmas berry because the bunches of bright red berries always ripen during the winter season and used as seasonal decorations. It is a common shrub of the dry chaparral hillsides throughout this area and brings a holiday joy to a drive along any road during late fall and early winter months. Toyon can grow to 15' or more with leathery, toothed, oblong leaves. The creamy white flowers bloom in large pyramidal terminal clusters. Hollywood, of Southern California fame, was originally named Hollywoodland for this shrub that grew in profusion on surrounding hillsides. The infamous Hollywood sign originally read Hollywoodland but after the last 4 letters fell away it was left as Hollywood. I photographed this bunch along Highway 299 West near Whiskeytown Lake.

TRAILING GOOSEBERRY, GROUND GOOSEBERRY
Ribes binominatum
Gooseberry family

STICKY CURRANT
Ribes viscosissimum
Gooseberry family

WESTERN SERVICEBERRY
Amelanchier alnifolia
Rose family

TOYON, CHRISTMAS BERRY, HOLLYWOOD
Heteromeles arbutifolia
Rose family

CASCADE MOUNTAIN ASH, MOUNTAIN ASH
Sorbus scopulina   Alternate leaves - 5 symmetrical petals ovary superior
Rose family

Hikers are likely to remember this tall (up to 12'), sprawling shrub by the deep gold foliage and brilliant oranges and reds of its berries in the fall of the year. It decorates entire mountainsides with color in places like Little Bear Lake and is one of the many things that make autumn in the high country so memorable. Masses of small white flowers bloom in flat-topped clusters beginning in late May, giving way to bunches of bright orange to deep red, berry-like pomes from late August into November. I photographed the flowers at Upper Albert Lake in the Russians in September and the berries at Little Bear Lake in the Trinity Alps in October.

LABRADOR TEA, TRAPPER'S TEA
Rhododendron columbianum   5 symmetrical petals forming a tube
Heath family

Labrador tea is a low growing, stiffly branched shrub that decorates the shorelines of lakes and edges of streams throughout the high country, often in large populations. The evergreen leaves are oblong, leathery, and crowded in tufts at the ends of branches. White, five petaled flowers bloom in rounded, compact clusters with conspicuous stamens. In protected pockets it can continue to bloom well into October. I photographed these at Log Lake in the Trinity Alps in July.

Note: Yuroks boil the leaves to make a medicinal herbal tea. For many years German brewers used a variety of it while brewing beer which they believed made it more intoxicating. Eventually this practice was forbidden by law because it supposedly led to increased aggression amongst imbibers.

WESTERN AZALEA
Rhododendron occidentale   5 symmetrical petals forming a tube
Heath family

Every wildflower is beautiful but in my book this one takes the prize. Azalea flowers are large, showy, and their fragrance is outrageously delightful. Walking through a patch of azalea along a high country trail on a warm afternoon is nothing short of intoxicating and, in my book, just about as close to heaven as you can get. Azaleas are most often associated with water and serpentine where they prefer stream banks, the shorelines of ponds and lakes, and marshy areas. They can also be found growing in highly mineralized sites at low elevations especially around Keswick and Shasta Lakes—often where copper mining was prevalent years ago. In the fall, leaves turn a beautiful gold to brilliant red. Goldenrod spiders (*Misumena vatia*) love the tubular shape of the flower because it provides a safe hiding place for the little critters. They are aggressive little spiders that defend their flowery homes with all the ferocity of a miniature charging bear. The one pictured in the inset dashed out and attacked my camera lens every time I got to within a couple of inches of the flower. The large photograph was taken along the Union Lake Trail in early June and the crab spider along the North Fork of Coffee Creek in July, all in the Trinity Alps.

CASCADE MOUNTAIN ASH
Sorbus scopulina
Rose family

LABRADOR TEA
TRAPPER'S TEA
Rhododendron columbianum
Heath family

WESTERN AZALEA
Rhododendron occidentale
Heath family

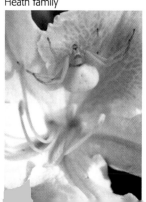

KLAMATH MANZANITA
Arctostaphylos klamathensis   5 petals joined into a bell
Heath family

This Klamath Mountain endemic is found mainly on serpentine soils and north facing or deeply shaded slopes between 5700' and 6500'. It associates with green-leaf and pinemat manzanitas but, unlike these two with their bright green leaves, has grayish to blue-green leaves. Another distinguishing feature is its intermediate size between greenleaf and pinemat—being between 1' and 2' tall. The diagnostic feature is the hairs that cover older twigs. New growth twigs are likewise hairy and often tipped with sticky resin. I had a devil of a time finding this one but once I took to heart the color of the leaves and size of the shrub it jumped right out at me. This species is only found within the range of this guide. I took these photographs on Scott Mountain in late April.

> The genus *Arctostaphylos* is a specialist within the California Floristic Province. In fact, 104 of the 105 *Arctostaphylos* species grow within this region, with only six extending beyond the boundaries. To learn more about this amazing group, see *Field Guide to Manzanitas*, also published by Backcountry Press.

PINEMAT MANZANITA
Arctostaphylos nevadensis   5 petals joined into a bell
Heath family

Though short in stature, this common manzanita covers a lot of ground laterally. On open ridge tops at higher elevations it rarely gets taller than your ankles and favors sunny, dry hillsides, ridgetops, and the understory of conifer forests. The leaves are small, oval, finely veined, tough, and leathery. The branches are likewise tough and resilient. The small white, urn shaped flowers often have a pinkish tinge and occur in small clusters at the ends of branches. I photographed this bunch above the shoreline of Doe Lake in early August.

GREENLEAF MANZANITA
Arctostaphylos patula   5 petals joined into a bell
Heath family

This shrub is common throughout the high country, often forming dense, impassible patches. This is the species that makes cross-country travel challenging. It prefers dry, open, and sunny sites where it grows to a height of 5'. It is an irregularly branched shrub with deep red bark that peels away to reveal new bark beneath that is bright green to yellow. Leaves are deep green, tough, oval, and finely veined. The flowers resemble tiny, upside down white to deep pink urns. Mealy reddish-brown fruits ripen late in the summer and are favored by bears—often seen in scat piled up on the trail. I photographed the white to pale pink flowers along the Union Creek Trail in the Trinity Alps in early June and the pink flowers on Scott Mountain also in June.

KLAMATH MANZANITA
Arctostaphylos klamathensis
Heath family

The photograph below illustrates the unique sticky hairs on the new twigs.

PINEMAT MANZANITA
Arctostaphylos nevadensis
Heath family

GREENLEAF MANZANITA
Arctostaphylos patula
Heath family

WHITELEAF MANZANITA
Arctostaphylos viscida
Heath family

5 symmetrical petals ovary inferior

This might be the earliest bloomer on the block, at least for regional shrubs. At lower elevations look for the bunches of white to pale pink flowers which open anytime after the middle of December. The leaves are tough and leathery and a paler grayish-green—which is how they got their name. As the shrub grows, its deep reddish-brown bark splits and reveals the new pale orange to yellowish-green bark beneath (see inset). The old bark curls up and eventually falls to the ground. The photograph of the flowers was taken near Shasta Lake but it is widespread throughout regional river canyons. The photograph of the peeling bark was taken above Lewiston Lake in late December.

ALPINE SPICY WINTERGREEN
Gaultheria humifusa
Heath family

5 petals joined into a bell

This is one inconspicuous wildflower growing only a few inches tall. To appreciate it you need to get down on your hands and knees and sometimes get wet because it frequents the shorelines of lakes and streams. The flowers are pea sized or smaller, snow white with deep red sepals and dark orange pistils. They generally hang face down from stout stems. The deep green leaves are oval, tough, and leathery. It is not deciduous hence the term "wintergreen." I took these photographs with my stomach submerged in Upper Albert Lake. My camera was on a table top tripod, also sitting in water. To get the photographs I had to shoot almost straight up into the small plant as it hung over a rock. In all my years visiting this lake I'd never seen them before.

SIERRA LAUREL
Leucothoe davisiae
Heath family

5 petals joined into a bell

The California endemic Sierra laurel can be found throughout the high country where it forms waste high thickets along shorelines of lakes, the edges of ponds, and banks of streams. Thick clusters of small, pendulous, white, urn-shaped flowers bloom on tall spikes from mid-summer well into the fall. The evergreen, oblong leaves are crowded along strongly upright stems. I shot the large photograph along the shoreline of Log Lake and the close-up image along the stream below Doe Lake, both in the Trinity Alps.

WHITELEAF MANZANITA
Arctostaphylos viscida
Heath family

ALPINE SPICY WINTERGREEN
Gaultheria humifusa
Heath family

SIERRA LAUREL
Leucothoe davisiae
Heath family

THIN-LEAF HUCKLEBERRY, BLACK HUCKLEBERRY
Vaccinium membranaceum   5 petals joined into a bell
Heath family

I remember a warm October afternoon backpacking to Little Bear Lake while enjoy-ing the intoxicating smell of ripe huckleberries. Every shrub was loaded with these little blue treasures—the taste as delicious as the smell. It was a bumper year for huckleberries with more than enough to go around—for the chipmunks, birds, bears, and humans alike. The shrubs grow to 3' or more and cover large areas. The leaves are larger and thinner that those of other huckleberries. I photographed the flowers at Big Duck Lake in the Russians and the fruit at Little Bear Lake in the Trinity Alps. In the fall they put on a beautiful display of brilliant red foliage in places like the East Weaver Lake basin.

A note about huckleberries and billberries: Several species of huckleberry are found throughout this area and distinguishing one from the other can be difficult, even for experts. Suffice to say you will likely run into any or all of them in different places as you hike these mountains. The two species illustrated in this guide (*V. circinatum* on page 234) are typical and most common. The fruits of all varieties taste excellent. Ponder the possibility of huckleberry pancakes on a chilly October morning in the high country!

SNOWDROP BUSH
Styrax redivivus   5 petals joined into a bell
Storax family

This low elevation shrub has to have some of the prettiest flowers around. Person-ally, I rank them right up there with the flowers of mock orange and Pacific dogwood for their graceful beauty. It is a shrub commonly found in open, dry, shaded forest slopes. The snow-white flowers hang in pendulous bunches, the petals fused at the base and flaring open at the tips to expose bundles of white stamens crowned with elongated, creamy-orange anthers. Leaves are round, leathery, dark green, yellow-green veined, and wavy at the margins. It is 8' to 12' in height. I photographed these on Bowerman Ridge in mid-June.

RED OSIER DOGWOOD, CREEK DOGWOOD
and MINER'S DOGWOOD, BLACKFRUIT DOGWOOD
Cornus sericea and *Cornus sessilis*   4 petals
Dogwood family

These two species nearly always have feet in water—sometimes forming dense stands next to streams, springs, and the shorelines of lakes. Multi-stemmed shrubs or small trees grow to 12' and are common at mid-elevations. Veins curve distinc-tively from leaf stem to tip. Flowers occur in loose, mounded clusters at the ends of the stems. The large white petaloid bracts of their larger cousin, Pacific dogwood, are absent from these species. Both species occupy similar habitat and, except for the fruit and twigs, are difficult to differentiate. The fruits of *C. sericea* are small and pale greenish-white and its twigs are red (top left inset). The fruits of *C. sessilis* arelarge, fleshy ,and blue-black (top right inset) with brown or gray twigs. The pho-tographs of *C. sericea* were taken along the shoreline of West Boulder Lake in the Trinity Alps in mid-July while the inset of the *C. sessilis* berries was taken along Slate Creek near the Kinney Camp Trailhead in the Trinity Alps in October.

THIN-LEAF HUCKLEBERRY
BLACK HUCKLEBERRY
Vaccinium membranaceum
Heath family

SNOWDROP BUSH
Styrax redivivus
Storax family

RED OSIER DOGWOOD
MINER'S DOGWOOD
Cornus sericea & *Cornus sessilis*
Dogwood family

WILD MOCK ORANGE
Philadelphus lewisii   4 petals
Hydrangea family

Mock orange is a common foothills shrub, up to 8' tall, loosely branched, and covered with small clusters of gorgeous white flowers. The flowers have four petals but, occasionally, five with prominent, creamy yellow anthers that give the blossoms a star-like quality. Older branches are gray while the younger ones, those nearest the flowers, are generally reddish green. The leaves are dark green, narrowly oval, pointed at the tips, and deeply veined with three main veins. Its preferred habitat is along streams, around fresh flowing springs, and in other places close to water. A good place to see it is along Canyon Creek Road on the way to the trailhead (where I shot the large photograph) and then along Canyon Creek Trail to a point about half a mile below Middle Falls (small photograph). Most literature says that when it's in full bloom the flowers give off a delightful fragrance reminiscent of orange blossoms—hence the name. I've never found the fragrance to be very strong but, subtle though it may be, it is quite pleasant.

BLUE ELDERBERRY
Sambucus nigra subsp. *caerulea*   5 symmetrical petals - ovary inferior
Muskroot family

This large fruiting shrub is found throughout the area covered by this book from the foothills to mid-elevation meadows and hillsides. The bushes can reach heights of 16' or more depending on location. The creamy white flower heads are large, compact, and have a pleasant smell. The fruit turns a dark blue by late summer and is often covered with a white, waxy bloom. The fruit of the blue elderberry is excellent for eating and can be included in pancakes, baked in pies, made into syrup and jams, and used to make wine. You have to beat the critters, as it is a favorite of bears, birds, chipmunks, and pine squirrels I photographed these along the road to the Deacon Lee Trailhead in the Russian Wilderness.

RED ELDERBERRY
Sambucus racemosa var. *racemosa*   5 symmetrical petals - ovary inferior
Muskroot family

This shrubby elderberry is commonly found at mid to higher elevations throughout the high country where it enjoys damp areas like the shorelines of lakes, streams, or near the edges of marshy meadows. The snow white flowers bloom in a small and compact bunches at the ends of the flowering stems. Late in the summer bright red berries ripen in large clusters but, unlike those of their cousin the blue elderberry, are not edible—even though they look absolutely delicious hanging from beautiful purple stems. I photographed the flowers on the shoreline of Buck Lake in August and the berries on the shoreline of Sugar Pine Lake in September, both in the Trinity Alps.

WILD MOCK ORANGE
Philadelphus lewisii
Hydrangea family

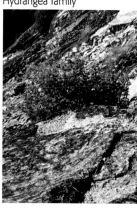

BLUE ELDERBERRY
Sambucus nigra subsp. *caerulea*
Muskroot family

RED ELDERBERRY
Sambucus racemosa var. *racemosa*
Muskroot family

LOVE HEATHER, WHITE HEATHER
Cassiope mertensiana   5 petals joined into a bell
Heath family

When this beautiful shrub blooms, it not only brightens up entire high elevation hillsides with its dainty white, bell shaped flowers but it also brightens your mood. It typically is small—usually no more than 1' to 3' tall—and thickly branched. Short, scale-like leaves encircle and hug each upright branch. It favors rocky outcrops and slopes, often gracing cliff faces. The nodding flowers, capped with bright red sepals, grow from the axils of the leaves and are approximately ¼" long. These photographs were taken at Big Duck Lake in the Russians but I've photographed them on the slopes above Salmon Lake and Upper Caribou Lake in the Trinity Alps as well.

FREMONT SILKTASSEL
Garrya fremontii   5 petals joined into a bell
Silktassel family

From a distance a silktassel looks a lot like a species of manzanita and most people pass it by as such. However, while its overall appearance might be similar, a closer inspection reveals some obvious differences. For one, silktassels are not as stout as manzanitas—meaning that wading through a patch won't leave you a bloody mess. For another, silktassel leaves are oppositely arranged along the branches while those of manzanita are alternate. What really gives them away are the flowers, which hang in long, pendulous catkins from the ends of the branches. Silktassels are also dioecious, meaning that any individual plant has all female or all male flowers. Typically, the flowers are white and pubescent but it is interesting to note that shrubs standing shoulder to shoulder often have flowers that appear to be different colors. Some appear yellowish while others almost purple. This difference is all in the color of the sepals. Bunches of flowers grow to 10" long if not longer, especially on the coast. In the fall they produce dark purple fruits much favored by bears. If you find yourself in the middle of a patch of ripening silktassel berries be on the lookout for furry foragers with purple lips. I shot both of these photographs within a few feet of each other on Weaver Bally in the Trinity Alps in late February and the photograph of the ripe fruit along the trail to Alpine Lake in September. If you make the hike up to the old Billy's Peak Lookout site above Coffee Creek in the fall when the silktassel is ripe, you might be rewarded with herds of grazing bears. Years ago I counted at least a dozen of them rummaging around in the bushes along the ridge.

LOVE HEATHER, WHITE HEATHER
Cassiope mertensiana
Heath family

FREMONT SILKTASSEL
Garrya fremontii
Silktassel family

CHAPARRAL CLEMATIS, PIPESTEM CLEMATIS
Clematis lasiantha   4 petals
Buttercup family

Years ago I came across a diary kept by a girl who, with her father, made trips into Redding to buy supplies for their homestead from the small community of Vollmers in the late 1800s. In it she often referred to her love of finding what she called "traveler's delight" twining through the brush alongside the road. What she described was chaparral clematis with its lovely creamy white flowers and prominent yellow stamens. They are easy to spot as the vines climb through brush to offer up their showy displays. Their preferred habitat is dry, brushy hillsides in full sun. In late summer the flowers are replaced with fuzzy seed heads that are just as interesting and showy as the flowers. I photographed these along Deadwood Road near Lewiston in June. **Note**: *Clematis ligusticifolia*, western virgin's bower, also grows in this area but along streams and near damp, shaded places. The flowers and seed heads are almost indistinguishable from those of chaparral clematis. In both species, the white "petals" are actually sepals.

WILD RASPBERRY, BLACKCAP RASPBERRY, WHITEBARK RASPBERRY
Rubus leucodermis   5 symmetrical petals - ovary superior
Rose family

Here is a treat for any woodland forager. The vines grow in profusion from low to mid-elevations throughout the foothills and mountains of this area. They are especially abundant in disturbed areas alongside roads and trails. If you can beat the animals to the fruit you are in for a tastebud delight. No matter where I am, and despite the situation, I am always sidetracked by the sight of the ripe raspberries where I stop to get my fill. The spiny vines grow in sprawling masses along the ground and, in May - July are covered with snow-white 5 petaled flowers typical of the rose family. Berries form soon afterwards and by the time late summer rolls around the tasty fruit is ready for harvest. They get their name blackcap raspberry because when picked they slip off like little beanie caps. I photographed the flowers along Trinity Mountain Road near VanNess Gulch in June and the fruit along the trail above Enni Camp on the way to Papoose Lake in the Trinity Alps in late August.

WILD CUCUMBER, COAST MAN-ROOT
Marah oregana   5 petals joined into a bell
Gourd family

This is one BAD cucumber, not cool at all, except to look at. The five petaled snow-white flowers form a bell or cup with the petals folding away from the center. A mass of deeply inset lemon yellow stamens occupy the center of the flower. Flowers are small but numerous, blooming in bunches all along the length of this climbing vine which can reach lengths of 20' or more. The large leaves are deeply lobed and smooth. On the coast the leaves are a deeper green, thicker, and more wrinkled. Large round to oblong glossy fruits begin to appear by late spring. They are light green with deep green stripes running the length and are, to varying degrees covered with prickly appendages. Fruits tend to be smaller than the coastal siblings and not as prickly. By late summer these "cucumbers" hang shiny and inviting—enticing the unwary to take a big bite. This is not a good idea as they are extremely bitter! It is common throughout this region from the coast to the foothills.

**CHAPARRAL CLEMATIS
PIPESTEM CLEMATIS**
Clematis lasiantha
Buttercup family

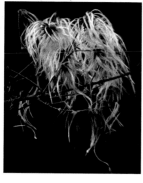

**WILD RASPBERRY,
BLACKCAP RASPBERRY**
Rubus leucodermis
Rose family

WILD CUCUMBER
Marah oregana
Gourd family

The view down Scott Mountain Creek towards the Upper Trinity River with Trinity Divide in the background.

Sulfur-flowered buckwheat (*Eriogonum umbellatum*) in bloom along the Deacon Lee Trail in the Russian Wilderness

BOG ASPHODEL
Narthecium californicum   3 or 6 petals
Bog asphodel family

Bog asphodel is a distinct wildflower that grows in wet meadows and marshy areas. The golden-yellow blooms are concentrated along a raceme that can grow to 16" tall, but often hidden in tall meadow grass. An interesting feature of these flowers is the woolly filaments topped with deep orange hook shaped anthers—the pollen-bearing parts of the stamens. I photographed this one in a wet meadow along the trail to Stoddard Lake, but I've also seen it in the meadow at L Lake, both in the Trinity Alps. **Note**: in the fall the once beautiful flowers go to seed and the seed heads are every bit as pretty and unusual as the blooms. For wont of a better analogy, they look a lot like the little hats artists feel somehow obligated to place on the heads of gnomes (see inset).

YELLOW TRITELEIA
Triteleia crocea   3 or 6 petals
Brodiaea family

The first thing you notice about this gorgeous *Triteleia* is the color. The deep, buttery yellow jumps out no matter the surroundings and, though it does not tend to bloom in large colonies, even alone it stands out. Each petal has a mid-vein of greenish-brown running the length. The anthers are snow-white. The plants range in height from 10" to 18". The leaves are almost as long as the flowering stalk but begin to wither and turn brown as the flowers mature. The number of flowers in each head ranged from five to more than a dozen. I photographed these on a flat alongside the road to the Poison Canyon Trailhead in the Trinity Alps in late May. **Note**: the blue version of *T. crocea* (also called yellow triteleia) is featured in the blue section of this guide (page 246).

PRETTY FACE
Triteleia ixioides subsp. *anilina*   3 or 6 petals
Brodiaea family

Pretty faces are common throughout the foothills and found in habitats ranging from dry and exposed to shaded and damp. The deep yellow, to straw colored blooms occur in loose clusters at the tops of stems that can reach 10" in height, sometimes taller. Each petal has a dark, reddish brown stripe down the center almost to the tip and in the center are several bright blue anthers. Flower buds are elongated and yellow with deep reddish brown stripes. I photographed these in Squirrel Gulch at the North end of Trinity Lake in June.

ARROW-LEAF BUCKWHEAT, COMPOSITE BUCKWHEAT, HEARTLEAF BUCKWHEAT
Eriogonum compositum var. *compositum*   3 or 6 petals
Buckwheat family

This is one of the largest buckwheats in this area—up to 2'—and thus easy to spot. The stems are stout and the basal leaves an elongated, heart shape, dark green above, and white-wooly beneath. The tiny white or yellow flowers bloom in compact heads that sit atop several elongated branches which in turn arise from the same spot at the top of the main stem. This flower arrangement is referred to as an umbel. It likes open rocky areas and meadows. I photographed the white one at Sapphire Lake in September and the yellow one along the highway between Gazelle and Callahan just before reaching the Scott Valley, in early August.

BOG ASPHODEL
Narthecium californicum
Bog asphodel family

YELLOW TRITELEIA
Triteleia crocea
Brodiaea family

PRETTY FACE
Triteleia ixioides subsp. *anilina*
Brodiaea family

ARROW-LEAF BUCKWHEAT
Eriogonum compositum var. *compositum*
Buckwheat family

CONGDON'S BUCKWHEAT
Eriogonum congdonii   3 or 6 petals
Buckwheat family

Congdon's buckwheat is one of the easiest buckwheats to identify. Unlike many other species in the genus, the branches of the flower clusters (inflorescences) are clearly visible above the small leaf-like bracts. The leaves are small, greenish-woolly above, densely white-woolly below, and curl under along the edges—making them appear narrow. The plants can be up to 12" tall, including the flowers. This species is endemic to serpentine, and is found in the Trinity Alps and along the Trinity Divide. It is one of the most common buckwheats in the Mt. Eddy to Scott Mountain area. I photographed these above Kangaroo Lake in Mid-July.

JAYNE'S CANYON BUCKWHEAT
Eriogonum diclinum   3 or 6 petals
Buckwheat family

This small buckwheat blooms at higher elevations throughout the mountains. The plants I've photographed have rarely been over 4" tall, including the blooms. The compact bunches of basal leaves are light green and covered with whitish hairs— almost cobwebby in appearance. I photographed these above the outlet of Sapphire Lake in late August.

LOBB'S BUCKWHEAT
Eriogonum lobbii   3 or 6 petals
Buckwheat family

This is also a fairly easy buckwheat to identify. The rounded heads of yellow flowers emerge from beneath the basal rosette of leaves and usually lie flat against the ground. The leaves are broadly oval, fuzzy, with white veins. It is common in granitic substrates, often in the cracks and fissures of outcrops. In late summer, in open exposed areas, the leaves and flowers turn a deep and vibrant red—especially true on the upper reaches of the Suicide Trail in the Trinity Alps. I photographed this one in late August above Upper Albert Lake in the Russians but have also photographed it above Lower Caribou Lake in the Trinity Alps.

SISKIYOU BUCKWHEAT
Eriogonum siskiyouense   3 or 6 petals
Buckwheat family

This is a small buckwheat that likes serpentine soils. The lemon yellow flowers bloom in small, tight clusters at the tops of strongly erect stems which arise from dense masses of tiny, succulent looking leaves. There is a single whorl of 3 leaf-like bracts about 2/3 of the way up the stems. I photographed these along the Pacific Crest Trail above Kangaroo Lake in mid-July.

CONGDON'S BUCKWHEAT
Eriogonum congdonii
Buckwheat family

JAYNE'S CANYON BUCKWHEAT
Eriogonum diclinum
Buckwheat family

LOBB'S BUCKWHEAT
Eriogonum lobbii
Buckwheat family

SISKIYOU BUCKWHEAT
Eriogonum siskiyouense
Buckwheat family

MT. EDDY BUCKWHEAT, SCOTT MOUNTAIN SULPHUR FLOWER
Eriogonum umbellatum var. *humistratum*   3 or 6 petals
Buckwheat family

Mt. Eddy buckwheat is similar to the more common sulphur-flowered buckwheats, of which there are close to 25 varieties. Its leaves are white-wooly both sides. It is found on serpentine at higher elevations from Mt. Eddy north to the Scott Mountains, and then west into the Trinity Alps, Russians, and Marble Mountains. I photographed these on Scott Mountain in mid-July.

SULPHUR-FLOWERED BUCKWHEAT
Eriogonum umbellatum   3 or 6 petals
Buckwheat family

When most hikers and backpackers think buckwheat and high country, this is the one that comes to mind. It is common and widespread at mid to high elevations on open, dry, exposed sites. The leaves are small, basal, and dark green on one side, light gray-green on the other. This buckwheat grows in large colonies and with so many flowers that they can color entire rocky hillsides. The lemon yellow flowers begin to turn a reddish-orange by late summer and the blooms persist into the early winter months. There are currently 25 varieties of this highly variable complex known from within California. Only *Eriogonum umbellatum* var. *humistratum* is listed as a separate entry here because it is a near endemic to the book's area. I photographed these in Bee Tree Gap at the head of Long Canyon in early August but one of the most gorgeous displays I've ever seen was the late season bloom along the Deacon Lee Trail in the Russians when all of the flowers had turned a deep reddish-orange.

YELLOW-LEAF IRIS, YELLOW-FLOWERED IRIS
Iris chrysophylla   3 or 6 petals
Iris family

This is an iris that, in some instances, can be confused with variations of the long-tubed iris because both have the same long corolla tube. Flowers are yellow or creamy white with a pale bluish tinge. The ones I've photographed along the Stoney Ridge Trail appear in two variations: the more common one having beautiful, soft yellow petals with minimal purple veining and a white patch extending to within an inch or so of the petal tip. The other having almost creamy white petals with prominent deep purple veining and a yellow stripe running the full length of the petals.

MT. EDDY BUCKWHEAT
Eriogonum umbellatum var. *humistratum*
Buckwheat family

SULPHUR-FLOWERED BUCKWHEAT
Eriogonum umbellatum
Buckwheat family

YELLOW-LEAF IRIS, YELLOW-FLOWERED IRIS
Iris chrysophylla
Iris family

GOLDEN EYED GRASS, YELLOW EYED GRASS, GOLDEN BLUE EYED GRASS
Sisyrinchium californicum   3 or 6 petals
Iris family

This distinctive member of the iris family can be found throughout the area covered by this guide—most often in wet meadows, near running or standing water. More common near the coast there are eastern populations on serpentines of the Klamath Mountains. The stems are strongly erect, to 24" tall, tough, and topped with a solitary bright yellow flower. The veins in the petals are usually brown. Based on these characteristics, it can't be confused with any other wildflower in the area. I found and photographed these in a wet meadow just off of Forest Highway 24 near Gumboot Lake in late June.

YELLOW FAWN LILY, GLACIER LILY
Erythronium grandiflorum subsp. *grandiflorum*   3 or 6 petals
Lily family

This little fawn lily emerges early in the blooming season, in open areas at the edges of melting snow banks and mesic sites in the middle to high elevations. There is no mistaking the bright yellow flowers with recurved petals, prominent stamens, and pistils—hanging from the ends of 6" to 7" stalks. At higher elevations you will find diminutive specimens blooming upright on the ends of almost non-existent stalks, nestled tightly into the green basal leaves. This photograph was taken along the Poison Canyon Trail below Lilypad Lake.

YELLOW BELLS, YELLOW FRITILLARY
Fritillaria pudica   3 or 6 petals
Lily family

I found this beautiful little fritillary growing on Scott Mountain at the edges of melting snow banks. A solitary deep, buttery yellow, bell shaped flower nods at the end of the flowering stem. The entire plant rarely exceeds 4"-6". I photographed this one on Scott Mountain next to receding snow banks in early July.

CREAM CUPS
Platystemon californicus   3 or 6 petals
Poppy family

This beauty is an early bloomer found from the floor of the Central Valley to the lower elevation foothills. It is variable in color—ranging from solid yellow to various combinations of yellow and white or orange and white. The flowers sit solitary atop 2½" to 4" stems and grow in profusion on exposed, sunny flats, and hillsides. There are six diamond shaped petals and the flowers can be up to ¾" in diameter. The beautiful golden-yellow and white version I found blooming in large colonies together with baby blue eyes up along Canyon Creek Road in mid-April. The mostly white version I photographed along Clikapudi Trail near Shasta Lake in late March.

GOLDEN EYED GRASS, YELLOW EYED GRASS
Sisyrinchium californicum
Iris family

YELLOW FAWN LILY, GLACIER LILY
Erythronium grandiflorum subsp. *grandiflorum*
Lily family

YELLOW BELLS, YELLOW FRITILLARY
Fritillaria pudica
Lily family

CREAM CUPS
Platystemon californicus
Poppy family

SIERRA WALLFLOWER
Erysimum perenne
Mustard family

4 petals

After trudging through knee deep snow above Foster Lake in late May, I came out upon the top of the ridge to find an amazing variety of wildflowers blooming in small areas of open ground. Front and center, was a gorgeous bunch of spreading phlox with a single Sierra wallflower blooming in the center—the two were meant to be together! I set up my camera gear and went to work in a thunderstorm—we wildflower photographers are nothing, if not fearless, in the face of being fried by lightning! I've photographed this wildflower in many other settings but this is the one that stays with me. This flower is easily recognized by the golden yellow blooms and its size—up to 24" tall. It is common throughout the area covered by this book.

CALIFORNIA POPPY
Eschscholzia californica
Poppy family

4 petals

This is our state flower. Easily recognized by its vibrant gold and orange blooms, it decorates roadsides and a myriad other open, sunny places at lower elevations throughout the state. You won't find it in the high country but it prospers along Highway 299 in the Trinity River Valley. The flowers spring from a mound of soft, grayish green, deeply dissected leaves. Each flower has four petals which form a broad cup flaring away at the tips. The center of the golden yellow flower is a darker orange. I photographed these on a flat between Rush Creek Road and the Trinity River near Lewiston in July.

CASTLE LAKE BEDSTRAW
Galium glabrescens subsp. *glabrescens*
Madder family

4 petals

The flowers of this species are tiny—no more than 1/4" across. The four greenish-yellow petals point straight out and form a cross (similar in appearance to the flowers of climbing bedstraw also pictured). The most distinctive feature is the hairy fruit, which looks silvery in the sunshine. This bedstraw is common from Castle Crags north to the Scott Mountains and west to the Trinity Alps, but can be confused—even by professional botanists—with the rare species *Galium serpenticum* subsp. *scotticum*, which inhabits the same area. This photo was taken above Kangaroo Lake on the Trinity Divide in late July. There are records of specimens from Stewart's Fork near Emerald Lake and from the Canyon Creek Lakes area in the Trinity Alps.

CLIMBING BEDSTRAW
Galium porrigens
Madder family

4 petals

Ever wonder the origin of the word the name "bedstraw?" Pioneers harvested huge bundles of this plant to "tick" their mattresses for cushioning. My great-grandmother told me stories of stuffing bedstraw into her own mattress as a little girl in Oklahoma in the late 1800s. This vine-like plant grows across the lower elevations, often climbing—or twining—through small bushes. The stems and leaves are Velcro-sticky to the touch and the tiny four-petaled yellowish-green flowers and white berries are inconspicuous. I photographed these one along Rush Creek near Lewiston.

SIERRA WALLFLOWER
Erysimum perenne
Mustard family

CALIFORNIA POPPY
Eschscholzia californica
Poppy family

CASTLE LAKE BEDSTRAW
Galium glabrescens subsp. *glabrescens*
Madder family

CLIMBING BEDSTRAW
Galium porrigens
Madder family

HOOKER'S EVENING-PRIMROSE
Oenothera elata subsp. *hirsutissima*   4 petals
Evening-primrose family

Here's a roadside wildflower that is particularly common along Highway 299 between Junction City and the Coast or the road to Kangaroo Lake on the Trinity Divide. It blooms mid to late summer at lower elevations. The tall stalks (to 5' or more) are crowned with large, lemon yellow flowers in a loose cluster. Each flower perches atop a red hypanthium. It can't be mistaken for anything else in this area. I photographed these along the road below Kangaroo Lake in July.

WESTERN BLADDERPOD
Physaria occidentalis subsp. *occidentalis*   4 petals
Mustard family

I've only found this tiny member of the mustard family on the serpentines of Scott Mountain. It is low growing—only about 4" high—with spoon shaped, fuzzy leaves from which stems arise carrying bunches of small, golden yellow, four-petaled flowers. Be careful where you walk, these are very inconspicuous. I photographed these in mid-July growing in rocky, exposed sites after an unusually heavy snow year.

MARSH YELLOW CRESS
Rorippa palustris   4 petals
Mustard family

Look for this tiny cress in open meadows shortly after the snow melts. It is a small wildflower, only reaching to about 8" in height, strongly upright with lance shaped leaves scattered along the length of the stem. The small, buttery yellow, four petaled flowers are tube shaped—flaring widely at the ends. I photographed these in the open, meadows below the Parker Divide in the Trinity Alps in late May.

MOUNTAIN JEWELFLOWER, SHIELDPLANT
Streptanthus tortuosus   4 petals
Mustard family

Mountain jewelflower is one you best get down on hands and knees and take a good look at. Beautiful yellow-green leaves almost completely enfold the upright stems and delicate, bell shaped flowers are scattered alternately at the tops of the stems. The flowers vary in color from yellow to a combination of cream, yellow, and red. When it goes to seed, dozens of elongated, lance shaped pods hang down which, together with the leaves, gives the plant its name—shieldplant (see inset). I took the large photograph on the ridge above Log Lake in July and the inset at the top of the pass between Ward and Salmon Lakes in mid-August—both in the Trinity Alps.

HOOKER'S EVENING-PRIMROSE
Oenothera elata subsp. *hirsutissima*
Evening-primrose family

WESTERN BLADDERPOD
Physaria occidentalis subsp. *occidentalis*
Mustard family

MARSH YELLOW CRESS
Rorippa palustris
Mustard family

MOUNTAIN JEWELFLOWER, SHIELDPLANT
Streptanthus tortuosus
Mustard family

NEVADA BIRD'S FOOT TREFOIL, SIERRA LOTUS, SIERRA NEVADA HOSACKIA
Acmispon nevadensis   5 irregular petals
Pea family

This member of the pea family grows in low mats in open, dry, and sunny areas. Five to twelve flowers bloom in compact clusters and are a bright buttery yellow. I have found mats of these plants 3' or more in circumference and absolutely covered with blooms—making it hard to miss. Stems and leaves are blue- or gray-green and covered with silvery hairs which make it soft to the touch. This is a native western species found from the Pacific Northwest into Baja California. I found it along the road to the Canyon Creek Trailhead.

MEADOW BIRDSFOOT TREFOIL
Hosackia pinnata   5 irregular petals
Pea family

The thick, rounded clusters of contrasting white and deep yellow blossoms make this lotus readily identifiable. The plants are between 5" and 16" tall and common alongside low elevation trails where there is plenty of moisture. Occasionally the lower portions of the petals are streaked with deep red. I photographed these along the road to the Stoddard Lake Trailhead in June.

SNUB PEA, SULPHUR PEA
Lathyrus sulphureus   5 irregular petals
Pea family

Young flowers, before they have fully opened, are a beautiful rusty orange on the backs of the petals. Fully opened flowers are white with brilliant lavender veins on the banner. This is a typical climbing pea and can be found at lower elevations throughout the area, generally in the front country of the Trinities. It prefers forested areas with a mix of sun and shade and likes to climb through brush. I photographed these near Shasta Lake but they are common throughout the region.

BIRD'S FOOT TREFOIL
Lotus corniculatus   5 irregular petals
Pea family

You can find this pretty little non-native weed from Eurasia across the region—from the coast to the inland foothills. It grows low to the ground in open, sunny areas and is common in disturbed areas along trails and roads. The bright masses of golden-yellow flowers make it easy to spot and identify. I photographed these along the Trinity River in late June.

NEVADA BIRD'S FOOT TREFOIL, SIERRA LOTUS
Acmispon nevadensis
Pea family

MEADOW BIRDSFOOT TREFOIL
Hosackia pinnata
Pea family

SNUB PEA, SULPHUR PEA
Lathyrus sulphureus
Pea family

BIRD'S FOOT TREFOIL
Lotus corniculatus
Pea family

MOUNT EDDY LUPINE
Lupinus croceus
Pea family

5 irregular petals

The compact buttery yellow flowers make it easy to identify in these mountains and hard to miss. People occasionally mistake yellow false lupine for this one but these plants have more than three leaflets per palmately compound leaf while yellow false-lupines have only three (like clovers). The plant grow to 18" and bloom in large colonies on multiple stems. I photographed these on the Stoney Ridge Trail in late June, but another good place to see them is along Blue Mountain Road between French Gulch and the East Fork of the Trinity River, especially in the vicinity of Blue Mountain.

YELLOW FALSE-LUPINE
Thermopsis gracilis
Pea family

5 irregular petals

It's easy to understand why, from a distance, this non-lupine might be confused with Mt. Eddy Lupine. Check it out up close, however, and the differences become apparent. These flowers are lemon yellow and loosely clustered along tall stalks, with only three leaflets per compound leaf. I photographed these along the lower part of the Boulder Creek Trail in the Trinity Alps in late June but they are common throughout these mountains.

STREAM VIOLET, SMOOTH YELLOW VIOLET, PIONEER VIOLET
Viola glabella
Violet family

5 irregular petals

This violet likes shade, water and—true to its name—grows along streams, near springs, and seeps. The heart shaped leaves are slightly cupped, finely toothed at the margins, and deep green. One to three flowering stalks arise from the rootstock bearing one lemon yellow to buttery yellow flower each leaf axil. The lower and two flanking petals are veined with deep purple and the flanking petals each have a slight yellow beard at the opening of the throat. *Viola glabella* can sometimes be confused with *Viola lobata* subsp. *integrifolia* because the leaf structure is similar. Look at the back of the flower—it's *V. glabella* if yellow and *Viola lobata* subsp. *integrifolia* if reddish or purplish. I took this photograph along the North Fork of Coffee Creek Trail in the Trinity Alps in early June.

PINE VIOLET
Viola lobata subsp. *integrifolia*
Violet family

5 irregular petals

Look for this violet in dry conifer or mixed-evergreen forests at low to mid elevations. The flowers range from bright lemon to a soft buttery yellow. The lower petal is veined with purple in the throat. The two flanking petals have a lemon yellow beard. The backs of the top two petals of both are deep, rusty red or sometimes purple. The big identifying factor when differentiating between the two subspecies is leaf structure. While the leaves of subsp. *lobata* are wide, and deeply divided, those of subsp. *integrifolia* are entire, triangular, and toothed. The two subspecies are common in this area and tend to grow in fairly large colonies, often together. I shot this photograph along the Stewart's Fork Trail in late May.

MOUNT EDDY LUPINE
Lupinus croceus
Pea family

YELLOW FALSE-LUPINE
Thermopsis gracilis
Pea family

STREAM VIOLET, SMOOTH YELLOW VIOLET
Viola glabella
Violet family

PINE VIOLET
Viola lobata subsp. *integrifolia*
Violet family

PINE VIOLET
Viola lobata subsp. *lobata*   5 irregular petals
Violet family

Look for this violet in dry, semi-open conifer or mixed forest stands at low to mid elevations. The flowers range from bright lemon to a soft buttery yellow. The lower petal is veined with purple in the throat. The two flanking petals have a lemon yellow beard. The backs of the top two petals of both are deep, rusty red or sometimes purple. The big identifying factor when differentiating between the two subspecies is leaf structure. While the leaves of lobata are wide, and somewhat deeply divided, those of integrifolia are entire, somewhat to sharply triangular and toothed. The two subspecies are common in this area and tend to grow in fairly large colonies, often mixed together. I shot this photograph near Big Carmen Lake on the Trinity Divide in mid-June.

ASTORIA VIOLET, UPLAND YELLOW VIOLET, CANARY VIOLET
Viola praemorsa subsp. *linguifolia*   5 irregular petals
Violet family

Here is another beautiful little violet that deserves close attention. While I've not found it there, Cal Flora recognizes a population along the Pacific Crest Trail on Scott Mountain... one of my perennial favorite hot spots for wildflowers. The flowers themselves look much like other yellow violets with maroon or deep reddish stripes emerging from the throat of the lower three petals and a yellow "beard" at the throat of the two flanking petals. The upper two petals are reddish or brownish purple on the backs. A single flower blooms at the top of a long, upright stem. The lance or oval shaped leaves are the interesting part - they can be either glabrous or covered in dense, silvery hairs giving them a furry look, the tips of which can be either pointed or rounded. I photographed these along Clikapudi Trail near Shasta Lake but will be actively pursuing the Scott Mountain population in the coming field seasons.

Note: *Viola praemorsa* subsp. *praemorsa* is also found throughout the Klamath Mountains but it is difficult to distinguish between the two.

SHELTON'S VIOLET, CUT-LEAF VIOLET
Viola sheltonii   5 irregular petals
Violet family

Shelton's violet is probably the earliest violet to bloom in these mountains. I have frequently found the plants emerging at low elevations in late February, with the flowers appearing around Shasta Lake in March and backcountry trails in mid-May. With its round and deeply divided blue-green leaves it is unmistakable. The flowers are bright yellow, with deep purple veining extending from the throat—especially on the lower petal. A sparse beard grows at the opening to the throat on the two flanking petals. The two top petals are purple on the backs. The ovary, deep inside the throat, is orange. I photographed this one along the North Fork of Coffee Creek Trail in the Trinity Alps in mid-May.

PINE VIOLET
Viola lobata subsp. *lobata*
Violet family

ASTORIA VIOLET, UPLAND YELLOW VIOLET
Viola praemorsa subsp. *linguifolia*
Violet family

SHELTON'S VIOLET, CUT-LEAF VIOLET
Viola sheltonii
Violet family

MOUNTAIN VIOLET, GOOSEFOOT VIOLET

Viola purpurea   5 irregular petals
Violet family

Of all the regional violets, none are as variable as the mountain violet. For that reason, I've included photographs and descriptions of the four variations I've found to be most common.

Top left: I photographed these in Whiskeytown National Recreation Area in early May. The deep green leaves are more or less heart shaped, deeply veined, with toothed margins. Several flowering stems arise from a single rootstock. The flowers are a beautiful golden yellow with dark purple veins extending from the throat on the lower petal. The two flanking petals have a sparse yellow beard just inside the throat. All of the petals are purple on the back. Look for this one on open, rocky flats in full sun or partial shade.

Top right: I photographed this one on the Stoney Ridge Trail in the Trinity Alps in late May. There were large colonies blooming at about 5000' in shaded sites all along the trail. Typically, the leaves are olive green, lance shaped, deeply veined, and lightly scalloped at the margins. The lemon yellow flowers all had a rounded look, with shortened petals veined with deep reddish-purple at the throat and a sparse yellow beard just inside the throat of the two flanking petals. The petals are purple on the backs.

Bottom left: I found this tiny mountain violet along the upper reaches of the Whorehouse Gulch Trail (now, for political expediency called "Lady Gulch") near the divide between Coffee Creek and the Salmon River. The dark green leaves are 1"-1¼" in diameter and shaped like the webbed foot of a goose, wavy on the margins, and deeply veined. The flowers are a deep, buttery yellow, with reddish purple veins extending from the throat of the lower petal and a yellow beard just inside the throat of the two flanking petals. The plants, including the flowering stalk, were less than 2" tall, growing in a large colony that extended for several yards along the trail. I've also found them along the trail to Parker Divide in the Trinity Alps.

MOST TYPICAL, Bottom right: This photograph, taken along the Stewart's Fork Trail in the Trinity Alps, represents what one will more typically find at low to mid-elevations in these mountains. The plants range in height from 4" to 7," with bright green, heart shaped leaves that are broadly scalloped at the margins. The flowers are almost lemon yellow with purple veining extending from the throat—more pronounced on the lower petal. Each flanking petal sports a lemon yellow beard just at the opening of the throat. This one likes damp, shaded sites and is commonly found alongside trails in the back country.

Whiskeytown National Recreation Area

Stony Ridge Trail in the Trinity Alps

Whorehouse Gulch (Lady Gulch) - Trinity Alps

Stewart's Fork Trail in the Trinity Alps

MOUNTAIN VIOLET, GOOSEFOOT VIOLET
Viola purpurea
Violet family

WESTERN BUTTERCUP
Ranunculus occidentalis
Buttercup family   5 symmetrical petals - ovary superior

This tall (12"- 20"), loosely branched wildflower is common at lower elevationsm where it prefers open, sunny areas. It sometimes begins to bloom in February in the foothills around the Sacramento Valley and in March the foothills surrounding the south and east facing slopes of the Trinity Alps. Like its cousin the alpine buttercup, this one is easily identified by its glossy yellow flowers that appear to have been waxed! I photographed these on Baxter Ridge above Trinity Lake in early June.

STICKY CINQUEFOIL
Drymocallis glandulosa
Rose family   5 symmetrical petals - ovary superior

The buttery-yellow flower petals fade to a light cream at the tips. The deep orange stamens in the center are what initially attract your eye to this beautiful little plant. Another identifying feature is the pale green calyx that shows between the petals. Unlike shrubby cinquefoil, this species has pinnately compound leaves. It is a slender, branching plant about 12" tall which prefers open, meadows, and slopes. These were photographed in the meadows below Long Gulch Lake in early August but you can find them throughout the high country at mid-elevations.

GORDON'S MOUSETAIL
Ivesia gordonii var. *ursinorum*
Rose family   5 symmetrical petals - ovary superior

I was sitting in camp at Summit Lake one afternoon glassing the serpentine slopes above the lake when this unusual splash of yellow caught my eye. I grabbed my camera and climbed around the outlet of the lake and up the slope to find this beautiful *Ivesia* in full bloom. It was growing in the jumbled rocks of the scree slope. It is characterized by heads of deep yellow flowers and thick bunches of dark green, deeply cleft leaves. In this area, I've only found it growing on exposed serpentine soils. Across other mountain ranges in the western United States it is the most widespread of the *Ivesias*. I photographed this bunch in a rocky cleft just below Lake Anna in July.

CREEPING SIBBALDIA, SIBBALDIA
Sibbaldia procumbens
Rose family   5 symmetrical petals - ovary superior

Sibbaldia is a world traveller—found throughout the northern latitudes on tundra and in alpine and sub-alpine regions. It forms multi-stemmed, low growing mats in open, gravelly areas. The grayish-green leaves are divided into three wedge shaped leaflets which have three teeth at the tips. Several flowering stalks arise from each plant and each hosts bunches of bright yellow flowers surrounded by hairy green bracts. I found and photographed this bunch in an open, exposed area just above Upper Caribou Lake in late August. It was common throughout the area.

WESTERN BUTTERCUP
Ranunculus occidentalis
Buttercup family

STICKY CINQUEFOIL
Drymocallis glandulosa
Rose family

GORDON'S MOUSETAIL
Ivesia gordonii var. *ursinorum*
Rose family

CREEPING SIBBALDIA, SIBBALDIA
Sibbaldia procumbens
Rose family

143

TINKER'S PENNY
Hypericum anagalloides
St. John's Wort family
5 symmetrical petals - ovary superior

Tinker's penny is most often found growing in small colonies alongside streams, the shorelines of lakes, and in wet meadows—almost always in full sun. Leaves are rounded, opposite, and clasp the short stems from top to bottom. Unlike other local St. John's worts, the stems are prostrate and mat-forming. Numerous deep yellow flowers (about ½" in diameter) open on each stem. It is a fairly inconspicuous plant. I photographed these at the outlet to Sapphire Lake in the Trinity Alps in September where they were hiding in tall grass.

KLAMATH WEED, COMMON ST. JOHN'S WORT, GOATWEED
Hypericum perforatum
St. John's Wort family
5 symmetrical petals ovary superior

First introduced to North America at the mouth of the Klamath River in the early 1900s, Klamath weed rapidly spread across California. By the 1950s it was found in over half of California's counties. It prefers disturbed areas from the coast to mid-elevations. It is poisonous to livestock and thus the subject of eradication efforts. It is a gangly, leggy, loosely branched plant with opposite stems and small, sharply oval leaves. It range from 2' to 3' tall. The yellow flowers have 5 petals which are sharply oval or lance shaped with numerous black spots along the edges. The stamens are numerous and prominent. It was used years ago during the Feast of St. John to ward off evil spirits and is also used as a treatment for depression. I photographed this plant along the road to the Stewart's Fork Trailhead in mid-June.

THE EDDYS STONECROP
Sedum kiersteadiae
Stonecrop family
5 symmetrical petals - ovary superior

This member of the stonecrop family is named after Julie Kierstead Nelson, a *Sedum* expert and one of this guide's contributors. Stonecrops are difficult to identify but the selection of species highlighted for this guide will make the task more approachable. *S. kiersteadiae* has numerous flowers blooming in loose bunches on an upright stalk. They are bright yellow, with sharply pointed petals, streaked with red down the center. When fully opened, the petals flare away from a reddish-orange ovary and stamens. The backside of the petals are also reddish-orange becoming more yellow towards the tips and edges. The basal rosette of leaves, as well as the stems, are succulent, fleshy, and a deep green to maroon. Smaller leaves, scattered along the flowering stem, appear grayish-purple. This photograph was taken above Upper Caribou Lake in the Trinity Alps in late August.

LANCE-LEAF STONECROP
Sedum lanceolatum
Stonecrop family
5 symmetrical petals - ovary superior

Of all the stonecrops this might be the easiest to identify. It is quite striking and blooms in abundance across open serpentine slopes. It is characterized by the reddish, succulent leaves and deep yellow flowers tinged with red. Flowering stalk are short with the flowers nestled in a compact bunch just above the leaves. This is a Scott Mountain favorite of mine—because that's the only place I've ever encountered it. I photographed these in early July following a particularly heavy snow year which delayed the usual earlier blooming season.

TINKER'S PENNY
Hypericum anagalloides
St. John's Wort family

KLAMATH WEED, COMMON ST. JOHN'S WORT
Hypericum perforatum
St. John's Wort family

THE EDDYS STONECROP
Sedum kiersteadiae
Stonecrop family

LANCE-LEAF STONECROP
Sedum lanceolatum
Stonecrop family

BROADLEAF STONECROP, PACIFIC SEDUM
Sedum spathulifolium   5 symmetrical petals - ovary superior
Stonecrop family

Look for this member of the stonecrop family at lower elevations throughout the region—often along back roads on shaded, steep, rocky hillsides. The perfect little flat rosettes of succulent leaves colonize large areas under proper conditions. The beautiful little deep yellow flowers bloom in widely branched bunches on stalks that sometimes reach 8" in height. I photographed these along the road to the Canyon Creek Trailhead in late May.

BLAZING STAR
Mentzelia laevicaulis var. *acuminata*   5 symmetrical petals ovary inferior
Blazing star or Loasa family

This 3' to 4' tall, stout, gangly plant decorates roadsides and disturbed areas at lower elevations throughout the area. Blazing star becomes a show stopper when it blooms with dozens of flowers on each plant. This lovely flower can be up to 6" across and a spectacular sunshine yellow. The slender, tapered petals flare away from a host of tall stamens when fully opened. The stems are light gray and the heavily toothed leaves a dull olive green. Look for it in mid-summer along Highway 299 between Weaverville and Big Bar or the Gazelle-Callahan Road as it descends into the Scott Valley.

AROMATIC SPRING-PARSLEY, NORTHERN INDIAN PARSNIP, TURPENTINE CYMOPTERUS
Cymopterus terebinthinus   5 symmetrical petals ovary inferior
Carrot family

This gregarious plant is common at lower elevations in the area covered by this guide. It is often found covering large sections of road-side slopes with its beautiful, deep green, fern-like foliage. Bright yellow flowers decorate large umbels, or umbrella shaped clusters of blooms. Thick stalks, that often reach 2' in height or more, support the flowers. The plant emits a strong anise smell that I find quite pleasant. I photographed these beautiful plants above the McCloud River along Gilman Road in early April but look for them across the region.

FOOTHILL LOMATIUM, SPRING GOLD
Lomatium utriculatum   5 symmetrical petals - ovary inferior
Carrot family

Foothill lomatium is common on open areas in the foothills in early spring. Being a member of the carrot family, it has leaves that are finely dissected and smell a bit like carrot leaves when crushed. The small bright yellow flowers bloom en masse in flat-topped clusters on top of stout stems. The entire plant rarely exceeds 6" or 7" in height. I photographed this one alongside the old road that runs through Bolt's Hill above Lewiston Lake in late May.

BROADLEAF STONECROP, PACIFIC SEDUM
Sedum spathulifolium
Stonecrop family

BLAZING STAR
Mentzelia laevicaulis var. *acuminata*
Blazing star or Loasa family

AROMATIC SPRING-PARSLEY
Cymopterus terebinthinus
Carrot family

FOOTHILL LOMATIUM, SPRING GOLD
Lomatium utriculatum
Carrot family

PURPLE SANICLE
Sanicula bipinnatifida   5 symmetrical petals - ovary inferior
Carrot family

This inconspicuous little plant could easily go unnoticed if not for the large, light, yellowish to olive green leaves. They are deeply cleft and toothed growing alternately along a central light reddish to gray-green stem. The tiny, ¼" to ½", purple (and sometimes yellow) flowers grow in several ball-shaped heads atop a long, thin stem. They occur in large populations and seem not to be picky about soil type. I photographed these on the Trinity Divide along Trinity Mountain road in late April and the yellow version along the road to the Lake Eleanor Trailhead in the Trinity Alps in late May.

HOWELL'S TAUSCHIA
Tauschia howellii   5 symmetrical petals - ovary inferior
Carrot family

The entire plant is usually less than 4" tall, with deeply dissected, spiny leaves that are taller than the flowering stems. The flowers are generally yellow and occur in loose clusters surrounded by leafy bracts. Two other *Tauschia* species could be mistaken for *T. howellii*. They are *T. glauca* and *T. kelloggii*, but they are typically much larger (4" to 20" in height) with flowers occurring in tighter bundles. It prefers dry, open sites with gravelly granitic soils at higher elevations. The best chance to find this rarity is along the high ridges of the northwestern portion of the Trinity Alps or the spine of the Russian Wilderness. I took this photograph while working with Julie Knorr documenting rare plants for the Klamath National Forest on the Siskiyou Crest in Siskiyou County. It has been found in the Marble Mountains but not, as far as I know, anywhere else.

COBWEBBY INDIAN PAINTBRUSH
Castilleja arachnoidea   5 irregular petals forming a tube
Broomrape family

I was lying in a huge, but scattered colony of this paintbrush shooting photographs when a couple of hikers wandered by and politely asked what I was doing (I've found this to be an all too common occurrence). When I pointed out that I was taking photographs of this beautiful little wildflower they were amazed that they had not seen them—yet there they were, right under their feet. Because the plants do blend with the color of the surroundings, they are easy to miss. The plants are about 12" tall, multi-branched, with stiff, light, gray-green leaves. The fuzzy flowers are light lemon yellow, orange, or reddish-pink. The photograph of the orange-yellow flowers was taken at Log Lake and the yellow ones in Doe Flat in the Trinity Alps in late August.

FIELD OWL'S-CLOVER
Castilleja campestris subsp. *campestris*   5 irregular petals forming a tube
Broomrape family

This tiny owl's-clover rarely gets over 3" tall and, because of its size, hides nicely in open, dry, or vernally damp grassy meadows. The inflated, lemon-yellow flowers (about ¼" across) form a tube with the three-lobed lower lip hanging down in a fan shape from the red spotted throat. The stems, leaves, and sepals are all fuzzy. I photographed these along the Kanaka Peak Trail in Whiskeytown National Recreation Area but I've also seen them along the lower stretches of the East Boulder Lake trail in the Trinity Alps.

PURPLE SANICLE
Sanicula bipinnatifida
Carrot family

HOWELL'S TAUSCHIA
Tauschia howellii
Carrot family

COBWEBBY INDIAN PAINTBRUSH
Castilleja arachnoidea
Broomrape family

FIELD OWL'S-CLOVER
Castilleja campestris subsp. *campestris*
Broomrape family

TOWERING LOUSEWORT
Pedicularis bracteosa var. *flavida*   5 irregular petals forming a tube
Broomrape family

This is the giant among louseworts—often reaching heights of 4' or more with flowers crowded along the upper fourth of the stalk.. My granddaughter insists the individual flowers look like miniature dolphins and not their namesake lice. Personally, I think she's right. Look for them in marshy areas or in wet meadows, often growing with corn lilies. I photographed these at the back of Upper Albert Lake in the Russians in September.

MOTH MULLEIN
Verbascum blattaria   5 irregular petals forming a tube
Figwort family

This is a common "weed" throughout this area and one than can be commonly seen along lower elevation roads and trails. The tall flowering stalks can be 5' in height and covered with beautiful yellow flowers on the upper third. The flowers are scarcely tubular and irregular, with petals that are united only at their bases. The plant may be a nuisance to some but the flowers are quite striking. Julie Kierstead Nelson says that she enjoys them growing and blooming in her garden because they are as beautiful as many plants for sale in nurseries—I agree. I photographed these alongside Highway 3 near Musser Hill just outside of Weaverville.

CHICKWEED MONKEYFLOWER
Erythranthe alsinoides   5 irregular petals forming a tube
Lopseed family

Look for crowded colonies of this tiny monkeyflower in rocky clefts near springs and seeps throughout the Trinity Alps. It makes up for its size in sheer numbers and is one small wildflower that you are unlikely to miss. The plants range anywhere from 3" to 6" in height with flowers that are a beautiful buttery yellow and about ¼" in diameter. Typically, you will find a few tiny red spots and one large red central spot on the lower petal. Occasionally, however, you will find them with no red spots at all or a solitary large red spot. I photographed these along the Canyon Creek Trail but have found them at Mill Creek Lake in the Trinity Alps as well—blooming from mid-June into July.

GIANT MONKEYFLOWER, COMMON MONKEYFLOWER, SEEP MONKEYFLOWER
Erythranthe guttata   5 irregular petals forming a tube
Lopseed family

Erythranthe guttata is a common monkeyflower and one most people are familiar with—it is pretty much universal in this area. It is found in wet areas from Pacific Ocean beaches, to low elevations in the Klamath, and even the floor of the Central Valley. The large, buttery yellow flowers congregate in large groups at the ends of the flowering stalks and have small red spots on the lower petal. The stems and leaves are hairy and somewhat sticky. They bloom en-masse wherever slow flowing or standing water is found (see inset). I photographed this pair along the Upper Trinity River in early July and the inset along the Mendocino coast in August.

TOWERING LOUSEWORT
Pedicularis bracteosa var. *flavida*
Broomrape family

MOTH MULLEIN
Verbascum blattaria
Figwort family

CHICKWEED MONKEYFLOWER
Erythranthe alsinoides
Lopseed family

GIANT MONKEYFLOWER
Erythranthe guttata
Lopseed family

151

MUSK MONKEYFLOWER
Erythranthe moschata   5 irregular petals forming a tube
Lopseed family

This little lemony-yellow monkeyflower, though sometimes more difficult to find, is easy to identify once you do. The flowers are tubular with fused petals that flare away at the tips. Three of the petals are lined with deep reddish brown stripes and are bearded in the throat. The shape of the flower, when looking directly into it, is round but each petal is slightly notched at the tips with slightly ruffled edges. The bright green leaves are more or less oval and can be slightly toothed at the margins. All the green parts of the plant are densely glandular and hairy making them sticky to the touch with a slightly musky smell. Plants tend to be shorter (10" to 12" in height) than what is described in other guides. They favor damp meadows and the edge of streams. I photographed these in the meadows surrounding Adams Lake in the Trinity Alps in September.

PRIMROSE MONKEYFLOWER
Erythranthe primuloides   5 irregular petals forming a tube
Lopseed family

A singular red spot centered at the throat of each of the three lower petals is indicative of this monkeyflower—some also have small red spots scattered in the throat. The petals are notched at the tips and rounded. Other traits to look for are the mats of oval or round leaves that can be either hairy or smooth. A single flower rises on a long, thin, and dark pedicel from short tufted stems. The plants are rarely over 5" tall. Look for it growing in dense colonies in rocky seeps or the edges of streams. It really likes crevices in cliff faces with sun and moisture. I photographed this one in shoreline grass at Stoddard Lake in the Trinity Alps in early September.

SHASTA LIMESTONE MONKEYFLOWER
Erythranthe taylorii   5 irregular petals forming a tube
Lopseed family

Climb around in the abundant limestone above Shasta Lake early in the season and you will be rewarded with finding this gorgeous little lemony-yellow monkeyflower. Small colonies grow and bloom in cracks and crevices throughout the area tending towards sunny exposures. This is a small monkeyflower, most reaching about 2" to 4" in height with deep reddish stems and gray-green fuzzy leaves which are toothed at the margins. The calyx tube is long with prominent red ridges and light red to pink between. Probably the most striking feature is the two bright red dots on the lower petal. Smaller red dots descend down into the flower tube as well. I photographed these above the McCloud arm of Shasta Lake in April. Now that extensive surveys have been done, this species has been found on substrates other than limestone but still geographically limited to the area around Shasta Lake.

TILING'S MONKEYFLOWER
Erythranthe tilingii   5 irregular petals forming a tube
Lopseed family

I've only run across this monkeyflower in one place—above Mill Creek Lake in the Trinity Alps. Here it was grows in thick masses in wet, rocky clefts. In size, they are halfway between the chickweed and giant or common monkeyflowers. Leaves are small, toothed, and a deep green. The flowers are more orange-yellow but spotted with red on the lower petal. Unlike the giant monkeyflower, the flowers are solitary in the leaf axil. I photographed these above Mill Creek Lake in the Trinity Alps in July.

MUSK MONKEYFLOWER
Erythranthe moschatus
Lopseed family

PRIMROSE MONKEYFLOWER
Erythranthe primuloides
Lopseed family

SHASTA LIMESTONE MONKEYFLOWER
Erythranthe taylorii
Lopseed family

TILING'S MONKEYFLOWER
Erythranthe tilingii
Lopseed family

153

CALIFORNIA STONESEED, CALIFORNIA PUCCOON
Lithospermum californicum   5 symmetrical petals forming a tube
Borage family

This is a common native plant that grows in profusion along the road to the Canyon Creek Trailhead where it blooms from late May well into June. The plants are tall, reaching 12" or so, and the leaves and stems are covered with soft hairs. The deep buttery yellow flowers are tube shaped and about ½" in diameter. Up close I find the plant very attractive, and I just like the name puccoon (say that 50 times fast!). Always curious about the origin of common names, I researched "puccoon" and found that it was derived from the Powhatan word "poughkone" in reference to this group of plants, especially the roots, which have been used for centuries to produce dyes. I photographed these along the road to the Canyon Creek trailhead in May.

NORTHERN SANICLE, SIERRA SANICLE
Sanicula graveolens   5 symmetrical petals ovary inferior
Carrot family

Northern sanicle grows in mats on open rocky slopes or in forested habitats throughout this area. It is found on a variety of substrates including serpentines and granites from low to high elevations. The pinnately compound leaves are dark green rimmed with purple and branch from purple stems. Several heads of dense, pale greenish-yellow flowers emerge in a loose group at the ends of the flowering stalks. I photographed this specimen near the upper end of its elevational range at about 6,500' near receding snowbanks above Foster Lake in the Trinity Alps in late May.

DALMATIAN TOADFLAX and COMMON TOADFLAX, BUTTER AND EGGS
Linaria dalmatica subsp. *dalmatica* and *Linaria vulgaris*   5 irregular petals forming a tube
Plantain family

This species is fond of open, sunny flats along the Trinity River and some of its southern tributaries. Considered a weed, imported from Europe and Asia, I still find the flowers beautiful. The buttery yellow, long-spurred flowers look like little snap-dragons and are arrayed along the upper half of a tall spike. **Note**: a second toadflax grows in the same neighborhood. *Linaria vulgaris,* or common toadflax, known as butter and eggs. The difference between the two is in the flower arrangement. Common toadflax has flowers arranged in a dense, almost whorled cluster at the tops of the flowering stem (see inset). The photograph of dalmation toadflax was taken along the Canyon Creek Road in mid-June while the inset of common toadflax was taken along the Trinity River near Douglas City in early July.

GRAY CUSHION PUSSYTOES, LOW PUSSYTOES
Antennaria dimorpha   Flowers in composite heads
Sunflower family

Every time I visit Scott Mountain I seem to make a new discovery, and this unusual little pussytoe was no exception. I found a small population of four plants growing in a low, 3" - 4" tall, spreading mound covering an area roughly two by three feet. The spoon shaped leaves, sharply up-turned at the margins, are green but covered with long gray hairs giving the plant a blue-green look. This species is dioecious meaning some plants are male and others female—these photographs are of the female plant bearing pistillate flowers. The Jepson eFlora describes these flowers as a dingy brown but those I found were definitely pale to dark yellow with prominent dark brown pistils. After an extensive search I found no other populations in this area. I photographed these in early June.

154

CALIFORNIA STONESEED
Lithospermum californicum
Borage family

NORTHERN SANICLE, SIERRA SANICLE
Sanicula graveolens
Carrot family

DALMATIAN TOADFLAX
Linaria dalmatica subsp. *dalmatica* & *Linaria vulgaris*
Plantain family

GRAY CUSHION PUSSYTOES, LOW PUSSYTOES
Antennaria dimorpha
Sunflower family

HEARTLEAF ARNICA
Arnica cordifolia   Flowers in composite heads
Sunflower family

The loose configuration of the ray flowers around the pale lemon yellow flower heads is one of the distinguishing features of this *Arnica*. The ray flowers can vary from oval to long and slender on the same head and have rounded notches at the tips. Leaves are opposite, heart-shaped, and toothed. They bloom in large colonies in shaded, damp sites at mid to high elevations. I photographed these along the trail above Lilypad Lake in the Trinity Alps in July but one of the most beautiful displays is along the Stewart's Fork trail below Nancy Creek. Also watch for them in Horse Heaven Meadows on the Trinity Divide.

RAYLESS ARNICA
Arnica discoidea   Flowers in composite heads
Sunflower family

This is a common *Arnica* at low elevations. The tall stems with bunches of lemon yellow, rayless flower heads are readily recognizable. Stems, leaves, and involucres are fuzzy. I photographed these on Bailey Cove Trail on Shasta Lake in May but I've seen them along Swift Creek near Preacher Meadows just outside the Trinity Alps. They like open, shaded areas and are especially abundant alongside trails.

CLASPING ARNICA
Arnica lanceolata   Flowers in composite heads
Sunflower family

Several species of *Arnica* are found in the area covered by this guide and are often difficult to tell apart—but leaf shape and habitat make identification fairly easy for Clasping arnica. The sharply toothed leaves are lance shaped, basal, and folded along the flowering stalks. For the most part, the plants are strongly upright found growing in rocky clefts near running water. The flowering stalks supports one to three buttery yellow composite flowers. The ray flowers are notched at the tips. I found and photographed these along Canyon Creek above Middle Falls and again at Upper Falls in late June.

BROAD-LEAVED ARNICA, MOUNTAIN ARNICA
Arnica latifolia   Flowers in composite heads
Sunflower family

Perhaps the best show of broad-leaved arnica, anywhere in this area, is along the last mile or so of the trail to Big and Little Duck Lakes. The shaded, moist meadows are loaded with them. As opposed to heartleaf arnica, these flowers often bloom in loose clusters at the tops of their tall stems. These were photographed just below Little Duck Lake in the Russians in early August.

HEARTLEAF ARNICA
Arnica cordifolia
Sunflower family

RAYLESS ARNICA
Arnica discoidea
Sunflower family

CLASPING ARNICA
Arnica lanceolata
Sunflower family

BROAD-LEAVED ARNICA, MOUNTAIN ARNICA
Arnica latifolia
Sunflower family

SEEP SPRING ARNICA, LONGLEAF ARNICA
Arnica longifolia
Sunflower family

Flowers in composite heads

Arnicas are difficult to identify to the species level. That being said, seep spring arnica—with beautiful golden yellow flowers found clustered in large patches next to flowing streams and springs—is one of the easier ones. They are especially beautiful along the upper reaches of Stony Creek (where I photographed these) in the Trinity Alps where they prefer stream-washed granite shelves and rocky outcrops alongside waterfalls. The paired leaves have lightly toothed margins, are long and narrow, and mostly fused along the flowering stems. Leaves and stems can be sticky. I photographed these in late July.

SHASTA COUNTY ARNICA
Arnica venosa
Sunflower family

Flowers in composite heads

The stem of this *Arnica* grows strongly upright, with narrowly oval leaves scattered in opposite pairs along the stems. The blooms lack ray flowers and have compact heads of upright deep yellow disk flowers. I photographed these along the shoreline of West Boulder Lake in the Trinity Alps in August. They are also found on Shasta Bally above Whiskeytown Lake, and north of Shasta Lake in the McCloud and Squaw Creek watersheds.

WESTERN HAWKSBEARD
Crepis occidentalis subsp. *conjuncta*
Sunflower family

Flowers in composite heads

This is another wildflower I've found in abundance on Scott Mountain. It grows in scattered locations preferring open, sandy to rocky sites on the south and west facing slopes. The leaves of this low growing plant are long, uniformly gray-green, and deeply cleft with wrinkled edges. Each plant that I found had several deep yellow flower heads with ray petals slightly toothed at the tips. This photograph was taken in early July.

BIGELOW'S SNEEZEWEED, SNEEZEWEED
Helenium bigelovii
Sunflower family

Flowers in composite heads

No matter where you go in the high country you are likely to find this plant somewhere along the way. It is mostly a meadow dweller but likes other wet areas as well. It tends to bloom in large colonies with dozens—if not hundreds of plants. It can reach a couple of feet in height and the flowers can be quite large. The most distinguishing feature of this flower is the large rounded knob of yellowish-orange disc flowers in the center surrounded by lighter, buttery yellow ray flowers. I might add that it is one of the most persistent of the late bloomers in the high country. I've found beautiful flowers well into the late fall season, even into early November. I photographed this bunch near Mt. Ashland in Southern Oregon in July.

SEEP SPRING ARNICA
Arnica longifolia
Sunflower family

SHASTA COUNTY ARNICA
Arnica venosa
Sunflower family

WESTERN HAWKSBEARD
Crepis occidentalis subsp. *conjuncta*
Sunflower family

BIGELOW'S SNEEZEWEED
Helenium bigelovii
Sunflower family

DELTOID-LEAF BALSAMROOT, SILKY BALSAMROOT and HYBRID BALSAMROOT

Balsamorhiza deltoidea
Balsamorhiza sericea and
Balsamorhiza sericea X deltoidea
Sunflower family

Flowers in composite heads

There is a place along the Upper Trinity River called Sunflower Flat which was probably named by miners or early settlers making their way up the old California-Oregon Trail over Scott Mountain in the mid to late 1800s. I am convinced this place name came from the balsamroot that blooms there in profusion. *Balsamorhiza* would have attracted the attention of those early travellers—it is a beautiful, bright and sunny wildflower when in full bloom and impossible to ignore. Today, as you drive along Highway 3 in the upper reaches of the Trinity River above Coffee Creek, it can still brighten your day, much as it would have years ago.

Deltoid-leaf balsamroot (*B. deltoidea*) is native to, and found throughout, California and not confined to any particular soil type. Silky Balsamroot (*B. sericea*) seems limited to the serpentine soils of the Klamath Mountains and is included in the California Native Plant Society list of Rare and Endangered Plants. I have no information about hybrid balsamroot (*sericea* x *deltoidea*), other than that it is found along with *B. deltoidea* and *B. sericea*.

While the flowers of all three are much the same, the leaves are quite different which makes identification fairly easy. The deep green leaves of *B. deltoidea* vary in size and, to a degree, shape. Typically, they tend to be large, wide at the base, tapering to the tip from which they gain their common name deltoid-leaf. The leaves of *B. sericea*, on the other hand, are gray-green, slightly fuzzy, pinnately compound, and deeply divided right down to the central stem. Leaves of the hybrid form (*sericea* x *deltoidea*) are a nice cross—being deep green, pinnately veined, and lobed.

DELTOID-LEAF BALSAMROOT
Balsamorhiza deltoidea
Sunflower family

HYBRID BALSAMROOT
Balsamorhiza sericea X deltoidea
Sunflower family

SILKY BALSAMROOT
Balsamorhiza sericea
Sunflower family

GREENE'S GOLDENBUSH
Ericameria greenei
Sunflower family   Flowers in composite heads

Greene's goldenbush is common and widespread plant throughout the area covered by this guide. Like *E. bloomeri*, this one displays lemon-yellow flowers that are structured with long, narrowly oval, and pointed ray flowers. The disc flowers are small but the stamens and anthers are prominent. All in all, when blooming, the plant has a decidedly shaggy look. In the area where I took this photograph the plants formed low, mounded bunches up to 12" in height and 24" in diameter. This *Ericameria* has an affinity for serpentine soils but they are not necessarily limited to that substrate. I photographed this bunch near the summit of Mt. Ashland in southern Oregon where it was blooming on gravelly soils.

FLEABANE DAISY, BLOOMER'S DAISY
Erigeron bloomeri
Sunflower family

Rayless heads of bright yellow disk flowers bloom atop short reddish stems which are surrounded by masses of long, very narrow leaves. The entire plant rarely exceeds 6" to 8" in height. It prefers open, rocky sites in full sun. I photographed this tiny daisy along the Pacific Crest Trail above Kangaroo Lake at the north end of the Trinity Divide in July. I've also seen it blooming atop the pass above Mumford Basin in the Trinity Alps.

ROCK DAISY
Erigeron petrophilus
Sunflower family   Flowers in composite heads

This tiny rayless daisy grows in open, rocky areas at mid to high elevations. In passing, the flowers resemble those of Bloomer's daisy (see above) but while this one has multiple flower heads per stem, *E. bloomeri* has one per stem. Also, this one has multiple leaves along the stem while the leaves of *E. bloomeri* are basal with no leaves on the stems. The flower heads are large, deep yellow, and bloom in small clusters at the tops of the stems. Both the leaves and stems are fuzzy. I photographed this small bunch on the ridge above Horseshoe Lake in the Trinity Alps in August.

CALIFORNIA HELIANTHELLA, CALIFORNIA LITTLE SUNFLOWER
Helianthella californica var. *shastensis*   Flowers in composite heads
Sunflower family

The tall, central flowering stalk is dark reddish-green and holds a singular, yellow-orange, compact, head of ray and disc flowers. Leaves are lance shaped, strongly upright, and in a basal mass surrounding the flowering stalk. They congregate in small colonies where it is shaded and damp at low to mid-elevations. I commonly find this wildflower blooming in the serpentine soils along the east side of the Trinity Alps, northern end of the Trinity Divide, as well as in the decomposed granitic soils on the south end of the Trinity Divide. I photographed these along the road to the Long Canyon Trailhead but look for them along Trinity Dam Boulevard near Lewiston and along Highway 3 as it skirts Trinity Lake in May and June.

GREENE'S GOLDENBUSH
Ericameria greenei
Sunflower family

FLEABANE DAISY, BLOOMER'S DAISY
Erigeron bloomeri
Sunflower family

ROCK DAISY
Erigeron petrophilus
Sunflower family

CALIFORNIA HELIANTHELLA
Helianthella californica var. *shastensis*
Sunflower family

COMMON WOOLY SUNFLOWER
Eriophyllum lanatum
Sunflower family

Flowers in composite heads

Several varieties of this species are found in the area, differing mostly in leaf color, hairiness, and degree of leaf lobing—thus I have included two photographs. These two photos show some of the variable features of this species. One I find commonly blooming from the floor of the Central Valley into the foothills of the surrounding mountains, and the other I find frequently at mid to higher elevations in the backcountry. The low elevation version is characterized by soft, fuzzy, gray-green leaves sprouting along a fuzzy, gray-green stems. The high country version is characterized by slightly fuzzy dark green leaves and nearly naked stems. The yellow blooms of both versions are almost identical in size although the disc flowers of those found in the high country tend to be a darker orange-brown. The low elevation version can be found blooming in large colonies where soil and moisture conditions are optimal or in scattered populations in places where they are exposed to dry and hot conditions—cut banks of roads for example. These bloom in early May and last well into August. I photographed these along Rush Creek Road near Lewiston in July. The high elevation version tends to bloom in small, scattered populations or individually at the edges of meadows near mixed-conifer stands. They begin their bloom at the end of July and continue well into September. I photographed this one along the trail below Sugar Pine Lake in the Trinity Alps in mid-September.

PRICKLY HAWKWEED, SHAGGY HAWKWEED
Hieracium horridum
Sunflower family

Flowers in composite heads

I found this tiny hawkweed blooming in open, exposed and sandy soil between rocky outcrops on the ridge between Sugar Lake and Little Duck Lake in the Russians. The flower heads are approximately ½" in diameter, the rays of which are squared and deeply toothed. The stems and leaves are deep green and covered with long white hairs. I took this photograph in early July after a heavy snow year.

COMMON MADIA
Madia elegans
Sunflower family

Flowers in composite heads

This is a common wildflower found from low to mid elevations throughout this area. The plants are tall and loosely branched with several flowers blooming along each stalk. The bright yellow ray flowers are deeply toothed, with or without faint to deep burgundy markings at the base surrounding the deep orange disc flowers. It's interesting to me that there is often a mix of flower coloration on each stalk—illustrates that nicely in this photo. This is one of those flowers that blooms early and stays late, often well into the fall. I photographed these along the road to the Stoney Ridge Trailhead in early June but you will see them blooming in large colonies next to roads and trails across the region.

164

COMMON WOOLY SUNFLOWER
Eriophyllum lanatum
Sunflower family

PRICKLY HAWKWEED, SHAGGY HAWKWEED
Hieracium horridum
Sunflower family

COMMON MADIA
Madia elegans
Sunflower family

THREADSTEM MADIA
Madia exigua
Sunflower family

Flowers in composite heads

This tiny wildflower is common and readily identifiable by its hairy bright green leaves, reddish stems, and tiny yellow flower heads. Flowers are ¼" to ½" across and scattered throughout the low growing plant. I photographed this inconspicuous plant along the Pacific Crest Trail west of Scott Mountain summit in July.

SLENDER TARWEED, GUMWEED
Madia gracilis
Sunflower family

Flowers in composite heads

Slender tarweed is just that—small, delicate, and less than 5" in height. The ray flowers are a pale lemon-yellow, deeply notched into threes, with each notch rounded at the tip. The disc flowers are dark and form a loose bunch in the center. Stems and leaves are fuzzy. I photographed these along the road to the Swift Creek Trailhead in early June.

WAXY CONEFLOWER, KLAMATH CONEFLOWER
Rudbeckia glaucescens
Sunflower family

Flowers in composite heads

This is a local giant among *Rudbeckias*. It blooms in damp, shaded meadows, and towers over most of the other plants in the neighborhood. Decorated stems range to almost 4' tall. The large, reflexed, deep yellow ray flowers drape away from the tall, cone shaped bunch of brownish disc flowers in the center. Each plant is crowned with a solitary flower head. The leaf margins of are mostly entire or minimally toothed. **Note**: There is a second species found in this area as well (*Rudbeckia klamathensis*). Except for the margins of the leaf flowers, the two closely resemble each other. Those of *R. klamathensis* are coarsely toothed or lobed. I photographed these one in a meadow along Horse Creek in the Trinity Alps in mid-July.

THREADSTEM MADIA
Madia exigua
Sunflower family

SLENDER TARWEED, GUMWEED
Madia gracilis
Sunflower family

WAXY CONEFLOWER, KLAMATH CONEFLOWER
Rudbeckia glaucescens or *klamathensis*
Sunflower family

SINGLE STEM BUTTERWEED, LAMBS-TONGUE RAGWORT
Senecio integerrimus var. *major*
Sunflower family

Flowers in composite heads

This is a hard-to-miss wildflower. It blooms from low to mid-elevations across these mountains—usually in open forested areas. Buttery yellow and orange clusters of ray and disc flowers form dense clusters atop tall, 1' to 2', stems. Stems and the mostly basal leaves are covered with whitish, cobwebby hairs. I photographed this bunch at the edge of an open meadow at Lower Albert Lake in the Russians, but along Highway 3 between Bowerman Ridge and Trinity Center is another good place to find them.

ARROWLEAF RAGWORT, ARROWHEAD BUTTERWEED
Senecio triangularis
Sunflower family

Flowers in composite heads

Arrowleaf ragwort resembles singlestem butterweed. While butterweed has hairy stems and leaves, the leaves of this one are not hairy and arrow shaped. The ray flowers are longer and more loosely arranged around the central cluster of orange disk flowers and the flowering heads are not as compact. The plants of both species are about the same height but grow in different habitats. *Senecio triangularis* prefers wet places while *Senecio integerrimus* prefers the understory of mixed conifer forests. Another ragwort, *Senecio aronicoides*, is common to the forested understory on Scott Mountain, and the Eddys (a small geographic subdivision on the Trinity Divide surrounding Mt. Eddy). I photographed these in an open wooded area below Sugar Pine Lake in late August.

WEST COAST CANADA GOLDENROD
Solidago elongata
Sunflower family

Flowers in composite heads

Goldenrod is common in lower elevation meadows and open, sunny places in the Trinity Alps and on the Trinity Divide. The tiny golden flowers bloom in elongated, dense clusters at the tops of leafy stems. The leaves get smaller the farther up the stem they grow. Plants can be 2' or more in height. I photographed these along Stewart's Fork where they are quite common not only in meadows but in areas where it is damp.

MULE'S EARS
Wyethia angustifolia
Sunflower family

Flowers in composite heads

Mule's ears are a low elevation, early spring favorite for Sunday drivers and hikers alike. The basal leaves are the most noticeable feature—large, upright, and shaped much like their namesake mule's ears. The showy, bright buttery yellow flowers stand out also. A single stem rises from the leaves to a height of about 16" with a single flower head that can be 8" in diameter. They are found in large colonies in open, sunny areas. I photographed this bunch along Highway 3 near Mule Creek.

SINGLE STEM BUTTERWEED
Senecio integerrimus var. *major*
Sunflower family

ARROWLEAF RAGWORT, ARROWHEAD BUTTERWEED
Senecio triangularis
Sunflower family

WEST COAST CANADA GOLDENROD
Solidago elongata
Sunflower family

MULE'S EARS
Wyethia angustifolia
Sunflower family

WATER PLANTAIN BUTTERCUP
Ranunculus alismifolius   Many petals
Buttercup family

This early season beauty is a common flower in wet meadows, along the edges of streams, and seeps across the region. The glossy, waxy, deep yellow flowers bloom on short stalks rising from dark green, basal, lance shaped leaves. You will often find it growing with marsh marigold, as the two like the same wet habitats. I photographed these in the marshy areas alongside the trail to Parker Divide in the Trinity Alps in early June.

YELLOW POND-LILY, BRANDY-BOTTLE, SPATTERDOCK, YELLOW COW-LILY
Nuphar polysepala   Many petals
Sunflower family

Yellow pond-lily is an aquatic perennial that blooms in low to mid-elevation mountain lakes and ponds throughout the area. Lilypad Lake takes its name from this plant which, by late summer, has covered most of the surface of the water with its large, heart-shaped leaves and gorgeous blooms. The flowers are cup shaped and buttery yellow with small scale-like petals surrounded by thick, showy sepals. By late summer the flowers and leaf stems have died back leaving only submerged, withered stems and rootstocks behind. I photographed this one at Horseshoe Lake in the Trinity Alps in August.

Big Boulder Lake in the Trinity Alps is a popular destination for day hikers and families backpacking with children. This gorgeous lake occupies a shallow basin surrounded by rich meadows and mixed conifers. There are many day hiking possibilities including Lost, Found, Tapie, and Little Boulder Lakes. In early summer, yellow pond lilies bloom along the shallow inlet side of the lake—a wealth of diverse wildflowers can be found in this basin.

WATER PLANTAIN BUTTERCUP
Ranunculus alismifolius
Buttercup family

YELLOW POND-LILY, BRANDY-BOTTLE
Nuphar polysepala
Sunflower family

Yellow pond lilies decorate shallow areas in Big Boulder Lake in the Trinity Alps.

DWARF OREGON-GRAPE
Berberis nervosa   3 or 6 petals
Barberry family

This is an interesting little plant found throughout the area in shaded sites, beneath a canopy of mixed conifer and hardwoods, at lower to mid-elevations. Its holly-like leaflets are evergreen, seven or more on the compound leaf, stiff, and spiny. Although the leaves can change color they are persistent through winter. It's a low growing plant, usually no more than 18" in height, with woody stems. In the spring, groups of yellow to yellow-green flowers form and are followed by dull blue fruit coated with a waxy whitish bloom. There are three species of Oregon-grape found in these mountains but this one is the one you are most likely to encounter. The berries in the small photograph actually belong to tall oregon grape (*Berberis aquifolium*) but look like those of *B. nervosa*. I photographed this bunch along Big French Creek in early September where the two can be found in close proximity. I photographed the flowers along the China Springs Trail to Grizzly Lake in August and the autumn red leaves along the Canyon Creek Trail in late September.

BUSH POPPY
Dendromecon rigida   4 petals
Poppy family

For most of the year this shrub is nondescript, with stiff branches and leathery gray-green leaves. But, in April and May, it explodes with beautiful, large golden yellow, bowl shaped flowers. It is a low elevation shrub that grows in exposed, dry sites, often alongside roads where the plants put on a magnificent display. I photographed these along Deadwood Road near Lewiston but look for them along Highway 106 near the north end of Trinity Lake.

SHRUBBY CINQUEFOIL
Dasiphora fruticosa   5 symmetrical petals - ovary superior
Rose family

This common cinquefoil grows throughout the mid-elevations of this area. It is a shrubby plant growing to about 2' in height with small, deeply divided leaves that have a rich, satiny feel. The brilliant yellow flowers bloom at the ends of branches or in the leaf axils. The petals are round with a crown of deep orange stamens and anthers in the center. I photographed these along the Fen Trail above Kangaroo Lake on the Trinity Divide in mid-July.

DWARF OREGON-GRAPE
Berberis nervosa
Barberry family

BUSH POPPY
Dendromecon rigida
Poppy family

SHRUBBY CINQUEFOIL
Dasiphora fruticosa
Rose family

ANTELOPE BRUSH, BITTER BRUSH
Purshia tridentata   5 symetrical petals - ovary superior
Rose family

This is a stout shrub of dry, open areas. It can be found on the north end of the Trinity Divide and along the spine of the Scott Mountains. I photographed this one on Scott Mountain where shrubs were between 4' and 6' in height. Stems are rigid and the twigs somewhat woolly. Leaves are gray-green, lightly hairy, alternate, wedge shaped, and notched at the ends. Like the twigs and leaves the flowers are woolly and yellow to cream colored. I find them to have a pleasant fragrance.

SKUNK BUSH
Rhus aromatica   5 symetrical petals - ovary superior
Sumac family

This shrub is deceiving. People who stumble into it often think they are wallowing in poison oak. Is it any wonder? Look at the way the leaves are grouped! To top it all off, they belong to the same family. Skunk bush is innocuous, however, and will not give you that itchy rash that follows exposure to poison oak. The deciduous leaves of skunk bush are not oily or shiny and are more elongated—but still in groups of three. The flowers are small, white to yellowish, and clustered at the ends of small, branched twigs. While the berries of poison oak are small and white, the berries of skunk brush are robust and orange to red. It is common at lower elevations throughout the area. I took the large photograph on Musser Hill near Weaverville in early July and the berries at Lowden Ranch near Lewiston in early October.

RUBBER RABBITBRUSH
Ericameria nauseosa   Flowers in composite heads
Sunflower family

Rabbit brush decorates open, sunny mountain slopes and flats throughout this area. It puts on quite a show when blooming in mid-summer—turning entire areas beautiful golden yellow. It forms thickets about 3' tall with narrow, entire, gray-green leaves, and dense heads of small golden yellow flowers. Look for it in areas that have been recently burned or that have a relatively persistent history of forest fires. I photographed these above Highway 299 near the French Gulch Turnoff where entire mountainsides were burned in 2007.

ANTELOPE BRUSH
BITTER BRUSH
Purshia tridentata
Rose family

SKUNK BUSH
Rhus aromatica
Sumac family

RUBBER RABBITBRUSH
Ericameria nauseosa
Sunflower family

BIRCH-LEAF MOUNTAIN-MAHOGANY
Cercocarpus betuloides var. *betuloides*   No obvious petals
Rose family

I can almost guarantee that it will not be the tiny flowers that first attract your attention to this shrub—it will be the clusters of long-tailed, fuzzy, snow-white seeds or achenes. In this area, birch-leaf mountain-mahogany rarely exceeds 15' in height but it can grow to around 40'. The broadly oval leaves are prominently veined, evergreen, and alternate with serrated margins in the upper half and smooth below. The trumpet shaped flowers are small and yellow with a reddish tinged base. There are no true petals on the flowers. It is a gnarly, rugged shrub that likes dry, sunny areas and is especially abundant on mid-to lower elevation mountain slopes. Look for it on hillsides along the Trinity River below Junction City and along the road to the North Fork of the Trinity River trailhead.

CURL LEAF MOUNTAIN MAHOGANY
Cercocarpus ledifolius   Alternate leaves & No obvious petals
Rose family

To pay homage to an expression from the 60s—this is one "gnarly" shrub. Winter storms with fierce winds and deep snow sculpt twisted, deeply furrowed trunks, rough bark, and tangled branches. In this area it rarely exceeds 15' and can be found at mid to high elevations throughout the Trinity Alps and Trinity Divide. It gets its name from the narrow, deep green leaves which roll under from the margins. The small and slightly tube shaped flowers vary from ¼" to ½" in diameter. They are white in with green centers, slightly reflexed, with prominent stamens and anthers. Like *C. betuloides*, the beautiful clusters of feathery, snow-white seeds or achenes will first catch your eye. In late summer they can turn the entire shrub a gauzy white. The large photograph was taken at the summit of Packer's Peak and the inset of the achenes above Mill Creek Lake—both in the Trinity Alps.

BUSH PENSTEMON
Keckiella lemmonii   5 irregular petals forming a tube
Plantain family

Talk about innocuous! The flowers of the bush penstemon are so small that hardly anyone ever notices them. And yet, when viewed up close, they are gorgeous. The plants themselves are hardly unassuming—some grow to over 4' tall overhanging low to mid-elevation trails. They prefer partially shaded areas where they grow at the edges of mixed conifer and hardwood forests. When viewed from the top, the flowers look like little brownish buttons but, if you get down on your hands and knees, it's a whole different story. The hairy and sticky yellow and cream colored petals are striped with deep maroon underneath—each has a prominent yellow staminode (sterile stamen) that is likewise hairy. Overall, the flowers are barely ¼" long and grow along the upper half of the stem. The species is found from the foothills of the Sacramento Valley—where I've encountered them next to trails near Keswick and Shasta lakes—to the upper elevations along the Fen Trail along the Scott Mountain Divide. I photographed these along Slate Creek on the Trinity Divide, but have found them blooming along the lower stretches of the trail to Duck Lakes in the Russians and along the Canyon Creek Trail in the Trinity Alps.

BIRCH-LEAF MOUNTAIN-MAHOGANY
Cercocarpus betuloides var.
betuloides
Rose family

CURL LEAF MOUNTAIN MAHOGANY
Cercocarpus ledifolius
Rose family

BUSH PENSTEMON
Keckiella lemmonii
Plantain family

A fen along the trail to Stoddard Lake in the Trinity Alps Wilderness holds showy raillardella and bog asphodel

Showy raillardella
Raillardella pringlei

LEOPARD LILY, CALIFORNIA TIGER LILY
Lilium pardalinum   3 or 6 petals
Lily family

This striking and graceful lily is a familiar sight along trails, streams, springs, and seeps throughout the high country. It is often falsely accused of being a tiger lily, which prompts me to remind people that tigers have stripes and leopards have spots. There are no stripes on this lily. This particular leopard, unlike its furry namesake, is not shy—sometimes blooming in huge colonies. There can be several flowers on stalks that reach over 6' if conditions are right. Conditions are always right above Papoose Lake where huge numbers of them bloom in August. Along the trail to Stoddard Lake in the Trinity Alps is where I shot the main photograph, the rocky slopes between Russian and Lower Russian lakes in the Russian Wilderness is where I took the smaller photograph. I was surprised to find them in bloom along the eastern shoreline of Lewiston Lake.

Note: There are 3 subspecies of *L. pardalinum* found in this area: leopard lily (*L. pardalinum* subsp. *pardalinum*), Shasta lily (*L. pardalinum* subsp. *shastense*) and Vollmer's lily (*L. pardalinum* subsp. *vollmeri*). Chances are good that you will run into all of them but differentiating between them is difficult.

WESTERN WALLFLOWER
Erysimum capitatum   4 petals
Mustard family

This wallflower is highly variable in terms of color—ranging from pale yellow to deep orange. The plants can be up to 2' tall though 1' is more typical. It is found at lower elevations than its cousin, the Sierra wallflower, and is common along roadsides in dry, open, mixed conifer forests from the coast to inland foothills. Look for the typical four petals and strongly erect central stamens. I photographed these along the lower reaches of the Swift Creek Trail in late May.

KLAMATH MOUNTAIN CATCHFLY, SALMON-FLOWERED CATCHFLY
Silene salmonacea   5 symmetrical petals - ovary superior
Pink family

These cartwheels are beautiful, but because of their size and coloration, frustratingly difficult to find. They don't hide, but rather grow in plain sight forming low mounds on exposed soils. There can be several 1½" to 2" salmon colored flowers blooming on each plant, each with five deeply cleft petals, and prominent stamens. The stiff, basal leaves are a light olive-green and covered with soft silvery hairs. They are restricted to northern Trinity County and inhabit openings in Jeffrey pine and incense-cedar woodlands. I've found and photographed them blooming along the road to the Lake Eleanor and Poison Canyon Trailheads in late May and early June. They seem to be especially fond of areas that have been recently logged (but not site prepped with herbicides) and exposed to lots of sun.

LEOPARD LILY
Lilium pardalinum
Lily family

WESTERN WALLFLOWER
Erysimum capitatum
Mustard family

KLAMATH MOUNTAIN CATCHFLY
Silene salmonacea
Pink family

COMMON FIDDLENECK, SMALL-FLOWERED FIDDLENECK
Amsinckia menziesii   5 symmetrical petals forming a tube
Borage family

The closer you get to this little wildflower the more beautiful and intriguing it is. Starting in late March and lasting through early June the deep, buttery yellow, and red spotted, trumpet shaped flowers open as the tightly wound flowering stems begin to unfurl (they really do look like fiddle necks). The plants are tall—up to 18″ but the individual flowers are small, perhaps ¼″ in diameter when fully opened. The stems are covered with coarse reddish-brown hairs. From a distance the small flower clusters are not showy but that changes when you get down at eye level with them. Look for them alongside roads and highways in the area. They prefer open, exposed sites on flats and hillsides. I photographed these along Clikapudi Trail near Shasta lake but they are common throughout the foothills. The small inset is a portion of a watercolor painting I did years ago.

SHOWY COLLOMIA, LARGE-FLOWERED COLLOMIA
Collomia grandiflora   5 symmetrical petals forming a tube
Phlox family

Showy or large-flowered collomia is a tall plant—up to 3′—that prefers dry, open, brushy, exposed sites. Trumpet shaped flowers bloom in compact bunches at the ends of the stems. The delicate salmon or pale yellow petals flare sharply away from the tube encasing a snow-white stigma and beautiful light blue anthers. I photographed these on a dry, sandy hillside on the divide between Bear and Black's Basins in the Trinity Alps in late July.

ORANGE AGOSERIS
Agoseris aurantiaca var. *aurantiaca*   Flowers in compact heads
Sunflower family

The rusty orange flowers of orange agoseris are a fairly common sight in dry, open areas at mid-elevations in the high country. I've never seen it in large colonies—and although you may find a lot of them in the same area, they do not seem to congregate. They are instantly recognizable, if not for the color, then for the long, rectangular and sharply toothed petals. Each flowering stalk is crowned with a single flower. I photographed this one on Mt. Ashland in Southern Oregon but look for them along the trail to Doe Lake and in places like Steveale Meadows in the Trinity Alps. As an interesting side note, this wildflower gets around. I've also photographed it high in the Grimmialp in Switzerland where it is called gold pippau.

COMMON FIDDLENECK
Amsinckia menziesii
Borage family

SHOWY COLLOMIA
Collomia grandiflora
Phlox family

ORANGE AGOSERIS
Agoseris aurantiaca var.
aurantiaca
Sunflower family

ORANGE HONEYSUCKLE
Lonicera ciliosa
Honeysuckle family

5 irregular petals forming a tube

Orange honeysuckle is fairly common in this area, at least in the Trinities. It is a wide-ranging vine often found clambering up trees and brush in protected and relatively damp sites. The brilliant reddish-orange blooms occur in bunches on short stalks arising from the centers of light green, conjoined oval leaves. There is no mistaking this for anything else in these mountains. I photographed the flowers along Canyon Creek on the way to the Canyon Creek Trailhead in June where they are especially abundant and the beautiful red fruit above Gray's Falls on the Trinity River. I've also found them blooming in various locations around Trinity Lake in mid-May.

SHOWY RAILLARDELLA
Raillardella pringlei
Sunflower family

Flowers in composite heads

This beautiful wildflower is endemic to serpentine soils in the north eastern Trinity Alps, the northern end of the Trinity Divide, and the Scott Mountains. I've never seen it bloom in abundance but have found it in isolated populations along the trail to Stoddard Lake, near Mill Creek Lake and in Mumford Meadows, all in the Trinity Alps. A single, tall, almost gangly stalk, grows from a group of basal, opposite, lanceolate leaves. The "single" flower blooming at the top of the stalk is made up of intense orange or yellowish orange ray flowers and a central bunch of similarly colored disc flowers. The flowers are large—almost 3½" across and in their prime in early June. It's a real treat to find these but watch where you walk as they prefer boggy (or should I say "fenny") as they share the same habitat as cobra lilies and bog asphodel places. I shot these photographs in a wet meadow alongside the road to Gumboot Lake on the Trinity Divide.

Canyon Creek in the Trinity Alps: Each stream pouring out of these mountains has its own special beauty and character. I have to say, I'm attracted to all of them for one reason or another. However, there is something about Canyon Creek that grabbed hold of me at an early age and has never let go. I think it's the granite. The granite that cradles it—that embraces it, that gives the water its clarity, its color, its definition. This stream flows through the heart of the White Trinities—the solid granite core of the Alps. This most solid of rocks, because of aeons of glaciation and erosion, seems to flow, along with the water, down from the highest peaks and ridges to the slicks and jumbled boulder fields before entering the Trinity River. In places, the rock is polished like glass. This interplay of water and granite is mesmerizing. I often take long pauses in my wanderings to just sit and watch this unique display. From the surrounding peaks to its confluence with the Trinity River, this drainage is a botanist's paradise presenting a staggering array of gorgeous wildflowers worthy of a day hike or a week spent backpacking. Anyone who enters will not be disappointed in the floristic diversity. Just remember to take time to while away a few hours creekside.

ORANGE HONEYSUCKLE
Lonicera ciliosa
Honeysuckle family

SHOWY RAILLARDELLA
Raillardella pringlei
Sunflower family

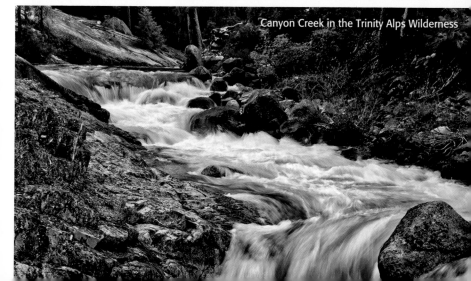

Canyon Creek in the Trinity Alps Wilderness

Taylor Lake in the Russian Wilderness with the Marble Mountains in the background.

Lewisia cotyledon x *whiteae* blooming above Upper Albert Lake in the Russian Wilderness

FIRECRACKER FLOWER
Dichelostemma ida-maia
Brodiaea family

3 or 6 petals

The nodding, clustered, bright red blooms of this wildflower are unmistakable and it is easy to understand how they got their common name. Locally they can grow to 3' in height with the 1" - 1½" long tubular shaped flowers blooming at the ends of the tall, naked stems. Look for them beside low elevation trails and roads throughout these mountains early in the spring. Trinity Mountain Road is a good bet for finding them in May as is Deadwood Road near Lewiston.

SCARLET FRITILLARY
Fritillaria recurva
Lily family

3 or 6 petals

The brilliant reddish-orange bell shaped flowers of this fritilary are an eye popper. You will find them alongside roads and trails throughout the area at lower to mid-elevations. Flowers bloom in the axils of long, lance shaped leaves along the upper portion of a stalk that can reach 30" in height. Its preferred habitats are shaded, moist sites where it can frequently be found growing on the cut banks of roads. I photographed these along the road to the Eagle Creek trailhead and Horse Flat Campground in late May. Look for them along the Stewart's Fork Trail, Rainier Road, or the Scorpion Creek Road to Bonanza King.

SIERRA ONION, DUSKY ONION
Allium campanulatum
Onion family

3 or 6 petals

This onion is tall (up to 20") and showy. Each long stem carries a large, loose ball or cluster of flowers numbering between 20 and 40. The flowers are mostly light magenta, with cream centers, ringed and spotted with a magenta, with a deep magenta stripe running the central length of each petal. Each plant has two or three flattened leaves, longer than the flowering stalks, which begin to turn brown and wither as the flowers open. I photographed this bunch in mixed oak fir and pine on the ridgetop along Trinity Mountain Road near Smith Trail in late May.

FALCATE ONION, SCYTHE-LEAVED ONION
Allium falcifolium
Onion family

3 or 6 petals

Falcate onion grows on the open, exposed serpentine slopes of Scott Mountain. Often, they are so abundant that those slopes appear vibrantly magenta at the height of the bloom. It is definitely a sight to see. The flowers bloom in a thick rounded bunch atop a 3" to 5" tall, thick, and flattened stem. I photographed these in mid-July on a slope below the Pacific Crest Trail before it crosses Highway 3.

FIRECRACKER FLOWER
Dichelostemma ida-maia
Brodiaea family

SCARLET FRITILLARY
Fritillaria recurva
Lily family

SIERRA ONION, DUSKY ONION
Allium campanulatum
Onion family

FALCATE ONION, SCYTHE-LEAVED ONION
Allium falcifolium
Onion family

DWARF ONION
Allium parvum
Onion family
3 or 6 petals

This is an early spring to late summer bloomer at mid to high elevations where it prefers exposed, rocky soils. The plants are tiny, hardly ever growing more than 2" in height, with dense clusters of creamy white flowers veined with red or pink. Often the only indication that you are in the area with them is the distinct onion smell released when crushed by a foot! This photograph depicts them at three times their actual size. Good places to find them are along the road to the North Fork of Swift Creek Trailhead and on the open gravelly slopes above Little Duck Lake where I photographed these.

PACIFIC MOUNTAIN ONION, WESTERN SWAMP ONION, TALL SWAMP ONION
Allium validum
Onion family
3 or 6 petals

This is the giant of the onion family in these mountains. I've found them up to 4' tall. They like their feet in water—preferring fens, wet meadows, seeps, and creek sides. The beautiful lavender flowers grow in loose clusters at the tops of the stems and have stamens and styles extending well beyond the petals, giving the flowers a ragged look. Step on one, or accidentally crush one and the onion smell will persist for the rest of the day! I photographed these in a fen along the trail to Stoddard Lake in August.

CALYPSO ORCHID, FAIRY SLIPPER
Calypso bulbosa
Orchid family
3 or 6 petals

Calypsos are among my favorite early wildflowers, often blooming in early May in moist, deeply shaded sites. A single flower blooms atop a naked stalk that reaches 4" to 5" in height, above a single, broad, basal leaf. The deep magenta sepals and lateral petals are alike—narrow and sitting like a crown above the same colored hood that lies over the top of the "moccasin" formed by the lower petal. The moccasin itself is whitish, hairy, and speckled with brownish-orange spots along the lower part of the lobe. Magenta spots descend into the throat. As is the case with other orchids—they should not be disturbed. Enjoy them but do not touch!

COMMON FIREWEED, TALL FIREWEED
Chamerion angustifolium subsp. *circumvagum*
Evening-primrose family
4 petals

This tall and showy fireweed is unmistakable. It can reach 5' or more in height and the tall stalks are crowned with large clusters of gorgeous, deep magenta-pink flowers beginning to bloom in July. It decorates meadows and the shorelines of lakes from the coast to the mountains throughout summer. They derive their common name by the fact that they are often the first plants to colonize an area after fire. Good places to see them are in Bear Basin, Horseshoe Lake, and along the Caribou Lakes Trail in the Trinity Alps, and Russian Lake in the Russian Wilderness.

DWARF ONION
Allium parvum
Onion family

PACIFIC MOUNTAIN ONION
Allium validum
Onion family

CALYPSO ORCHID, FAIRY SLIPPER
Calypso bulbosa
Orchid family

COMMON FIREWEED, TALL FIREWEED
Chamerion angustifolium subsp. *circumvagum*
Evening-primrose family

RED RIBBONS
Clarkia concinna subsp. *concinna*   3 or 6 petals
Evening-primrose family

Here is a beautiful flower that graces exposed, dry, and rocky cutbanks in the lower elevations along the south side of the Trinity Alps. It can grow to 2' in height and is loosely branched with a multitude of flowers on each plant. The olive-green leaves are 2" to 3" in length and oval to linear. The blooms are striking—deep pink to red with some pale pink striping. There are four petals, each divided into three segments—the middle segment being wider at the ends than the other two and all are ruffled at the tips. Good places to see them are along the French Creek and Canyon Creek roads in spring. I photographed these along Canyon Creek Road in June.

WINECUP CLARKIA, FOUR-SPOT
Clarkia purpurea subsp. *quadrivulnera*   4 petals
Evening-primrose family

This little *Clarkia* likes damp meadows where it hides among tall grasses. Stems are erect, leaves are long, lance-shaped, and hairy. The four fan shaped lavender to wine purple petals are small with a darker purple spot near each tip. The edges of the petals are slightly ruffled. A good place to look for them is along Rush Creek Road, Canyon Creek Road, and on Musser Hill near Weaverville.

FAREWELL-TO-SPRING, DIAMOND CLARKIA
Clarkia rhomboidea   4 petals
Evening-primrose family

Farewell-to-spring (my favorite name for this *Clarkia*) is a common wildflower in the foothills throughout this area. The plants can be tall and spindly—often reaching 2'—with small, lavender to wine-colored flowers blooming along the stems. The petals are narrow at the base and rhomboid shaped at the tips, spotted with deep magenta and white near the centers. You can find them along Rush Creek Road and along the Trinity River in May and early June.

RED RIBBONS
Clarkia concinna subsp. *concinna*
Evening-primrose family

WINECUP CLARKIA
purpurea subsp. *quadrivulnera*
Evening-primrose family

FAREWELL-TO-SPRING
DIAMOND CLARKIA
Clarkia rhomboidea
Evening-primrose family

CALIFORNIA-FUCHSIA, ZAUSCHNERIA
Epilobium canum subsp. *latifolium*   4 petals
Evening primrose family

The distinguishing feature of this gorgeous *Epilobium* are the long, tubular shaped, brilliant red flowers. At the tips, the petals flare slightly with red stamens and a single red style extending well beyond. Leaves are deep green and both flowers and leaves are hairy. In the Trinities I've always found them growing on rocky outcrops and talus slopes at elevations of 6,000' or more. The only other wildflower this could be mistaken for is the redbush beardtongue (page 236). The inferior ovary and eight stamens distinguish this species from the beardtongue. A great place to see these is around Sapphire and Mirror Lakes in the Trinity Alps where they bloom in late summer and early fall. To save a backpacking trip into the high country, you can find them blooming in the gardens of the Redding Arboretum. I photographed these above the shoreline of Sapphire Lake in mid-September.

DESERT WILLOWHERB, SLENDER ANNUAL FIREWEED
Epilobium minutum   4 petals
Evening primrose family

I found and photographed this tiny *Epilobium* along the trail to the summit of Packer's Peak in late June. There were scattered colonies blooming in the serpentine soils beginning at about 5,800' to just below the summit at almost 8,000.' As you can see, the teeny flowers (a little over 1/10" in diameter) ranged from white to deep pink and occur mostly on pairs of stems originating in the leaf axils. Their preferred habit seems to be open and dry but also around vernal pools and disturbed areas. They frequently populate areas after fire.

SISKIYOU FIREWEED, ROCK FRINGE
Epilobium siskiyouense   4 petals
Evening-primrose family

You will find this beautiful little *Epilobium* growing in the crevices of serpentine rock outcrops and cliff faces above 5,500'. It rarely exceeds 10" in height. Leaves are a bluish-green, thick, oval, with pointed tips, crowded along the stems, and usually coated with a light waxy bloom. One of the best places to see them is along the Fen Interpretive Trail (where I photographed these) above Kangaroo Lake from mid-July and on into early August. You will also find them in Bear Basin and on the slopes surrounding Seven-up Lake in the Trinity Alps.

CALIFORNIA-FUCHSIA ZAUSCHNERIA
Epilobium canum
subsp. *latifolium*
Evening primrose family

DESERT WILLOW HERB
Epilobium minutum
Evening primrose family

SISKIYOU FIREWEED
Epilobium siskiyouense
Evening-primrose family

CALIFORNIA CENTAURY, CHARMING CENTAURY
Zeltnera venusta   4 petals
Gentian family

This is a low elevation, early spring flower. The deep reddish-purple, lance shaped petals flare away from the center revealing a cluster of bright yellow spirally twisted anthers. There are several flowers in a bunch at the top of stems that can reach 7" in height. Look for them in open, grassy, vernally wet areas along Rush Creek Road and around Bolt's Hill above Lewiston Lake.

OREGON ROCKCRESS
Arabis oregana   4 petals
Mustard family

Like other rockcresses, this one also likes cracks and crevices in rocky outcrops. I've always found it in areas where shade is abundant along stream drainages near water although it does like some sun exposure. The plants themselves are about 7" to 8" tall with rosettes of large, fuzzy, basal leaves and smaller, lance-shaped leaves developing alternately along the tall flowering stalk. The small flowers bloom in the upper portion of the stalk, are 4 petaled, and range in color from light to dark lilac. I photographed these on a rocky outcrop in the Clear Creek Gorge south of Redding but I have also found them along French Gulch Creek near the community of French Gulch.

SHASTA ROCKCRESS
Boechera breweri subsp. *shastaensis*   4 petals
Mustard family

This is a small rockcress thought to be endemic to the limestones surrounding the McCloud Arm of Shasta Lake. Interestingly, I have photographed a rockcress similar in appearance on the limestone around Natural Bridge south of Hayfork. Like Brewer's rockcress, the flowers are lilac purple and bloom on a tall stalk emerging from a basal rosette of fuzzy gray-green leaves. Smaller, lance shaped leaves grow alternately along the flowering stalk. I photographed these in the crevices of limestone above the McCloud Arm of Shasta Lake but I might note that limestone occurs throughout the western half of the Trinity Alps so the probability of finding this species elsewhere is quite high.

CALIFORNIA CENTAURY
CHARMING CENTAURY
Zeltnera venusta
Gentian family

OREGON ROCKCRESS
Arabis oregana
Mustard family

SHASTA ROCKCRESS
Boechera breweri subsp. *shastaensis*
Mustard family

PACIFIC BLEEDING HEART
Dicentra formosa   4 petals
Poppy family

Bleeding hearts begin their bloom in the foothills in early May and continue well into August in the higher elevations. I have even found them blooming in late September below Mirror Lake in the Trinity Alps. The rose pink flowers resemble fat, little, elongated hearts—growing in tight clusters at the tops of their stems. The leaves are thin and deeply dissected, appearing fern-like. Look for them in pockets along streams like along the Upper Trinity River, Boulder Creek, Union Creek, and along the shoreline of West Boulder Lake in the Trinity Alps.

FEW-FLOWERED BLEEDING HEART
Dicentra pauciflora   4 petals
Poppy family

This diminutive bleeding heart loves serpentine and I've found vast carpets of it on open slopes around Union Meadows and Union Lake. The feathery-leaved plants grow from 2" to 5" in height. Each plant holds one to four nodding flowers ranging in color from near white, rose to pink, and deep purple. Each bloom resembles a tiny heart with petals sharply reflexed at the ends. The prominent pistil is covered by the larger heart shaped petals, and extends beyond the flower as the seed pod matures. They are early bloomers, often appearing as snow banks melt beginning in mid-May at around 5,000'. I photographed these near Union Lake in the Trinity Alps in late May and early June.

FRINGE POD, HAIRY LACEPOD, SAND FRINGEPOD
Thysanocarpus curvipes   4 petals
Mustard family

This member of the mustard family is one of those that, until it goes to seed, is fairly unassuming. It is a leggy plant, often growing to more than 30" but 15" to 24" is more common. The tiny white flowers bloom in an open raceme followed by seed pods that are as beautiful as they are interesting. The pods form a translucent elongated oval with a central yellowish-green pod from which short green ribs radiate outward turning magenta toward the edges. The intervening space between the ribs form small openings near the central pod, are closed, and white or light pink as they near the edge. They are showy and put on a beautiful display when backlit by the sun. I photographed these along the Trinity River near Junction City in late June.

RIBBED FRINGE POD, SHOWY FRINGEPOD, SHOWY FRINGE POD
Thysanocarpus radians   4 petals
Mustard family

This leggy wildflower is common in open areas throughout the valleys and foothills. The tiny greenish-white flowers will not initially attract your attention but the pretty little seed pods, from which it gets its common names, will. The pods hang down from the ends of alternating reddish stems, are round, translucent, with green ribs radiating from a central yellowish-green pod outward to a thickened, deep magenta rib. The intervening space between the green ribs and the outer magenta rib are mostly white. I took this photograph at Lowden Ranch along the Trinity River in early July.

PACIFIC BLEEDING HEART
Dicentra formosa
Poppy family

FEW-FLOWERED BLEEDING HEART
Dicentra pauciflora
Poppy family

FRINGE POD, HAIRY LACEPOD
Thysanocarpus curvipes
Mustard family

FRINGE POD, RIBBED FRINGE POD
Thysanocarpus radians
Mustard family

199

RED LARKSPUR, CANYON LARKSPUR
Delphinium nudicaule　　　　　　　　　　　　　　　5 irregular petals
Buttercup family

This is a wildflower that frequents the sides of roads in the foothills and low elevation back country trails throughout the area. It prefers damp, shaded hillsides and mossy rock outcrops. The flowers are ¾" to 1" long, deep orangish-red, with a long spur at the back. The petal-like sepals flare at the tips. Good places to see these are along Rainier Road above Trinity Lake, the road to the Stewart's Fork trailhead, and in the limestone surrounding the McCloud Arm of Shasta Lake.

SIERRA MILKWORT
Polygala cornuta　　　　　　　　　　　　　　　　5 irregular petals
Milkwort family

The closer you get to this tiny wildflower the more beautiful it is. The white and magenta-purple flowers, each with two wing-like sepals, are gathered in loose clusters at the ends of short stems. Stamens and pistils are hidden by closely folded petals. The leaves are dark green and oval. I've found it in various lower elevation locations throughout the Trinity Alps. I have also found it blooming alongside trails above Keswick Lake in the Sacramento River Canyon. I photographed these at the East Fork Stewart's Fork Trailhead in July.

SIERRA PEA
Lathyrus nevadensis var. *nevadensis*　　　　　　5 irregular petals
Pea family

This little pea grows in large, scattered populations along trails and roads at low to mid-elevations throughout the area. The blossoms are a delicate pinkish-magenta and the leaves are pinnately compound. Stems are jointed in a slight zig-zag shape between the leaves. They grow or sprawl low to the ground in areas with some tree cover but with adequate exposure to the sun where they twine through downed branches and brush. Mumford Meadows in the Trinity Alps is a good place to see them as are the roadsides leading to the Granite Peak Trailhead along Buck Ridge (where I photographed these).

SHASTA CLOVER
Trifolium productum　　　　　　　　　　　　　　5 irregular petals
Pea family

The descending tubular shaped, white to red flowers of Shasta clover bloom in compact heads atop tall, naked stalks in damp, open locations at higher elevations. The flowering heads can be up to 1½" long. The leaves are long and oval with toothed margins. I've found it throughout the Trinities and Russians. I photographed these in the wet meadow at the back of Big Duck Lake in the Russian Wilderness.

RED LARKSPUR, CANYON LARKSPUR
Delphinium nudicaule
Buttercup family

SIERRA MILKWORT
Polygala cornuta
Milkwort family

SIERRA PEA
Lathyrus nevadensis var. *nevadensis*
Pea family

SHASTA CLOVER
Trifolium productum
Pea family

CHICK LUPINE
Lupinus microcarpus   5 irregular petals
Pea family

The tiers of deep pink flowers are arranged along a fairly tall, reddish-brown, stalk about 12" to 18" in height. The leaves are also tinged with red at the margins. This is the only pink lupine in this area and, therefore difficult to mistake. It is widespread throughout California with populations across Trinity and Siskiyou counties. I originally found this species near Natural Bridge south of Hayfork and also along the road to the Canyon Creek trailhead—which is where this photo was taken..

RED COLUMBINE, SITKA COLUMBINE
Aquilegia formosa   5 symmetrical petals - ovary superior
Buttercup family

This wildflower does not need an accompanying description as it looks like no other found in this area. It is common from the low elevation foothills around Shasta Lake to mid-elevations in the mountains. In the foothills the species favors north-facing, shaded, damp sites. At higher elevations it prefers wet, shaded, meadow areas. A great place to see them in the high country is along the trail to Big and Little Duck lakes in the Russians where they grow in profusion along with dozens of other wildflowers. I photographed these about one mile below Little Duck Lake.

FENDLER'S MEADOW-RUE
Thalictrum fendleri   5 symmetrical petals - ovary superior
Buttercup family

This unusual wildflower is one that many hikers will never see. It grows in plain sight in wet, shaded areas. In the jungle-like mass of vegetation this one doesn't particularly stand out. This is a dioecious species, where one individual plant has female flowers and another plant only male parts—each are very distinctive. Surprisingly, male flowers are more likely to catch your eye because of their dangling clusters of stamens waving in the slightest breeze. If you find one, you will also find the other because they often grow entangled with each other. Overall, the plants can reach 24" in height and are loosely branched. I photographed these in the wet meadows and thickets below Middle Bowerman Meadows in the Trinity Alps around the 4th of July.

PIPSISSEWA, PRINCE'S PINE
Chimaphila umbellata   5 symmetrical petals - ovary superior
Heath family

Pipsissewa usually forms large thickets with plants up to 8" tall. The plant is evergreen with stiff stems and deep-green, toothed, oval leaves. Flowers bloom in clusters and are mostly pink. The petals arch away and form small "hoods" over the prominent wide stigma and ten stamens. It prefers deep, shaded conifer woods and is quite common throughout these mountains—mostly at lower to mid-elevations. I photographed these above Sugar Pine Lake in late September.

CHICK LUPINE
Lupinus microcarpus
Pea family

RED COLUMBINE, SITKA COLUMBINE
Aquilegia formosa
Buttercup family

FENDLER'S MEADOW-RUE
Thalictrum fendleri
Buttercup family

PIPSISSEWA, PRINCE'S PINE
Chimaphila umbellata
Heath family

HARSH CHECKERBLOOM
Sidalcea asprella
Mallow family

5 symmetrical petals - ovary superior

Harsh checkerbloom likes much the same habitat as Oregon checkermallow—wet places in meadows, on brushy hillsides, and alongside trails. The deep rose flowers bloom on a tall stalk and can be found even into October in protected areas. Look for it all over the high country. I photographed these in Long Canyon Meadows in the Trinity Alps in August.

OREGON CHECKERMALLOW, OREGON CHECKERBLOOM
SPICATE CHECKERMALLOW
Sidalcea oregana
Mallow family

5 symmetrical petals - ovary superior

You can find this mallow blooming all summer long in the high country—even into October in protected areas. It likes wet places and can be found on hillsides, meadows, and along trails. It grows to 3' tall and is usually found blooming in large colonies. I photographed these near Big Carmen Lake on the Trinity Divide but look for them in moist areas like Bowerman or Long Canyon meadows in the Trinity Alps or along the Paynes Lake trail in the Russians.

RED MAIDS
Calandrinia menziesii
Miner's lettuce family

5 symmetrical petals - ovary superior

This brilliantly colored wildflower likes open, sunny places where it blooms in large numbers. The deep rose colored flowers are about the size of your little fingernail and sit singly atop a short stem bracketed by small, pointed leaves. The basal leaves are stout, fleshy, club shaped, narrow, and becoming oval at the tips. All of the leaves are ciliate, or hairy at the edges. It occurs commonly at lower elevations throughout the area and can be found along trails and roads. I photographed these alongside Clikapudi Trail near Shasta Lake in late May and have also found them along Highway 299 near Trinity Dam Boulevard and alongside the road leading to Buckhorn Dam on Grass Valley Creek on the Trinity Divide.

HAIRY ROCKROSE
Cistus incanus
Rock-rose family

5 symmetrical petals ovary superior

Here is another naturalized, non-native wildflower found in this area. Initially it was introduced by the California Department of Transportation as part of highway beautification projects. It now seems that, over time, it has adapted and spread to other areas. The numerous large, showy flowers have a texture like crumpled tissue paper, are light purple with deep orange pistils and anthers, and can be seen from a distance. The shrubby plants grow to 3' and have leaves and stems that are somewhat grayish-green. They thrive in disturbed areas and can be especially invigorated by wildfire. I photographed these along Packer's Bay Road above Shasta Lake but you will find them blooming along Highway 299 West along the Trinity River in mid- June.

HARSH CHECKERBLOOM
Sidalcea asprella
Mallow family

OREGON CHECKERMALLOW
Sidalcea oregana
Mallow family

RED MAIDS
Calandrinia menziesii
Miner's lettuce family

HAIRY ROCKROSE
Cistus incanus
Rock-rose family

ONE-SEEDED PUSSYPAW
Calyptridium monospermum   5 irregular petals - ovary superior
Miner's lettuce family

This pussypaw has one deep green, elongated, spoon shaped rosette of leaves (with small leaves present along the flowering stem) and two or more flowering stems per rosette. Flowers bloom in dense rose to white clusters at the ends of the stems which hug the ground at night and rise a few inches off the ground in full day-light. Typically the flowering heads are no more than 2" across but I have seen some giants that exceeded 6" on the upper reaches of the Suicide Trail and at Horseshoe Lake, both in the Trinity Alps. Look for them throughout the summer wherever you find exposed sandy flats. I photographed these on Mt. Ashland in July but they are common throughout the area.

PUSSYPAW, UMBELLED PUSSYPAW
Calyptridium umbellatum   5 irregular petals - ovary superior
Miner's lettuce family

Umbelled pussypaws typically have two or more clustered rosettes of deep green, elongated spoon shaped leaves with no leaves on the flowering stem. There is one flowering stem per rosette and the flowers are typically white but can age to pale pink. The plants rarely exceed 5" in height. Flower stalks are long and each is topped with a round ball of compact flowers about 2" in diameter. When cool, stalks lie flat to the ground but as the day heats up the stalks rise until some of them are almost vertical. They prefer dry, sandy soils and can be found throughout the area from low to sub-alpine elevations. I photographed these along the Siskiyou Summit in South-ern Oregon but they are common throughout the area. A good place to find them is near Middle Falls along Canyon Creek where they are abundant on the sandy flats between granite outcrops.

INDIAN PINK, CALIFORNIA PINK
Silene laciniata subsp. *californica*   5 irregular petals - ovary superior
Pink family

These beautiful wildflowers are early bloomers in the foothills. Look carefully and you will find them decorating cut-banks along Highway 299, Highway 3, Trinity Mountain, and Rush Creek Roads. The brilliant red flowers cannot be mistaken for any other in the area. They are about 1" across, with five deeply cleft petals and a prominent bunch of stamens rising from the center. The plants are loosely branched with long stems, but spread laterally along the ground usually not more than 7" or 8" tall. I photographed these along Highway 299 near Buckhorn Summit in May. Why is it called a "pink" when the flower is red? The answer is simply that it belongs to the Pink family and that the color of the flower has nothing to do with the name.

ONE-SEEDED PUSSYPAW
Calyptridium monospermum
Miner's lettuce family

PUSSYPAW
Calyptridium umbellatum
Miner's lettuce family

INDIAN PINK
Silene laciniata subsp. *californica*
Pink family

ROSEROOT STONECROP, PACIFIC ROSEROOT, KINGSCROWN
Rhodiola integrifolia subsp. *integrifolia*   5 irregular petals - ovary superior
Stonecrop family

Roseroot stonecrop grows in pocket meadows, on cliffs, talus, and subalpine ridges. It is a small succulent with light green leaves growing in whorls up the flowering stem. The flowers are deep magenta-red and yellow and bloom in a tight, flattened cluster at the tops of the stems. Most wildflower books portray the flowers as less-than-spectacular but this is an absolutely gorgeous stonecrop and possibly the most beautiful of the entire lot! The only place I've seen this species is at Big Duck Lake in the Russian Wilderness

COBRA LILY, COBRA PLANT, CALIFORNIA PITCHER PLANT
Darlingtonia californica   5 irregular petals - ovary superior
Pitcher plant family

Here's a little meat eater for you! One of those vicious little plants that attracts bugs, invites them into its inner workings, and then slowly eats them. The modified leaf that forms the plant resembles a hollow tube. It is narrow at the bottom, rising from the rootstock, widening as it ascends, folding over at the top in a shape that resembles a rearing cobra—replete with leafy appendages flaring away from the opening at the bottom of the head that one could construe as fangs.

The plant varies in color from a light green to a mottled yellow-green with numerous maroon spots as they age. They range to about 18" tall and are often crowded in huge colonies. The trap, or opening, by which insects are enticed to enter, is hidden beneath the downward pointing "head" and behind the "fangs." Once the insects are inside, numerous translucent windows along the leaves allow light in and confuse them (much like the windows in our houses attract flies). Also inside, are stiff, downward pointing hairs and a secreted lubricant, both of which are designed to prevent escape. Pooled at the bottom of the stem is an enzyme-laden liquid that, once encountered by the hapless insect, begins the digestion process. Nutrients from the insects provides the plant with resources not available from the serpentine soils on which it grows.

In late spring and early summer, large, deep red, inverted, vase-shaped flowers nod gracefully at the ends of tall red-green stems and are surrounded by pale yellow-green sepals. Cobra lilies are a "flagship" species throughout the serpentine country described in this guide, growing in huge colonies in fens (peatlands fed by groundwater) and hillside seeps where the peat buildup required to make a fen is not present. They are hard to miss and good places to see these carnivores at work are along the Swift Creek Trail in the Trinity Alps, the Parks Creek Road on the Trinity Divide, and along the Fen Trail above Kangaroo Lake in the Scott Mountains.

Note: There is a *Darlingtonia* fen located along the upper reaches of the trail to Bear Lakes in the Trinity Alps. What makes it interesting is the fact that there isn't an ounce of serpentine in the area. The substrate is entirely granitic.

ROSEROOT STONECROP
Rhodiola integrifolia subsp. *integrifolia*
Stonecrop family

COBRA LILY, COBRA PLANT, CALIFORNIA PITCHER PLANT
Darlingtonia californica
Pitcher plant family

GLAUCOUS TAUSCHIA
Tauschia glauca   5 irregular petals - ovary superior
Carrot family

This wildflower is distinguished by the tall reddish-green stems which are topped with radiating clusters of tiny deep rose-purple flowers. Pistils and stamens extend well beyond the petals. The opposite leaves are pale light green, deeply cleft, and toothed along the margins. This is a common wildflower of open, grassy or rocky areas in serpentine at lower elevations. I photographed this one along the road to the Lake Eleanor Trailhead in June.

WOODLAND STARS
Lithophragma (several species)   5 irregular petals - ovary superior
Saxifrage family

The star-like, deeply divided, pale pink or creamy white flowers bloom on simple, tall stems. Each of the five petals are lobed, so the flower has a ragged look. Woodland stars bloom in early spring at lower elevations along the Trinity River—around Lewiston and Rush Creek for example. Several species of woodland stars occur in the area and are challenging to distinguish from one another. One such is the Hill star which is also found at mid-elevations and frequents the sides of trails along Stewart's Fork and Canyon Creek. I took this photograph on the Stewart's Fork Trail in early June.

FRAGRANT FRINGECUP
Tellima grandiflora   5 symmetrical petals - ovary inferior
Saxifrage family

Botanical manuals indicate that the flowers of this plant are usually white but that there are red and pink variations. I've never seen one with white flowers in this area, only pink but I will keep looking! Sniff as hard as I might—I've never detected any fragrance from this wildflower.

This is one wildflower you have to get up close and personal with to appreciate its delicate beauty. It grows in damp, shaded places and—because the flowers are so tiny—it blends in with the background foliage. The flowers are somewhat cup shaped with reflexed, deeply cleft, and sharply pointed petals. They are scattered along stalks that in some places are 12" to 16" tall. Leaves, which cover the lower third of the stalk, are large, palmately lobed, veined, and almost heart shaped. The photograph on the left was taken along Stewart's Fork Trail and the one on the right along VanNess Creek above Trinity Lake, both in mid-May.

APPLEGATE'S INDIAN PAINTBRUSH - RED AND YELLOW VARIATION
Castilleja applegatei   5 irregular petals forming a tube
Broomrape family

This paintbrush is one of the most common species at middle to higher elevations throughout these mountains. You will find it growing in dry, open, exposed and sandy sites—like ridge tops. It is both gregarious and found in small, scattered groups. I photographed the red and yellow flowers on the rocky slopes above Upper Albert Lake in the Russian Wilderness in late September.

GLAUCOUS TAUSCHIA
Tauschia glauca
Carrot family

WOODLAND STARS
Lithophragma (several species)
Saxifrage family

FRAGRANT FRINGECUP
Tellima grandiflora
Saxifrage family

APPLEGATE'S INDIAN PAINTBRUSH
Castilleja applegatei
Broomrape family

211

SCARLET INDIAN PAINTBRUSH, GREAT RED INDIAN PAINTBRUSH
Castilleja miniata subsp. *miniata*   5 irregular petals forming a tube
Broomrape family

This one truly is a giant with large, bright red flowering heads that will keep you entertained throughout the summer and early fall. It tends to favor wet, open, sunny slopes. Because of its size and extended season (some continuing to bloom well into October) you will not confuse this paintbrush with any other and it is the one you will most likely encounter. I photographed this one in Long Canyon Meadows in late September.

FROSTED INDIAN PAINTBRUSH
Castilleja pruinosa   5 irregular petals forming a tube
Broomrape family

Trying to identify the variety of *Castilleja* species in the region is a difficult task. There are too many species to illustrate here—that's what the gigantic eight pound botanical manuals are for! Frosted Indian paintbrush is a common, low growing paintbrush that you will find in abundance blooming in places like Union Meadows in late May and June. I've found hundreds of them there and none ever taller than 7". I photographed these along the Union Lake Cut-off trail in early June.

SPLITHAIR INDIAN PAINTBRUSH
Castilleja schizotricha   5 irregular petals forming a tube
Broomrape family

The plants are 3" to 6" in height with narrow three-lobed leaves scattered along the upright stems. The flowers are pale to dusty red and softly hairy. The entire plant is covered with white-woolly hairs. This one favors dry, open, rocky, and sandy sites in full sun. Places to look for it are on the slopes above Black's Basin in the Trinity Alps and below Twin Lakes in the Russians. I photographed this in August below Dogwood Lake in the Marble Mountains but you will find it throughout the Trinities and the Russians.

SISKIYOU MOUNTAINS OWL'S-CLOVER
Orthocarpus cuspidatus subsp. *cuspidatus*   5 irregular petals forming a tube
Broomrape family

The most distinguishing feature of this particular owl clover is the prominent white and inflated lower lip. The other petals are a light pinkish magenta. Unlike Copeland's (next page) in which the flowers grow in a long tube shaped cluster, this one is shorter and more squat, flaring at the center to give the flowering head a triangular shape. It has similar tastes in habitat, preferring relatively dry, open areas at mid to high elevations. I photographed this one on Mt. Ashland in Southern Oregon but look for it all summer in places like High Prairie and Mary Blaine Meadow in the Trinity Alps and along the upper reaches of the Paynes Lake Trail in the Russians.

SCARLET INDIAN PAINTBRUSH
Castilleja miniata subsp. *miniata*
Broomrape family

FROSTED INDIAN PAINTBRUSH
Castilleja pruinosa
Broomrape family

SPLITHAIR INDIAN PAINTBRUSH
Castilleja schizotricha
Broomrape family

SISKIYOU MOUNTAINS OWL'S-CLOVER
Orthocarpus cuspidatus subsp. *cuspidatus*
Broomrape family

COPELAND'S OWL'S-CLOVER
Orthocarpus cuspidatus subsp. *copelandii*   5 irregular petals forming a tube
Broomrape family

This owl's-clover blooms throughout the summer in the high country where it prefers dry, exposed, rocky meadows, and openings. The plants are loosely branched but strongly upright with reddish stems that can reach 12" in height. The flowers are deep rose in color with the lower lip white and inflated. I photographed these in Bear Basin in the Trinity Alps in late August. Other places to look for them are in Elderberry Duff and Parker Meadows in the Trinity Alps and Horse Heaven Meadows on the Trinity Divide.

LITTLE ELEPHANT HEADS, BABY ELEPHANT HEADS
Pedicularis attollens   5 irregular petals forming a tube
Broomrape family

This wildflower is definitely cute—with tiny light to dark pink flowers that look like little elephant heads. The upper petals are narrow and recurved from a protruding bulge that resembles an elephant's trunk. The lower petals spread away and droop forming the ears. There are many flowers in a compact head blooming near the top of a nearly leafless stalk. Leaves are linear, finely divided, and mostly basal. They prefer wet meadows, fens, and stream banks at mid to high elevations. Look for them around Caribou Lake (where I photographed these) from late July through September.

INDIAN WARRIOR, WARRIOR'S PLUME
Pedicularis densiflora   5 irregular petals forming a tube
Broomrape family

Indian warrior blooms early at low elevations, often competing with milkmaids and manzanita to be the first to show. I've found them in full bloom in mid-January in some years but, more typically in late February. Low elevation warriors are larger and stand taller than those you will find in higher elevations. Lower down they can reach heights of 12" or more but higher rarely exceed 6". Flowers are a deep vibrant red or orange and the leaves long, deeply dissected, and fern-like. I shot this photograph along Scorpion Creek below Bonanza King Lookout in early June, but look for them along the Swift Creek trail as well, especially between the trailhead and the turnoff to Granite Lake. As an interesting side-note, I recently found and photographed a group of beautiful, buttery yellow warriors (see inset) along Highway 36 west of Platina—life is full of surprises!

LEAFY LOUSEWORT, PARROT'S BEAK
Pedicularis racemosa   5 irregular petals forming a tube
Broomrape family

It wasn't until I began putting this guide together that I'd ever heard these called parrot's beaks—which they in no way resemble. They are more commonly called elephant heads because of the overall shape of the flower. Common names aside, this pretty wildflower is found throughout the Trinities, Russians, and the Marbles at mid to high elevations—especially around water. The leaves are undivided, lance-like, and finely toothed. I photographed these at the outlet to Buckhorn Lake in the Marble Mountain Wilderness in mid-August.

COPELAND'S OWL'S-CLOVER
Orthocarpus cuspidatus subsp. *copelandii*
Broomrape family

LITTLE ELEPHANT HEADS
Pedicularis attollens
Broomrape family

INDIAN WARRIOR, WARRIOR'S PLUME
Pedicularis densiflora
Broomrape family

LEAFY LOUSEWORT, PARROT'S BEAK
Pedicularis racemosa
Broomrape family

215

PINK-FLOWERED STICKSEED
Hackelia mundula   5 irregular petals forming a tube
Borage family

This uncommon stickseed grows in small, scattered, and isolated colonies around the edges of wet meadows, near springs, and along the banks of streams. The soft pink flowers are large, up to ½" across, and bloom in loose clusters at the tops of tall stems. Plants can reach heights of 3'. It is the only pink stickseed in these mountains. Look for them along the Pacific Crest Trail above West Boulder Lake and along the trail between South Fork Lakes and Saloon Creek (which is where I photographed these) in the Trinity Alps in July.

BITTER DOGBANE
Apocynum androsaemifolium   5 irregular petals forming a tube
Dogbane family

Dogbane loves open, sunny, and rocky slopes as well as disturbed sites. It is a low, spreading plant with long, opposite, oval leaves, that are dark green above and pale beneath. In late summer, at higher elevations, the entire plant turns a brilliant red while, at lower elevations it tends to be more yellow. The white to pinkish, tubular flowers resemble those of manzanita and can cover almost the entire plant. Like milkweed, dogbane exudes a milky substance when its stems are broken. I photographed this bunch near the top of the Long Canyon Trail below Bee Tree Gap but it is common throughout.

SHOWY MILKWEED
Asclepias speciosa   5 irregular petals forming a tube
Dogbane family

This milkweed is commonly found along the edges of roads, highways, and on dry, open flats throughout. The plants can approach 4' in height with several globose heads of large beautiful pink and magenta flowers. The leaves are large, fuzzy and gray-green. A milky sap appears when stems are broken and is very sticky. Butterflies are drawn to milkweed and for some species it is a primary food source. *Asclepias fascicularis*, a similar milkweed, also grows in this area and, except for the linear shaped eaves, might be mistaken for *A. speciosa*. I photographed these on a flat near Junction City just above the Trinity River in late June.

PINK-FLOWERED STICKSEED
Hackelia mundula
Borage family

BITTER DOGBANE
Apocynum androsaemifolium
Dogbane family

SHOWY MILKWEED
Asclepias speciosa
Dogbane family

PURPLE MOUSE-EARS, DOUGLAS' MONKEYFLOWER, BROWNIES
Diplacus douglasii   5 irregular petals forming a tube
Lopseed family

Here's a tiny monkeyflower that often hides in plain sight. The 3" to 4" plants like dry, exposed rocky sites at lower elevations. A solitary magenta-purple flower opens atop a short stalk that rises from a basal rosette of light green and deeply veined leaves. The upper two petals of the flower are the largest and give rise to one of its best common names—purple mouse-ears. The lower petals are shorter and less prominent. They should not be confused with dwarf monkeyflower (described below) which it can be distinguished from by the broad inflated throat at the base of the petal lobes. I photographed these alongside the road to the Big French Creek Trailhead in the Trinity Alps in late June.

KELLOGG'S MONKEYFLOWER
Diplacus kelloggii   5 irregular petals forming a tube
Lopseed family

This tiny magenta-purple monkeyflower resembles the Douglas' monkeyflower (mentioned above) except that the flowers lack large upper petals and have a well developed lower petal lobes. Two or three flower bearing stems rise out of the basal leaf cluster, each stem with a solitary flower at the top. The flower is tubular with the petals opening away from the throat. The throat itself is yellow and spotted with deep magenta. The leaves are olive green with reddish tinted veins and purple underneath. I photographed this one along the Park's Creek Road just off Highway 3 in mid-June.

DWARF MONKEYFLOWER
Diplacus nanus var. *nanus*   5 irregular petals forming a tub
Lopseed family

This really is a dwarf wildflower, barely over two inches tall and easy to miss while trudging uphill on a hot day under the weight of a loaded pack. My observant grandson Nico first found them on a backpacking trip into West Boulder Lake and brought them to my attention. In that particular location, individual plants were scattered and blooming in the open on light colored granitic sand—making them difficult to see until I dropped my pack and started crawling around in the dirt taking photographs. The beautiful deep pink corolla is trumpet shaped with petals that flare away from the center exposing a deep yellow throat spotted with pink. The compact leaves are olive-green, covered with minute hairs, and narrowly oval. I photographed these little bloomers on sandy flats along the Pacific Crest Trail above West Boulder Lake in the Trinity Alps in August.

LAYNE'S MONKEYFLOWER
Diplacus nanus X *layneae*   5 irregular petals forming a tube
Lopseed family

Another tiny monkeyflower—this species is so small and delicate that a backpacker might never see it. The long, tube shaped flowers are beautiful pink with white and yellow throat spotted with a deeper magenta. Petals fan away from the throat in a perfect circular shape. Leaves, stems, and sepals are all hairy. I've never seen it much over 3" tall. The species seems to grow in colonies on dry, exposed, sandy sites. My grand-daughter Cristan discovered it on a pack trip into the area around Horse Creek in August which is where I photographed these.

PURPLE MOUSE-EARS
Diplacus douglasii
Lopseed family

KELLOGG'S MONKEYFLOWER
Diplacus kelloggii
Lopseed family

DWARF MONKEYFLOWER
Diplacus nanus
Lopseed family

LAYNE'S MONKEYFLOWER
Diplacus layneae
Lopseed family

BREWER'S MONKEYFLOWER
Erythranthe breweri   5 irregular petals forming a tube
Lopseed family

The plants hug the ground, growing to 2" tall. The pink to deep rose, tube shaped flowers are minute, 1/8" across, blooming in dense colonies in open and sandy meadows at mid to high elevations. A close-up inspection reveals classic monkey-flower structure—with recurved upper petals, three lobed petals that form a lower lip, notched at the tips. Look for them in places like Doe Flat, (where I photographed these), along the PCT between Doe and Little Granite Lakes, or the dry meadows at the head of Horse Creek in the Trinity Alps from mid-summer to mid-fall.

CRIMSON MONKEYFLOWER, SCARLET MONKEYFLOWER, CARDINAL MONKEYFLOWER
Erythranthe cardinalis   5 irregular petals forming a tube
Lopseed family

This has got to be the most brilliantly colored of all the monkeyflowers. Striking red and yellow streaked flowers bloom at the ends of tall, upright stalks that can reach 24" in height. Stalks, leaves and sepals are all covered with very sticky hairs. Look for them in moist, sandy areas along the Trinity River and around springs and seeps at lower elevations. Along the river they are often partially submerged by rising spring run-off. They can bloom all summer long. I photographed these near the mouth of Indian Creek on the Trinity River in late July.

LEWIS' MONKEYFLOWER
Erythranthe lewisii   5 irregular petals forming a tube
Lopseed family

This is a large, beautiful, and showy monkeyflower. It graces areas where there is running water including the shorelines of lakes, the edges of seeps, and snow melt ponds early in the blooming season—anywhere from early July to late August depending on elevation. The brilliant pink flowers are ¾" in diameter on plants ranging from 12" to 24" in height. Because of their size and color, they cannot be confused with any other monkeyflower in this area. I photographed these in the steep, wet meadows at the back of Grizzly Lake in August but another good place to look for them is in the upper bowl of Long Canyon at the base of the climb to Lake Anna.

NETTLELEAF HORSE MINT, GIANT HYSSOP
Agastache urticifolia   5 irregular petals forming a tube
Mint family

This is a common wildflower through the mountains of northern California and southern Oregon. You will find it in mid-elevation wet meadows where it grows to 6' tall. The lilac, purple, and white flowers are long, tubular and bloom in dense, 3" to 6" spikes. The plant has a strong odor. I took this photograph in a meadow on Mt. Ashland in Southern Oregon.

BREWER'S MONKEYFLOWER
Erythranthe breweri
Lopseed family

CRIMSON MONKEYFLOWER
Erythranthe cardinalis
Lopseed family

LEWIS' MONKEYFLOWER
Erythanthe lewisii
Lopseed family

NETTLELEAF HORSE MINT, GIANT HYSSOP
Agastache urticifolia
Mint family

NEWBERRY'S PENSTEMON, MOUNTAIN PRIDE, DAVIDSON'S PENSTEMON
NEWBERRY'S-DAVIDSON'S PENSTEMON HYBRID

Penstemon newberryi, Penstemon davidsonii
and *Penstemon newberryi* X *davidsonii*　　　　5 irregular petals forming a tube
Plantain family

All of the Newberry's variations, including those that are blue and bluish purple are included here for ease of comparison.

Newberry's penstemon is highly variable with tubular shaped flowers ranging in color from electric pink to deep magenta with yellow spots around the flower's opening. Long hairs decorate the throat. Its leaf structure varies as well and all this because it hybridizes with Davidson's penstemon. Newberry's is rangy with larger leathery leaves toothed at the margins while Davidsons forms dense mats with smaller leaves likewise toothed. Davidson's flowers typically are tubular, small and soft mauve on the outside, lighter in the throat which is trimmed with white hairs. Davidson's and the Newberry's/Davidson's hybrid both lack the yellow spots found on Newberry's. Newberry's can be found throughout a variety of habitats but almost always around rocks and rocky outcrops at mid-to higher elevations. The Davidson's I've found have been occupants of higher elevation exposed ridgetops. Flowers of the hybrid version tend to be light to dark blue sometimes tinged with a bit of magenta and, in shape, more closely resembling Newberry's. The hybrid can be found in association with Newberry's and I have found a mix of pink and blue flowers on the same stalk.

I photographed the vibrant pink Newberry's above the shoreline of Doe Lake in the Trinity Alps. The photograph of the Davidson's was taken on the ridgetop between Trail Gulch and South Fork Lakes in the Trinity Alps. I photographed the blue hybrid above Upper Albert Lake in the Russian Wilderness. They bloom from July into September.

PRIDE OF THE SIERRAS

Penstemon newberryi var. *newberryi*　　　　5 irregular petals forming a tube
Plantain family

Recognized more by its color than anything else this *Penstemon* is a real standout. Except for color it closely resembles its cousin Newberry's penstemon. Newberry's, however, is typically a lighter shade of pink and not the deep, electric rose-red of this one. The plants of both are similar—forming low growing evergreen mats with deep, leathery green leaves that are toothed at the margins. Both inhabit dry, rocky places such as granite outcrops and crevices where, as one Yosemite naturalist notes, "it looks impossible for flowers to grow." I found and photographed these blooming in serpentine outcrops along the Pacific Crest Trail below Deadfall Lakes on the Trinity Divide in early August.

NEWBERRY'S PENSTEMON
Penstemon newberryi
Plantain family

DAVIDSON'S PENSTEMON
Penstemon davidsonii var. *davidsonii*
Plantain family

DAVIDSON'S-NEWBERRY'S PENSTEMON HYBRID
P. newberryi X *davidsonii*
Plantain family

PRIDE OF THE SIERRAS
Penstemon newberryi var. *newberryi*
Plantain family

FOXGLOVE
Digitalis purpurea
Plantain family

5 irregular petals forming a tube

We usually think of foxgloves as being a coastal flower, but there is a small population up along the North Fork of Coffee Creek. It is a non-native that is highly poisonous to livestock as well as humans. I have a hunch that the folks who built their homes (think Hodges Cabin) along the creek in the early 20th century probably planted foxgloves in their gardens and those now growing are garden escapes. It grows up to 6' or 7' tall with deep rose-purple (sometimes white), tubular flowers clustered along the upper portions of the stem. The throat of each flower is speckled with white and deep purple. They typically bloom in July. **Note**: The North Fork of Coffee Creek was ravaged by the Coffee Fire in the summer of 2014 and much of the drainage went up in flames. Although the foxgloves I photographed there were found along the creek, they might now be gone.

NOTHOCHELONE, TURTLEHEAD, WOODLAND PENSTEMON
Nothochelone nemorosa
Plantain family

5 irregular petals forming a tube

Nothochelone is found throughout the Russian Wilderness at higher elevations. It favors shaded sites and is typically found on the north sides of mountain peaks, around rocky outcrops, and scree slopes. The hairy flowers bloom in loose clusters and are mostly creamy pink on the outsides of the petals to deep purple in the throat. The genus name comes from the Greek word for "false turtle" which refers to the corolla that supposedly looks like a turtle's head. I've photographed plenty of turtles through the years, but I fail to see the resemblance. I took this photograph on the ridge between Big Duck and Eaton Lakes in mid-July but you can find them blooming well into September.

VARIABLE-LEAF COLLOMIA
Collomia heterophylla
Phlox family

5 irregular petals forming a tube

This beautiful little *Collomia* is anything but shy. The small, tubular, brilliantly deep pink flowers have centers of white and yellow, and bloom en-masse from tufts of leaves at the tops of short, branched stems. Though only a few inches tall, the color is so intense that they are hard to miss. The lobed leaves distinguish this from other annual *Collomia* species. Large colonies bloom from May into June in sandy soil alongside low elevation trails throughout these mountains. I photographed these along the Boulder Creek Trail in the Trinity Alps in late May.

TRACY'S COLLOMIA
Collomia tracyi
Phlox family

5 symmetrical petals forming a tube

These little wildflowers were blooming all along the trail to the top of Packer's Peak in the Trinity Alps in late June. There were hundreds of tiny bunches growing in the direct sun, on the open, exposed slopes in serpentine soils. Flowers can range from white to lavender, with white edging on the petals. The flowers are ¼" in diameter or smaller. Pollen on the anthers is bright blue. It is a multi-branched plant with several reddish-purple stems crowded with lance shaped, hairy leaves.

FOX GLOVE
Digitalis purpurea
Plantain family

NOTHOCHELONE, TURTLEHEAD
Nothochelone nemorosa
Plantain family

VARIABLE-LEAF COLLOMIA
Collomia heterophylla
Phlox family

TRACY'S COLLOMIA
Collomia tracyi
Phlox family

225

SCARLET GILIA, SKY ROCKET
Ipomopsis aggregata   5 symmetrical petals forming a tube
Phlox family

I like the name "sky rocket" for this brilliant red wildflower. It's entirely fitting because of the long, funnel shaped flowers that flare sharply at the ends revealing long stamens topped with brilliant yellow anthers. With a little imagination they look just like exploding sky rockets—the 4th of July kind. It can be found from mid to high elevations throughout these mountains preferring exposed, dry, sandy sites, often in the company of spreading dogbane. It grows in profusion along the upper portions of the trail between Syphon and Russian Lakes in the Russian Wilderness, Mt. Ashland in Southern Oregon, and along the Pacific Crest Trail through the north end of the Trinity Alps.

MIDGET PHLOX, SLENDER PHLOX
Microsteris gracilis   5 symmetrical petals forming a tube
Phlox family

I first found this tiny phlox growing on steep cutbanks and cliffs alongside Canyon Creek Road in mid-April. They were scattered throughout the area and numerous in shade as well as sun. The petals are delicate lavender-pink with darker areas of purple near the lower portion of the petals and greenish-white near the center of the corolla. The plants are small, 2" to 4" tall on average, and the flowers about 1/8" across. The plants I photographed were multi-branched with several flowers on each plant. You really have to look for this one as it tends to hide down in and amongst other plants, especially heron's bill which—from a distance—the flowers resemble.

SPREADING PHLOX
Phlox diffusa   5 symmetrical petals forming a tube
Phlox family

This was my mother's favorite high country flower and, through the years, has remained one of mine as well. It blooms in large colonies in open, sunny areas popping up as the winter snows melt. The beautiful deep lavender-pink flowers crowd the plants and fade to near white as they age. The mats of leaves are needle-like with the flowers blooming in low mounds over the tops. They are found all across the mid to higher elevations and good places to find them in late spring and early summer are between Union Meadows and the Parker Divide, along the Swift Creek Trail, and in the basin surrounding Gray Rocks Lakes on the Trinity Divide. I shot the large photograph above Horse Creek Meadows in early July and the smaller one along Swift Creek, in late May. It is not unusual to still find blooms in September in protected places at higher elevations.

SCARLET GILIA, SKY ROCKET
Ipomopsis aggregata
Phlox family

MIDGET PHLOX
Microsteris gracilis
Phlox family

SPREADING PHLOX
Phlox diffusa
Phlox family

SHOWY PHLOX
Phlox speciosa   5 symmetrical petals forming a tube
Phlox family

Showy phlox is one of those wildflowers you will find blooming early in May in foothills around the Central Valley and through early June at mid to high elevations such as on Scott Mountain. The large, deep pink flowers grow in clusters on loosely branched plants that can grow to 7" tall—sometimes climbing up into the low branches of surrounding brush. Look for them along the cutbanks of roads and highways, which always seem to be the best place to locate them. I photographed these along Highway 299 West on the west side of Buckhorn Summit in June.

MOSQUITO BILLS, SAILOR CAPS, HENDERSON'S SHOOTING STAR
Primula hendersonii   5 symmetrical petals forming a tube
Primrose family

This, the most common of shooting stars in our area, grows in the lower elevations in the foothills. They are also among the earliest bloomers, arriving in late January or early February in the foothills of the Sacramento Valley. The plants are usually 4" and 7" tall with loose clusters of deep magenta to light purple flowers at the tops of reddish stems. As with all shooting stars, the flowers are easily identified and Henderson's is especially so because of its size and the rounded, oblong leaves. I've found it blooming along the lower ends of the Swift Creek and Stewart's Fork Trails in May and early June.

SIERRA SHOOTING STAR, JEFFREY'S SHOOTING STAR
TALL MOUNTAIN SHOOTING STAR
Primula jeffreyi   5 symmetrical petals forming a tube
Primrose family

This is the giant among local shooting stars with stalks as tall as 24." You will find it in wet meadow, alongside streams, springs, and seeps. It likes its feet in the water! The only other shooting star that grows this large is the Alpine shooting star (shown below). The pale lilac flowers bloom in a loose cluster at the tops of the stems. Look for it along the road to the Tangle Blue Trailhead and along the Stoddard Lake Trail, both in the Trinity Alps.

ALPINE SHOOTING STAR
Primula tetrandra   5 symmetrical petals forming a tube
Primrose family

The pink blooms of this shooting star make identification easy. It is only found in wet meadows and open areas at higher elevations in the area covered by this guide. It can grow to 20" but most often 7" to 12". I photographed this one near the outlet of Lois Lake in the Trinity Alps, but have found it around Little Bear Lake, in the meadows around Upper Caribou Lake in the Trinity Alps, as well and in rocky areas on the south side of Big Blue Lake in the Russians.

SHOWY PHLOX
Phlox speciosa
Phlox family

MOSQUITO BILLS, SAILOR CAPS
Primula hendersonii
Primrose family

SIERRA SHOOTING STAR, JEFFREY'S SHOOTING STAR
Primula jeffreyi
Primrose family

ALPINE SHOOTING STAR
Primula tetrandra
Primrose family

SIERRA PRIMROSE
Primula suffrutescens   5 symmetrical petals forming a tube
Primrose family

This is one of our true alpine wildflowers. It can be found at higher elevations grow-ing among the rocks on scree slopes, along the bergschrund line on rocky shelves, and beneath the tallest peaks above Papoose, Caribou, and Grizzly Lakes. In my years in the high country I have never encountered it anywhere else, although Marla Knight notes a possible occurrence in rocks alongside the new Caribou Lakes Trail below Little Caribou Lake. The flowers are unmistakable, with five deep magenta pink petals surrounding a yellow center blooming on stems up to 7" tall. The stiff leaves form a rosette, appear wrinkly, are elongated, and toothed on the margins. I photographed these just below the granite peaks above Upper Caribou Lake in mid-August.

HAIRY-FRUIT VALERIAN, MOUNTAIN VALERIAN
Valeriana pubicarpa   5 symmetrical petals forming a tube
Valerian family

I found and photographed this gorgeous little valerian blooming in decomposed granite at the top of the ridge between Little Duck Lake and the Sugar Creek drain-age. All of the populations were in mostly shaded sites on the west and northwest facing part of the ridge. Typically, the plants were no more than 12" tall with deep green, round basal leaves and smaller, opposite, lance shaped leaves growing more scattered the farther up the flowering stalk they grew. Beautiful light pink to magenta flowers bloom in clusters along the upper third of the stalk with prominent stamens.

WESTERN PEONY, BROWN'S PEONY
Paeonia brownii   Flowers in composite heads
Peony family

This is the sole member of the Peony family found in this area and restricted within the boundaries set in this guide with isolated populations from Weaverville, Doug-las City, and Hayfork areas. The plants are bushy with several stems rising from a common rootstock between 12" and 20" in height. The leaves are divided with oblong, rounded leaflets that, because of a waxy powder, have an bluish appear-ance—especially in the older leaves. One or more flowers nod at the ends of tall, thick red stems with spreading, deep reddish-green to purplish sepals edged with yellow-gold. Sepals and petals appear much the same. Fleshy, elongated pistils are surrounded by numerous stamens. I photographed this one along Highway 97 east of Weed in early May.

WESTERN EUPATORY, WESTERN SNAKEROOT
Ageratina occidentalis   Flowers in composite heads
Sunflower family

Look for this beautiful little plant along streambanks, the shorelines of lakes, and around springs at mid to high elevations throughout these mountains. It can reach heights of 4' but is more commonly 2' tall with strongly erect, hairy stems arising from a woody base. Leaves are arrowhead shaped, finely toothed, and alternate along the stems. The flowers occur in elongate clusters of heads, can be white, pink, or light purple and are characterized by prominent style branches, which give the clusters a fuzzy look. I've only found light pink or light purple forms in the high country—never the white version. I photographed these along the outlet stream of Big Boulder Lake in the Trinity Alps in late July.

SIERRA PRIMROSE
Primula suffrutescens
Primrose family

HAIRY-FRUIT VALERIAN, MOUNTAIN VALERIAN
Valeriana pubicarpa
Valerian family

WESTERN PEONY. BROWN'S PEONY
Paeonia brownii
Peony family

WESTERN EUPATORY, WESTERN SNAKEROOT
Ageratina occidentalis
Sunflower family

ROSY PUSSYTOES, ROSY EVERLASTING
Antennaria rosea
Sunflower family

Flowers in composite heads

The deep green leaves of this pretty little pussytoe are longer, more upright, stiffer, and not nearly as fuzzy as other *Antennaria* species—also, they clasp the flowering stalk along its entire length right to the base of the flowering head. Like all pussytoes, the little flowers bloom in a compact head at the tops of the stems, but these are graced with a beautiful rose-pink mass of ray flowers surrounding a Q-tip-like white button of disc flowers top and center. I do not encounter many of these on my high country adventures but I did find and photograph this bunch on a rocky ledge just above Doe Lake in the Trinity Alps in mid-September.

BREWER'S SWAMP THISTLE
Cirsium douglasii var. *breweri*
Sunflower family

Flowers in composite heads

This is a common native thistle found in damp environments at middle to high elevations throughout the area. It is slender-stalked, covered with white woolly hairs, and growing to 3' in height. The lavender to pink flower heads are 1" long and bloom in small clusters. It is spiny and, unless you enjoy excruciating pain, should never reach out and grab one. Spines occur along the stems, leaf margins, and bracts below the flowers. I photographed this one near Elderberry Duff in the Trinity Alps in late August.

RED THISTLE, SHOWY THISTLE
Cirsium occidentale var. *candidissimum*
Sunflower family

Flowers in composite heads

This is the showiest of all the thistles and you don't need to get out of your car to find them. They are a roadside attraction from low to mid elevations throughout the area where they bloom on open, dry, rocky slopes. The entire plant, including stems and leaves, are cobwebby white. The large flower heads are an intense and striking red. They cannot be confused with any other thistle in this area. I photographed this one along Highway 3 near Callahan in August.

PHILADELPHIA FLEABANE
Erigeron philadelphicus
Sunflower family

Flowers in composite heads

This is a common fleabane that occurs on open, rocky sites, along streams, and in other damp places throughout the mid-elevations. It can grow in huge colonies and flower heads can be up to 1" across with a multitude of long, pinkish to blue slender ray flowers surrounding each compact head of yellow disc flowers. A single stem arising from the rootstock loosely branches midway to support several flower heads. Leaves to 6" long clasp the stalks. I photographed these in Long Canyon Meadows in the Trinity Alps.

ROSY PUSSYTOES, ROSY EVERLASTING
Antennaria rosea
Sunflower family

BREWER'S SWAMP THISTLE
Cirsium douglasii var. *breweri*
Sunflower family

RED THISTLE, SHOWY THISTLE
Cirsium occidentale var. *candidissimum*
Sunflower family

PHILADELPHIA FLEABANE
Erigeron philadelphicus
Sunflower family

WOODLAND WIRE LETTUCE
Stephanomeria lactucina
Sunflower family

Many petals

I look at these two photographs and see different wildflowers but I am assured by my coauthors that they are, indeed, the same species. The basic plant structure is identical with thin flowering stems, about 24" long, trailing along the ground with the combined weight of leaves and flowers. Leaves are gray-green, long, and lance shaped. Flowers are variable, from purple-violet or mauve fading to a creamy-white center with several prominent cream colored stamens topped with dark mauve anthers. Individual petals are rectangular, squared, notched at the tips, and rimmed with a thin creamy white band. Seed heads are fuzzy white. I found both specimens in late September within 60' of each other in full bloom along the Deacon Lee Trail in the Russians.

Note: In 2014 the July Fire burned a large area of the Russians, including the stretch of the Deacon Lee Trail where I had previously found this species. On a trip into Russian Lake in 2015 I found no sign of the plants or flowers—the entire area severely burned and thick with bracken fern.

The Stony Ridge Trail is one to savor throughout the backpacking season but especially in early summer—when the entire trail is alive with an amazing variety of wildflowers. Through the years I have found and photographed over 54 species along the road to the trailhead or on the trail itself. On a dayhike in late July of 2017 I found 30 species in bloom.

This is a hike I do often, not only for the opportunity to photograph wildflowers, trees, and lichens—but for the stunning scenery as well. The view from Stonewall Pass westward over VanMatre Meadows to Stewart's Fork with the White Trinities beyond is as beautiful as any in the Trinity Alps (see title page). The view back down over Red Mountain Meadows to Granite Peak and Trinity Lake isn't bad either!

WOODLAND WIRE LETTUCE
Stephanomeria lactucina
Sunflower family

The **Stony Ridge Trail** ascends through Red Mountain Meadows towards Stonewall Pass.

SISKIYOU LEWISIA, CLIFF MAIDS, HECKNER'S LEWISIA
Lewisia cotyledon var. *heckneri*
Miner's lettuce family

many petals

All *Lewisia* species are beautiful but the way this one graces rocky outcrops makes it hard to beat. The candy-striped pink and white flowers are large and numerous, blooming in loose bunches at the tops of long, reddish stems early in the season. Leaves are large, pale green, and crowded in a basal rosette. There are three varieties; var. *heckneri* (pictured on the opposite page) has sharply toothed leaves, var. *howellii* has wavy-edged leaves and var. *cotyledon* has leaf margins that are entire. A good place to see var. *cotyledon* is on the scree slopes and cliff faces above Upper Albert Lake in the Russians.

QUILL-LEAVED LEWISIA, LEE'S LEWISIA
Lewisia leeana
Miner's lettuce family

many petals

The deep pinkish-purple flowers of Lee's lewisia are tiny but bloom in large clusters at the tops of branched stems which make them easy to spot. The leaves form basal tufts, are linear, fleshy, and pointed. It prefers sunny, open rocky areas. A great place to see this species is at Little Duck Lake in the Russian Wilderness. They bloom in abundance around the lake but are common through the high country. I photographed these in rocks above Lion Lake in the Trinity Alps in late May. Also pictured (in the inset) is a white variation of this *Lewisia* which I found on the slopes above Salmon Lake in the Trinity Alps in early September.

LEWISIA COTYLELEDON / LEWISIA LEEANA HYBRID
Lewisia X *whiteae*
Miner's lettuce family

many petals

Flowers of this *Lewisia* are vibrant pink, ½" wide, sometimes with a deeper red vein down the center of each petal, blooming in loose clusters along red stems. Several stems arise from each leaf cluster. The leaves are narrow, succulent, and form dense basal tufts. They prefer rocky outcrops and talus slopes. This species is a hybrid between Siskiyou lewisia and Lee's lewisia. The hybrid has narrower leaves and smaller flowers than Siskiyou lewisia. I photographed these just below Upper Albert Lake in the Russians in September.

WESTERN STAR FLOWER
Lysimachia latifolia
Myrsine family

many petals

These little beauties love the deep shade and lingering spring moisture provided by an overhanging forest canopy. They are common throughout the entire area and, when blooming, really do look like little stars. Each plant is about 6" tall, with five leaves in a whorl around the strongly ascending stem. Each can have as many as three bright pink flowers with deep yellow anthers—though usually there is only one. The flowers fade to white as they age. I photographed these along the Swift Creek Trail but you will find them along many of the lower elevation trails like Stewart's Fork.

SISKIYOU LEWISIA, CLIFF MAIDS
Lewisia cotyledon var. *heckneri*
Miner's lettuce family

QUILL-LEAVED LEWISIA, LEE'S LEWISIA
Lewisia leeana
Miner's lettuce family

LEWISIA
Lewisia X *whiteae* (*L. cotyledon*/*L. leeana* hybrid)
Miner's lettuce family

WESTERN STAR FLOWER
Lysimachia latifolia
Myrsine family

WESTERN REDBUD
Cercis occidentalis
Pea family

5 irregular petals

These beautiful shrubs can grow into small trees nearly 20' in height. They bloom in early spring on bare twigs and are covered from top to bottom with delightful pink pea-shaped flowers—which begin to fade as the leaves open. Being in the pea family, the seeds mature in long, reddish-brown pea-like pods. The leaves are mostly round and silver dollar sized or larger. You will see them along almost every road in this neck of the woods. They are a popular spring-time attraction with Sunday drivers but, as pretty as the springtime show is, the colorful autumn leaves can be just as stunning. When weather conditions are just right the leaves turn beautiful shades of gold and deep red.

BALDHIP ROSE
Rosa gymnocarpa
Rose family

5 symmetrical petals - ovary superior

Flowers of the baldhip rose are not as large as those of the sweet-briar rose (below), but they are every bit as beautiful. The flowers tend to be 1" to 1½" across and a deep magenta or pink. The distinguishing feature of this rose is that the sepals tend to fall off as the hip (seedpod) develops, making the fruit look like a berry and leading to the name "baldhip" rose. I've found that it grows in shaded or semi-shaded areas dominated by mixed conifers and hardwood stands at mid-elevations as opposed to the sweet-briar rose which frequents open and sunny foothill and valley locations. Good places to see these are along the Canyon Creek Road to Ripstein Campground and along the trail to Duck Lakes in the Russian Wilderness. I photographed the flowers along Canyon Creek Road in June and the "hips" along the trail to Stoddard Lake in the Trinity Alps in early September.

SWEET-BRIAR
Rosa rubiginosa
Rose family

5 symmetrical petals - ovary superior

This non-native forms large thickets in open, sunny, foothill and valley locations often forming large mounds 6' or more in height and several feet across. Clusters of large, beautiful pink flowers up to 2½" across cover the bushes and are very fragrant! My grandmother loved roses and dug up and transplanted dozens of these to places around her house in Lewiston where, 50 some odd year later, they still thrive. **Side note**: in the smaller photograph you can see several small black beetles that have attached themselves to the stamens and anthers. I've found this to be a fairly common relationship along Rush Creek Road where I took these photographs.

WESTERN REDBUD
Cercis occidentalis
Pea family

BALDHIP ROSE
Rosa gymnocarpa
Rose family

SWEET-BRIAR
Rosa rubiginosa
Rose family

DOUGLAS SPIRAEA, HARDHACK
Spiraea douglasii
Rose family

5 symmetrical petals - ovary superior

The dark to light rose pink flowers of Douglas spiraea bloom in narrow, elongated clusters on tall, upright stems from a loosely branched shrub that sometimes approaches 6' tall. Prominent stamens give the flower clusters a decidedly fuzzy look. This is a shrub that likes semi-shade and moisture so look for it in damp meadows, around springs and along the banks of creeks in places like Big Boulder (where I photographed these) and Log Lakes.

Note: Intrigued by strange common names, I've always wondered where the term "hardhack" came from. A search of the Kinnikinnick Native Plant Society web site out of Northern Idaho gave me the answer. It seems that early settlers in the Northwest gave it that name because it was found in dense stands or clusters that were hard to hack through while clearing land or, I suppose, while travelling. Also, it is interesting to note that the scientific name *Spiraea* comes from the Greek word for wreaths or garlands for which reason species of *Spiraea* are often called bridal-wreath shrubs.

ROSE MEADOWSWEET, MOUNTAIN SPIRAEA
Spiraea splendens
Rose family

5 symmetrical petals - ovary superior

The fuzzy looking flat-topped clusters of deep pink flowers on this shrub give it away. The flowers bloom at the tops of tall stems that can reach to 3' in height. The leaves are oval and scalloped, densley arrayed on the bottom halves of the plant, and only sparsely up the flowering stalk. This *Spiraea* likes semi-shade and moisture, so look for it in damp meadows, around springs, and along the banks of creeks and lakes. You will find it at higher elevations in places along Canyon Creek, Long Canyon, and Sugar Pine Lake in the Trinity Alps. I photographed this one in a wet meadow near Gumboot Lake on the Trinity Divide in July. I have found it blooming around Mirror Lake and in the meadows above Sapphire Lake in the Trinity Alps in September.

MOUNTAIN PINK CURRANT
Ribes nevadense
Gooseberry family

5 symmetrical petals - ovary inferior

This loosely branched shrub is hard to miss when it's blooming. Reaching to 4' to 5' in height, it has wrinkled leaves that resemble those of the maples. The flowers bloom in a brightly colored raceme of deep pink, with slightly reflexed sepals surrounding white, tube shaped petals that effectively hide the stamens and anthers. They can be found throughout the mountains from low to mid-elevations in moist, shaded sites. The fruit of the currant is not sticky so it cannot be confused with gooseberries, to which they are related. The deep, blue-black berries ripen in bunches and are almost always coated with a bloom—a light blue to gray color which can be easily wiped away. A similar species, *Ribes sanguineum*, is also present in the book area. It differs in having larger flowers with more reflexed sepals. I photographed the flowers along the trail to Duck Lakes and the berries along the Deacon Lee Trail in September both in the Russians.

DOUGLAS SPIRAEA
HARDHACK
Spiraea douglasii
Rose family

ROSE MEADOWSWEET
MOUNTAIN SPIRAEA
Spiraea splendens
Rose family

MOUNTAIN PINK CURRANT
Ribes nevadense
Gooseberry family

SIERRA GOOSEBERRY
Ribes roezlii   5 symmetrical petals - ovary superior
Gooseberry family

It is difficult to mistake this one! The thorny shrub is loaded with pendulous, velvety, red and pink flowers in the spring and sharp, prickly fruits in the summer and fall. It grows in dry sites, along the edges of meadows, around the trunks of trees, and in rocky places. If you can get your fingers past the spines, the fruit is delicious and worth the effort to husk at least one. Harvesting enough for a pie is another task all together. I should know—my grandmother often sent me on gooseberry picking expeditions when I was a kid. While I had the bloody fingers to prove it, the effort was worth it when biting into the golden brown crust and steaming, sweet filling! I'm waiting for one of my grand kids to mimic the efforts of my early days, as I have not had such a pie since my grandmother passed. I photographed the flowers along the North Fork of Coffee Creek in late May and the fruit in Cabin Meadow below Sugar Pine Lake in September—both in the Trinity Alps.

PINK MOUNTAIN HEATHER
Phyllodoce empetriformis   5 petals joined into a bell
Heath family

This might be the quintessential wildflower of the high mountains. Scottish Highlanders are especially enamoured with them—inspiring songs and poetry like no other flower (except maybe the rose) through the centuries. When it flowers in mid-summer, mountainsides and the shorelines of lakes are alive with its color.

It is a shrubby plant that grows to 4' tall, with lance shaped, bristly leaves along the entire stem. Beautiful bunches of small, pink, urn shaped flowers hang from the stems in thick bundles. You will find them throughout the high country growing at the edges of meadows or next to rocky outcrops. In the fall, flowers remain on the stems, turning golden brown. Excellent places to see them include Caribou Lake in the Trinity Alps and Little Duck Lake in the Russians. I shot the large photograph behind Big Duck Lake in the Russians and the late season flowers at Little Bear Lake in the Trinity Alps in early October.

DWARF BILBERRY
Vaccinium cespitosum   5 petals joined into a bell
Heath family

This delightful little bilberry (aka huckleberry) is a low, ankle high shrub which forms dense thickets in shaded, semi-damp areas throughout the Trinity Alps, the Trinity Divide, and Russian Wilderness. It rarely grows over 20 inches in height, has small, mostly oval leaves lightly serrated on the margins, and greenish stems. When ripe, the tasty little blue-black berries are a favored snack for birds and chipmunks. Human foragers will rarely find enough for a batch of morning pancakes. I photographed the flowers along the Bear Basin Trail in late August and the developing fruit at Log Lake, both in the Trinity Alps. The inlet side of Eaton Lake in the Russians is carpeted with them.

SIERRA GOOSEBERRY
Ribes roezlii
Gooseberry family

PINK MOUNTAIN HEATHER
Phyllodoce empetriformis
Heath family

DWARF BILBERRY
Vaccinium cespitosum
Heath family

RED BUSH BEARDTONGUE, REDWOOD PENSTEMON
Keckiella corymbosa   5 irregular petals forming a tube
Plantain family

This species loves hot, dry, exposed places. So much so, that it blooms long after other flowers have gone into summer dormancy. The flower tubes are bright red and upwards of 2" long. The lower petal is deeply incised, folded down at the tip, with an upper petal forming a hood extending out over the lower one. The entire plant, including the flowers, is hairy and sticky. Besides low elevation, back county trails, the best place to see this gorgeous red *Keckiella* is along Highway 299 between Junction City and Willow Creek or Canyon Creek Road on the steep rocky cutbanks. I photographed these near the turn-off to Helena along Highway 299 in mid-July.

Note: If you are driving 299, rubber necking for flowers along the way is NOT a good idea. It's a dangerous winding roadway—leave the wildflower viewing to your passengers!

SWAMP LAUREL
Kalmia polifolia   5 petals joined into a bell
Heath family

Kalmia Lake near the head of Canyon Creek in the Trinity Alps is named for this beautiful shrub. Like so many alpine lakes in this area, its shoreline is decorated with stands of *Kalmia*—creating a gorgeous setting. The flowers are a striking pink, deeper in hue at the ends of the petals, and almost white in the centers. Each lightly cupped flower has a prominent, deep magenta pistil and ten white stamens with anthers aging blue. It grows to about 4'. Look for it at Little Duck Lake in the Russian Wilderness and Virginia Lake in the Trinity Alps. It has a long blooming season, often extending well into September and I have even found it blooming in a small, protected pocket along the shoreline of Little Bear Lake in mid-October.

Little Duck Lake: This lake is one of the jewels of the Russian Wilderness. It is surrounded by open, glacially polished granite slabs and peaks, meadows, stands of subalpine fir, and rich with an amazing variety of wildflowers. *Anemone, Montia, Valerian,* and *Lewisia* are just a few of the genera found here. The lake, like many in the high country, is alive with rough-skinned newts (*Taricha granulosa*) or "mud puppies" as we called them when I was growing up. These brown and orange newts (see inset) are oodles of fun for kids to find and play with but deadly poisonous if eaten! There is enough toxin in the skin of just one of these little critters to decimate at least a dozen people. Play yes—taste no! Notice the thick stands of low growing swamp laurel that decorate the shoreline in the picture. In late July and August it is absolutely gorgeous.

RED BUSH BEARDTONGUE
REDWOOD PENSTEMON
Keckiella corymbosa
Plantain family

SWAMP LAUREL
Kalmia polifolia
Heath family

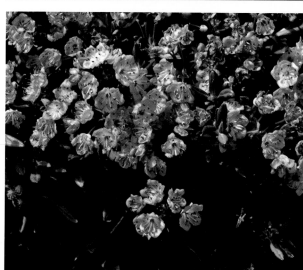

CREEPING SNOWBERRY & COMMON SNOWBERRY
Symphoricarpos mollis (left) and
Symphoricarpos albus var. *laevigatus* (right)
Honeysuckle family

5 irregular petals forming a tube

What most people immediately recognize about both snowberry species is not the flower but the white berries that mature late in the summer and fall. The inconspicuous, reddish pink flowers begin to show in early May and are hidden away beneath the leaves. While the berries might look delicious, they are poisonous.

The woody, vine-like stems of creeping snowberry (*S. mollis*) are typically reddish brown, grow low to the ground, or up surrounding brush while covering shaded areas from the foothills to the mountains. I've found it along trails above Shasta Lake and along mid-elevation trails in the Trinity Alps.

Common snowberry (*S. albus* var. *laevigatus*) is a stout, erect shrub frequently found in forested areas. It prefers deep shade at lower elevations growing to 4" or more in height. It can be found in abundance in places like Clear Creek Campground or along East Weaver Creek.

I photographed the creeping snowberry flowers (on the left) above the East Weaver Creek Campground near Weaverville in June and the berries along the trail to Stoddard Lake in the Trinity Alps in September. I photographed the common snowberry fruit (right) in October in Clear Creek Campground on the Trinity Divide.

CALIFORNIA SPICEBUSH, CALIFORNIA SWEET-SHRUB
Calycanthus occidentalis
Sweet shrub family

Many petals

This shrub is a long-time favorite of mine. When it blooms in late spring it is often covered with large and beautiful, deep burgundy flowers. From a few feet away the flowers look velvety soft, but in actuality, are quite rigid. It is not uncommon for the sharply pointed petals to be capped with brown at the tips. The leggy shrubs grow quickly to heights of 12' or more and can form dense thickets around springs and along streams throughout the lower elevations. The large, deep green leaves are more-or-less elliptic with a rounded base, a pointed tip, and slightly hairy beneath. I photographed the flower along VanNess Creek above Trinity Lake in June and the seed pod near Clear Creek Campground in October.

CREEPING SNOWBERRY
Symphoricarpos mollis
Honeysuckle family

COMMON SNOWBERRY
Symphoricarpos albus var. *laevigatus*
Honeysuckle family

CALIFORNIA SPICEBUSH, CALIFORNIA SWEET-SHRUB
Calycanthus occidentalis
Sweet shrub family

PINK HONEYSUCKLE, HAIRY HONEYSUCKLE
Lonicera hispidula
Honeysuckle family

5 irregular petals forming a tube

This is a difficult wildflower to classify by color. As you can see from the photographs, some of the flowers are white, some are white with a pink tinge at the base of the petals, and others are definitely pink. At lower elevations, where I shot these photographs, the majority of flowers are white with a light pink tinge. One of the best indicators that you are indeed looking at a honeysuckle are the opposite, oval leaves which, at the ends of the stems, become fused—appearing to wrap around the long, trailing stems. Bright red berries ripen later in the summer. This honeysuckle prefers dry, shaded sites. I photographed these along Big French Creek in the Trinity Alps in June and the berries above Gray's Falls on the Trinity River in late October.

TWIN FLOWER
Linnaea borealis var. *longiflora*
Twin flower family

5 petals joined into a bell

Twin flowers inhabit deeply shaded, damp forest floors—in settings where you might expect to find faeries or gnomes. The plants are small, rarely exceeding 6" in height and form dense, ground covering mats when conditions are favorable. The top of the central stem gives rise to two smaller stems that emerge upward at a perfect 45° angle with two delicate, pink and white flowers hanging at another 45° angle outward from the end of each. The pendant flowers are bell-shaped and about ½" long. A prominent white pistil extends beyond the petals and forms a perfect little clapper to the bell of the flower. I shot the large photograph along Mule Creek at the foot of the Trinity Alps and the smaller photograph along the Boulder Creek Trail—both in mid-July. There is a section of the Stewart's Fork Trail, near the upper end of Oak Flat where these little beauties can be found en-masse. **Note**: The genus is named after the 'father' of modern plant taxonomy, Carl von Linne, also known as Linnaeus. The same species grows in Sweden, where he lived and worked.

The Dorleska Mine: In its day this was probably one of the richest mines in the Coffee Creek area. It sported a cookhouse, dining hall, workings covered by snow sheds, and tons of heavy equipment. Remnants of that by-gone era are readily evident in this basin and a reminder to wilderness enthusiasts that this country once hummed with human activity. Except during hunting season, not many people visit here but it is well worth the effort. There is a tiny lake in this basin that my friend Roger Parks unofficially named Redbud Lake. The name has stuck through the years but unless you're a heavy sleeper you probably won't want to camp by it. It is home to thousands of frogs and they will drive you nuts all night long with their singing and croaking (I know this from personal experience). This is serpentine country so wildflower hunting is excellent throughout the late spring and early summer season and the scenery is stunning.

PINK HONEYSUCKLE
HAIRY HONEYSUCKLE
Lonicera hispidula
Honeysuckle family

TWIN FLOWER
Linnaea borealis var. *longiflora*
Twin flower family

A boiler, once used to power mining equipment at the Dorleska Mine, sits abandoned in this photograph taken looking across tailing piles to the northeast. It is just one piece amidst huge piles of old equipment left behind after the mine was abandoned.

An afternoon thunderstorm breaks over the Trinity River along Highway 299.

Silver bush lupine
Lupinus albifrons

CROWN BRODIAEA
Brodiaea coronaria
Brodiaea family

3 or 6 petals

This is another *Brodiaea* that favors dry, open places and shares similarities in basic structure with dwarf brodiaea (*Brodiaea minor*), except for height. The deep bluish purple flowers of crown brodiaea, however, tend to be more upright and almost funnel shaped. I photographed this bunch on a dry flat along the upper Trinity River in June. Alice Jones reports it from several areas in Trinity County, around Weaverville for example, and also near Trinity Center in Norwegian Meadows. (don't go looking for them in Norwegian Meadows however—it is private property).

BLUE DICKS
Dichelostemma capitatum
Brodiaea family

3 or 6 petals

Blue dicks are perhaps the earliest of the brodiaeas to bloom in this area, often appearing on sun-warmed hillsides and exposed roadside cut-banks in early February. They are characterized by the long flowering stalks that are often 18" or more in height. Each stalk is topped with a tight group of upright, bell-shaped, light to dark blue (sometimes even light violet) flowers. The weight of the flowers at the tops of those tall, slender stems can cause the stem to bend or undulate, sometimes clear to the ground. I photographed this one above Clear Creek in Whiskeytown National Recreation Area but it is common at lower elevations throughout this area.

FORK-TOOTHED OOKOW
Dichelostemma congestum
Brodiaea family

3 or 6 petals

The flowers of fork toothed ookow bloom in compact heads at the tops of naked stems that can reach 3' in height. They are about ¾" long, range in color from deep blue to purple, are bell shaped, pinched in the middle above the ovaries, then flaring at the tips. Each flower has three fertile stamens and three forked, tooth shaped projections in the center, surrounding the stamens. The leaves are deeply grooved down the center. I photographed these in a meadow below Rush Creek Road in mid-May.

WILD HYACINTH
Dichelostemma multiflorum
Brodiaea family

3 or 6 petals

This is one of the earliest wildflowers to bloom in the lower elevations throughout this area. It decorates hillsides from the Central Valley to the hills surrounding the Trinity River and Trinity Alps. Flowers have compact heads of beautiful blue to light lilac nodding at the tops of stems that can reach 2' in height. Their nectar is a favored food source for pipevine swallowtail butterflies. The leaves are grass-like and are almost the same length as the flowering stems. I photographed these along the Trinity River near Lewiston.

CROWN BRODIAEA
Brodiaea coronaria
Brodiaea family

BLUE DICKS
Dichelostemma capitatum
Brodiaea family

FORK-TOOTHED OOKOW
Dichelostemma congestum
Brodiaea family

WILD HYACINTH
Dichelostemma multiflorum
Brodiaea family

YELLOW TRITELEIA, TRINITY MOUNTAINS PRETTY FACE

3 or 6 petals

Triteleia crocea
Brodiaea family

But, it's not yellow you say! So why is it called yellow triteleia when it is clearly not yellow? Well, it's just another of those common name anomalies that drives amateurs, like myself, nuts. I am assured by the editors of this guide, however, that they are one and the same—genetically identical. With its clusters of white, deep blue and soft purple blooms it only resembles its yellow namesake in overall structure and habitat requirements. The stems are strongly erect, to 2' in height, and supporting terminal clusters of gorgeous flowers. I've found it in scattered populations exclusively in serpentine soils and only along a short stretch of the road to the North Fork of Swift Creek Trailhead in the Trinity Alps in late May. These were blooming just a few miles from the area where I photographed the yellow version (page 120).

BOWL-TUBED IRIS, GROUND IRIS

3 or 6 petals

Iris macrosiphon
Iris family

Members of the Iris family are a beautiful addition to late spring and early summer hikes. But, like most irises, bowl-tubed iris are highly variable in terms of color including flowers that are cream to yellow to deep blue/purple. The key characteristic is the bowl shaped bulge at the top of the long corolla tube. It is a low growing iris, only to about 6" high, and common throughout the lower to mid-elevations. I photographed this near Natural Bridge in Trinity County but have also found it along the North Fork of the Trinity River Trail.

WESTERN BLUE FLAG

3 or 6 petals

Iris missouriensis
Iris family

This iris species is tall, with each beautiful soft purple flower blooming at the top of a 24" to 36" stiff stem. It looks a lot like a domestic iris that has invaded a high mountain meadow. Because of their size, they can't be confused with any other native iris in the area covered by this guide. Locally, they can be found growing in large areas of vernally wet to dry meadows. I photographed these above Mill Creek Lake in the Trinity Alps.

BLUE-EYED GRASS, IDAHO BLUE-EYED GRASS

3 or 6 petals

Sisyrinchium bellum and *Sisyrinchium idahoense*
Iris family

Blue-eyed grass is a common wildflower but just inconspicuous enough to make it easy to miss. The flowers bloom in clusters at the tops of flattened, grass-like stems, are a light blue, with deep blue veining, a yellow spot at the base, and a sharp pointed tip. *S. idahoense* grows in moist areas around meadows, streams, and springs from mid to high elevations while *S. bellum* grows at lower elevations. Both species vary in color from light to dark blue to pale lilac. The combination of the Latin word sus (meaning pig) and the Greek word rhynchos (meaning snout) allude to swine digging the roots of some bulbous plant for food which is spoken of in the writings of Pliny and Theophrastus. To the best of our knowledge, the reason for applying the name to a genus of New World irises was arbitrary. I've photographed blue-eyed grass from the Trinity Alps to South Carolina—where I heard locals refer to them as meadow stars. I photographed *S. bellum* on Musser Hill near Weaverville and the inset of *S. idahoense* in Mumford Meadows along Swift Creek in the Trinity Alps.

YELLOW TRITELEIA, TRINITY MOUNTAINS PRETTYFACE
Triteleia crocea
Brodiaea family

BOWL-TUBED IRIS, GROUND IRIS
Iris macrosiphon
Iris family

WESTERN BLUE FLAG
Iris missouriensis
Iris family

BLUE-EYED GRASS, IDAHO BLUE-EYED GRASS
Sisyrinchium bellum and *Sisyrinchium idahoense*
Iris family

CAT'S EARS, PUSSY EARS
Calochortus elegans and *Calochortus tolmiei*
Lily family

3 or 6 petals

Cat's ears might well be regarded as the true harbingers of spring. There are other wildflowers that bloom earlier but not quite the way these do. Huge areas in open woods and hillsides will be covered with these gorgeous little fuzzy flowers in April in the lower elevations. The blooming season extends itself well into late August into the high country. Because they are such variable species, I've included the more common color variations here. The two species vary in the degree to which the fine hairs cover the top and sides of the petals. *C. tolmiei* has fine hairs that don't extend to the tip of the petals while *C. elegans* has fine hairs that extend to the tip of the petals. The flowers range in color from white to purplish-blue with all sorts of variations in between. The stalk can grow to around 12" or so and can host several flowers. A single, long, and arching lance-shaped leaf precedes the bloom with a single leaf along the flowering stem. The large photograph of *C. elegans* was taken along Highway 3 near Covington's Mill and the smaller one on the Swift Creek Trail in the Trinity Alps, in late June and early July. The large photograph of *C. tolmiei* was taken alongside Weaver Bally Road near the East Weaver Lake trailhead in June and the small one in a meadow below Doe Lake in August, both in the Trinity Alps.

NAKED MARIPOSA LILY, NAKED STAR TULIP
Calochortus nudus
Lily family

3 or 6 petals

These flowers are found at mid-elevations in grassy meadows throughout the Trinities. They are small, not getting much over 8" tall with pale lilac petals and distinctive blue anthers. This tiny relative of the pussy ear is much favored by goldenrod spiders, who frequently take protective custody of the flowers just as they begin to open. They guard their little homes with a vengeance, rushing to the edges of the petals with little legs waving a warning to anyone or anything intruding too closely. I've actually had them attack my camera lens! Look for them and their tiny guardians in places like Bowerman Meadows (where I photographed these) and along the Pacific Crest Trail above Kangaroo Lake on the Trinity Divide.

Note: Goldenrod spiders are variable with regards to color—they can be yellow, white, or brown.

CAT'S EARS, PUSSY EARS
Calochortus tolmiei
Lily family

CAT'S EARS, PUSSY EARS
Calochortus elegans
Lily family

NAKED MARIPOSA LILY
NAKED STAR TULIP
Calochortus nudus
Lily family

GREEN-GENTIAN, WHITESTEM FRASERA
Frasera albicaulis subsp. *nitida*   4 petals
Gentian family

This is a common wildflower that I've found blooming at lower elevations in the foothills along the Sacramento River as well in the high meadows below Red Mountain in the Trinity Alps. Regardless of the elevation, it seems to bloom everywhere in June. It is readily identifiable by its long, grass-like, opposite leaves rimmed with silvery white. The flowers have four whitish-blue petals striped and spotted with purple with a green gland at the base of each. The petals are pointed and extend slightly cupped to the sides. The stamens are light lilac. I photographed these in an open brushy area alongside the upper reaches of the Stony Ridge Trail in the Trinity Alps in June, where they were often interspersed with bear-grass.

EXPLORER'S GENTIAN, BLUE GENTIAN, MOUNTAIN BOG GENTIAN
Gentiana calycosa   4 petals
Gentian family

Except possibly for pink mountain heather, I don't think there is a wildflower more symbolic of the high country than explorer's gentian. The deep, electric blue flowers occur in large colonies and grace mid to high elevation trails and meadows throughout the area. Their deep, urn-shaped blooms are easily recognized. There is one area in the Trinity Alps where I have found a persistent population of a deep and vibrant pink version. I've photographed these in several areas including Upper Wright Lake in the Marble Mountains and Grizzly Lake in the Trinity Alps.

FRINGED GENTIAN, HIKER'S GENTIAN, ONE-FLOWERED GENTIAN
Gentianopsis simplex   4 petals
Gentian family

Fringed gentian takes its name from the toothed edges of the four deep slate-blue petals forming the flower tube. This graceful little wildflower rarely exceeds 8" tall and hides in deep, wet, grassy meadows. The leaves on the lower stem are about 1" long and spoon shaped—often dried by the time flowers appear. I photographed these in the meadows below Trail Gulch Lake in the Trinity Alps in July. I've also found them around Diamond Lake and in the meadows along the trail to Stoddard Lake—where you will also find a consistent white form interspersed with the blue.

BREWER'S ROCK CRESS
Boechera breweri   4 petals
Mustard family

This rock cress is a small inconspicuous wildflower only reaching to about 8" in height and found in open, dry, rocky areas. Lance shaped leaves are scattered the length of the hairy stem. The tube shaped flowers are small, have four deep purple petals and flare widely at the tips. Flowers that I've photographed rarely exceed ½" in diameter. I photographed these on a rocky outcrop just above Stewart's Fork. You will also find them blooming in serpentine soils just below Parker Divide in the Trinity Alps and in the granite outcrops around Big Blue in the Russians.

GREEN-GENTIAN, WHITESTEM FRASERA
Frasera albicaulis subsp. *nitida*
Gentian family

EXPLORER'S GENTIAN, BLUE GENTIAN
Gentiana calycosa
Gentian family

FRINGED GENTIAN, HIKER'S GENTIAN
Gentianopsis simplex
Gentian family

BREWER'S ROCK CRESS
Boechera breweri
Mustard family

DAGGERPOD, PHOENICAULIS, WALLFLOWER PHOENICAULIS
Phoenicaulis cheiranthoides   4 petals
Mustard family

At the very top of Packer's Peak (7,828') in the Trinity Alps, on a cold, windy day in May with snow and rain showers moving across the high country, I found a small population of this gorgeous wildflower blooming in protected rocky crevices. Even though I did a wide search around the summit I found no others. It is common throughout the Pacific Northwest across a variety of habitats. It is found on volcanic and sandy soils, in rocky areas, in meadows, and sagebrush scrub above 3,000'. The light green and fuzzy leaves form a small and mostly upright basal rosette. Lance shaped leaves occur alternately along the flowering stem. Beautiful purple flowers cluster at the tops of the stems.

MONKSHOOD
Aconitum columbianum   5 irregular petals
Buttercup family

Monkshood is common throughout this area where it favors wet meadows and stream banks at mid-elevations. Typically the flowers are a deep blue or purple but it is not uncommon to find large colonies of white ones as well. The distinctive hood shape makes it unmistakable for any other flower. They can grow to 5' tall. I photographed the purple ones in Long Canyon and the white one near the inlet to Rush Creek Lake (on the north side of the Trinity Alps).

GIANT LARKSPUR, TALL LARKSPUR, MOUNTAIN LARKSPUR
Delphinium glaucum   5 irregular petals
Buttercup family

This larkspur is easily identifiable by sheer size alone, with plants reaching 8' in height. Upper stems are covered by crowded deep blue to purple flowers. The stems and deeply divided leaves are pale whitish-green. It favors wet meadows or the edges of running water. I have found them below Buck Lake in the Trinity Alps and in the meadows surrounding Deep Lake in the Marble Mountain Wilderness. I photographed these in Bear Basin in the Trinity Alps.

DWARF LARKSPUR, NUTTALL'S LARKSPUR
Delphinium nuttallianum   5 irregular petals
Buttercup family

This is another of the earliest bloomers at lower elevations and can be found in sunny sites from the foothills to mid-elevation meadows. The plants grow to 16" tall with rounded leaves that are palmately divided. Several deep blue to purple flowers bloom along an erect stem. The petal-like sepals fan away from the center and the upper petal has a toothed and white decoration that forms a "hood" which arches over the stamens and pistils. The spur at the back of the flower is about ½" long. I photographed these along Canyon Creek in late May but look for them along almost any trail in the area. I photographed this one in Union Meadows.

Note: Goldenrod spiders are fond of this wildflower.

DAGGERPOD, PHOENICAULIS
Phoenicaulis cheiranthoides
Mustard family

MONKSHOOD
Aconitum columbianum
Buttercup family

GIANT LARKSPUR, TALL LARKSPUR
Delphinium glaucum
Buttercup famil

DWARF LARKSPUR, NUTTALL'S LARKSPUR
Delphinium nuttallianum
Buttercup family

WOOLY-POD MILKVETCH, PURSH'S MILKVETCH

Astragalus purshii   5 irregular petals
Pea family

This tiny plant is as pretty when it goes to seed as it is when it's in full bloom. It is so small that I've seen people walk right over whole patches of it without realizing it was there. It grows on open and exposed serpentine flats and slopes is especially abundant on Scott Mountain where you can find it along the Pacific Crest Trail. The deep pink-purple flowers, about ½" long, and the fuzzy, globose seed pods are its most prominent features. The pinnately compound leaves are gray-green, fuzzy, and grow low to the ground. Step carefully and go slowly—t's the only way you will ever see them. I photographed these along the road to Big Carmen Lake on Scott Mountain in early June.

SILVER BUSH LUPINE

Lupinus albifrons   5 irregular petals
Pea family

This wildflower is a winner in the roadside attraction category. It is found throughout the area and, because of its woody stems up to 3' tall, the masses of deep purple flowers, and gorgeous silver foliage, it is unmistakable. It is one of my favorite early bloomers and one that seems to do well in native plant gardens. A great place to enjoy them is at the Whiskeytown National Recreation Area Visitor Center where they have included them in their landscaping. I photographed these along the Trinity River below Lewiston.

MINIATURE LUPINE, TWO-COLORED LUPINE

Lupinus bicolor   5 irregular petals
Pea family

This diminutive lupine is an early bloomer, often found in early May, preferring grassy flats and hillsides. It rarely grows above 6" in height with deeply cleft, dark green leaves along the lower portion of the stem. The flowers are deep bluish purple with a white patch on the upper flag decorated with tiny purple spots and bloom scattered along an erect stem. I photographed these near Squirrel Flat on the north end of Trinity Lake in early June.

BREWER'S LUPINE

Lupinus breweri var. *breweri*   5 irregular petals
Pea family

Brewer's lupine is small (4" to 6" in height) including the flowers which bloom in little compact heads, forming extensive, and dense mats at higher elevations. The stout leaves of this lupine are covered with silvery hairs. A few years ago, while hiking along the ridge top from Upper Albert Lake to Taylor Lake in the Russians, I found populations that covered acres of exposed decomposed granite soils. And then, a couple of years ago I found the same thing on the Bear Creek trail between East Weaver Creek and Monument Peak in the Trinity Alps. I photographed this one on the ridge above Twin Lakes in the Russians in late August. A penny amidst the plants gives some indication of size.

WOOLY-POD MILKVETCH
Astragalus purshii
Pea family

SILVER BUSH LUPINE
Lupinus albifrons
Pea family

MINIATURE LUPINE, TWO-COLORED LUPINE
Lupinus bicolor
Pea family

BREWER'S LUPINE
Lupinus breweri var. *breweri*
Pea family

BROAD-LEAVED LUPINE
Lupinus latifolius   5 irregular petals
Pea family

This is a common trailside lupine that you will find growing throughout the area at low to mid-elevations. The flowering stalks can reach to 2' in height and flowers tend to a light lilac with deep lilac accents. I photographed these along the trail to Big Duck Lake in the Russian Wilderness.

LOBB'S LUPINE
Lupinus lepidus var. *lobbii*   5 irregular petals
Pea family

Lobb's lupine is low growing and forms dense mats on sandy soils at higher elevations. It favors decomposed granite flats and slopes in open sun at or near the tops of ridges. The light blue to deep purple flowers form compact heads approximately 2" in diameter and 2" tall. Leaves are stiff, deeply cleft, and covered with fine hairs giving them a silvery cast. Easily mistaken for Brewer's lupine, Lobb's lupine are more sprawling, taller, and not as compact overall. I photographed these on the broad ridge between Lost Lake and Cub Wallow in the Trinity Alps in early August.

VELVET LUPINE
Lupinus leucophyllus   5 irregular petals
Pea family

This is one unique and recognizable lupine. Tallest plants grow to about 24" and to fully appreciate them you really need to get up close and personal. It is soft, fuzzy, and silvery white—tinged slightly with magenta on the stems and leaf petioles. The petals are creamy white to light purple or lavender, and age to a pale brown. When I say that the plant is fuzzy and soft I mean it—kitten soft. It's one of those plants you want to pet! I have photographed these along Highway 3 near Stewart's Fork and along the road to the Stoney Ridge Trailhead. Rarely growing in abundance, both of these populations include only a few dozen specimens. I have also found scattered populations along Highway 3 between Sunflower Flat and the lower stretches over Scott Mountain.

VALLEY SKY LUPINE, SKY LUPINE
Lupinus nanus   5 irregular petals
Pea family

This might be the most recognizable lupine anywhere in this area. Beginning in late March it can light up vast areas of the landscape in clouds of blue from the floor of the Central Valley to the foothills of the Trinities. This lupine ranges from 8" to 12" in height and likes open, sunny areas. You don't even have to get out of your car to appreciate it. Driving along Interstate 5, Highways 299, Highway 3, or even up Canyon Creek Road—you will recognize it instantly.

BROAD-LEAVED LUPINE
Lupinus latifolius
Pea family

LOBB'S LUPINE
Lupinus lepidus var. *lobbii*
Pea family

VELVET LUPINE
Lupinus leucophyllus
Pea family

VALLEY SKY LUPINE, SKY LUPINE
Lupinus nanus
Pea family

BIGLEAF LUPINE
Lupinus polyphyllus   5 irregular petals
Pea family

This is, perhaps, the showiest of all the lupines in the high country—mainly because of its size. It is especially abundant in wet meadows in the Russian Wilderness. I photographed these in the meadow above Lower Albert Lake in September where I literally found hundreds of them blooming. In this particular place, the flowering stalks were reaching heights of 4' with beautiful, almost geometrically arranged, spikes of white (near the base) to purplish-blue flowers near the top.

WESTERN DOG VIOLET, EARLY BLUE VIOLET
Viola adunca subsp. *adunca*   5 irregular petals
Violet family

These little violets can bloom as early as late April in vernally damp places in the High Country, but late May is a better bet. They are definitely a "get down in the dirt" wildflower if you really want to check them out. The little elliptic and cupped leaves are first to show as the ground warms in the spring, soon followed by flowering stalks 1" to 1 ½" tall, topped with a single pale blue, dark blue, or deep purple flower. I photographed the deep purple flowers along the road to the Lake Eleanor/Shimmy Lake Trailhead in late May in the Trinity Alps. The same violet appears a light blue along Union Creek and in Bullard's Basin in the Trinity Alps.

LYALL'S ANEMONE
Anemone lyallii   5 symmetrical petals - ovary superior
Buttercup family

If you want to see this beautiful little anemone walk the trail to Little Duck Lake in the Russians in early summer—it's the only place in this area I've ever seen it. The little flowers, 1" to 1 ½" in diameter, have 5 to 6 sepals that resemble petals and, in this area, range from pale blue, a light purple, to a beautiful deep magenta. The predominant color, however, is a pale bluish-purple. Lyall's has fewer than 35 stamens as opposed to more than 35 for Oregon anemone which, in all other aspects, it resembles. The flowering stalks are tall with a single large basal leaf that is divided into three leaflets and then divided again. It is often withered by the time the plant flowers. There are three additional whorled 'leaves' along the stem below the flowers, called bracts, which look similar to the basal leaf. It grows in proximity to Columbia windflower, which is snow white. I took this photograph on the trail to Little Duck Lake in July.

OREGON ANEMONE, BLUE WINDFLOWER
Anemone oregana var. *oregana*   5 symmetrical petals - ovary superior
Buttercup family

At first glance you would think that this little anemone is identical to the Lyall's anemone and, indeed, there are many similarities. One big difference is in the number of stamens—Oregon usually has more than 35 and Lyall's less. This is not a hard and fast rule but, on average it works. Recently I counted them on about 30 individuals and found that the number ranged from about 33 to more than 45. The single leaf is basal, divided into three and then divided into three again. Just below the single flower are three 3-parted bracts that look like leaves. The flowers are up to 1 ¼" in diameter—some a bit larger. I photographed these on Scott Mountain in the middle of May.

BIGLEAF LUPINE
Lupinus polyphyllus
Pea family

WESTERN DOG VIOLET, EARLY BLUE VIOLET
Viola adunca subsp. *adunca*
Violet family

LYALL'S ANEMONE
Anemone lyallii
Buttercup family

OREGON ANEMONE, BLUE WINDFLOWER
Anemone oregana var. *oregana*
Buttercup family

WESTERN BLUE FLAX
Linum lewisii var. *lewisii*   5 symmetrical petals - ovary superior
Flax family

This is an iconic wildflower of the dry and open high country meadows. The graceful and large blue flowers bloom loosely at the top of tall, erect stems, up to 14" or more in height and clothed with short, narrow leaves. The dish-shaped flowers are about 1" to 1 ¼" in diameter and have five petals that are striped lengthwise with a deeper blue, with a yellow spot at the center and strikingly white anthers. I photographed these in Siligo Meadows in the Trinity Alps in early August.

PALE PENNYROYAL, COYOTE-MINT, WESTERN MOUNTAIN BALM, PALE MOUNTAIN MONARDELLA, PALE MOUNTAIN MINT
Monardella odoratissima   5 irregular petals forming a tube
Mint family

I find pennyroyal to be one of the most delightful plants in this book. You know immediately when you're in the vicinity of a population by the strong smell of mint. It grows everywhere from the foothills surrounding Shasta Lake to higher elevations in the back-country and prefers areas that are relatively dry and sunny. The plant itself is loosely structured, about 8" to 10" tall, with stiff stems, and lanceolate leaves that can range from deep to a lighter grayish-green. Crush the leaves and the mint smell can stop you in your tracks. Flower heads tend to be flat to slightly globose with dozens of individuals beginning their bloom around the edges and gradually working towards the center. Individual buds (which are hairy) and flowers vary from lilac to light magenta to almost white. All in all, this is a hard one to miss. I photographed these below Josephine Lake in the Russians in mid-August.

SELF-HEAL
Prunella vulgaris subsp. *lanceolata*   5 irregular petals forming a tube
Mint family

This low growing member of the mint family likes moist, shaded sites in deep woods, wet meadows, along streams, and around springs. It is common at mid to higher elevations throughout the area. The two-lipped flowers bloom in densely packed spikes and are mostly pinkish magenta fading to white at the edges. The upper lip forms a concave cover over the lower lip which hangs down. I photographed this one near the outlet to Sapphire Lake but the meadows along the trail to Stoddard Lake and Horse Heaven Meadows are good places to look as well.

CREEPING SAGE, SONOMA SAGE
Salvia sonomensis   5 irregular petals forming a tube
Mint family

This is a low elevation wildflower, forming large colonies in open, rocky sites. The plants are about 6" to 8" tall with stout, strongly erect stems, encircled with whorls of sticky bracts and dozens of light lilac-blue flowers. The lower petal of each flower extends well beyond the others and is cleft and ruffled, with deep purple filaments topped with bright yellow anthers extending well beyond the flower. Bees love these flowers. I photographed this alongside the road to the Granite Peak Trailhead on Buck Ridge.

WESTERN BLUE FLAX
Linum lewisii var. *lewisii*
Flax family

PALE PENNYROYAL, COYOTE-MINT
Monardella odoratissima
Mint famil

SELF-HEAL
Prunella vulgaris subsp. *lanceolata*
Mint family

CREEPING SAGE, SONOMA SAGE
Salvia sonomensis
Mint famil

NOSE SKULLCAP, SNAPDRAGON SKULLCAP
Scutellaria antirrhinoides
Mint family
5 irregular petals forming a tube

This tiny skullcap can be easily missed because they tend to occur as scattered individuals but larger populations are not uncommon. The stems are strongly upright, about 6" to 8" tall, with two oval leaves arranged in opposite pairs along the stem. One deep blue to rose-purple flower blooms in each leaf axil, so that the flowers are paired up the stem. They like grassy meadows and full sun. I photographed this one alongside the trail through Mumford Meadows above Swift Creek in the Trinity Alps in late August.

GRAY-LEAVED SKULLCAP
Scutellaria siphocampyloides
Mint family
5 irregular petals forming a tube

This is a strongly erect skullcap, often reaching 12" in height with narrowly oval, smooth leaves scattered along the stem. The purple flowers are borne in the leaf axils and are strongly tubular until the upper third when the petals begin to flare. The upper petal narrows to form a small rounded protuberance that over arches the lower petal. The lower petal flares outwardly and has a clear, rectangular white spot in the center. They are common throughout the area covered by this guide. I photographed this one in the wet meadows along the Lake Eleanor trail in the Trinity Alps.

DANNY'S SKULLCAP, TUBEROUS SKULLCAP
Scutellaria tuberosa
Mint family
5 irregular petals forming a tube

Like the other regional skullcaps this one is small, growing to 8" tall with stems that are hairy and red. The leaves, are oval and hairy like the flowers. Flowers bloom out of the leaf axils and are deep purple to blue. The upper petal forms a hood that over arches the lower petal which is flared, ruffled, with a white patch filled with purple spots. I photographed this one in the drier part of the meadow surrounding upper Twin Lake above Swift Creek in July.

LARGE-FLOWERED BLUE-EYED MARY
Collinsia grandiflora
Plantain family
5 irregular petals forming a tube

Even though these are larger than Torrey's blue-eyed Mary, they are still difficult to spot. The plants are up to 10" in height, loosely branched, with flowers scattered throughout. The upper two petals of the flowers are white with a tinge of purple. The lower three petals are dark bluish-purple and rarely more than 1/4" in diameter. They like open, sunny, sandy areas and blend in nicely with their surroundings. I photographed these on a sandy bench just above Canyon Creek in early June.

NOSE SKULLCAP, SNAPDRAGON SKULLCAP
Scutellaria antirrhinoides
Mint famil

GRAY-LEAVED SKULLCAP
Scutellaria siphocampyloides
Mint family

DANNY'S SKULLCAP, TUBEROUS SKULLCAP
Scutellaria tuberosa
Mint family

LARGE-FLOWERED BLUE-EYED MARY
Collinsia grandiflora
Plantain family

271

TORREY'S BLUE-EYED MARY
Collinsia torreyi var. *latifolia*
Plantain family

5 irregular petals forming a tube

This is the tiniest blue-eyed Mary—only a few inches tall, loosely branched, with flowers that are less than ¼" in diameter. The top two petal lobes are white, the lower lip is deep electric blue, and deeply cleft into three lobes—the central lobe of which is small and sharply pointed. Look closely for it in sandy soils alongside trails throughout these mountains because it is difficult to spot. Delicate blue-eyed Mary is similar but smaller and not pictured here. I photographed these above Little Granite Lake on the trail from Doe Lake in late August.

SISKIYOU BEARDTONGUE
Penstemon anguineus
Plantain family

5 irregular petals forming a tube

This is a common *Penstemon* at lower elevations in the mountains that blooms in moist, shaded areas. The plants can reach 1' in height with loosely scattered whorls of pale lavender flowers along the top third of the stem. Stems and leaves are somewhat hairy. I took this photograph along the Bowerman Meadows Trail in the Trinity Alps in July.

AZURE PENSTEMON
Penstemon azureus
Plantain family

5 irregular petals forming a tube

Penstemons are perennial favorites of mine—their neon blues and pinks decorating trails and hillsides from early spring into late fall. This one is large, standing to 30" tall in the lower elevations and 8" to 10" higher up. The flowers have deep lavender tubes opening into azure blue lips, from yellowish buds. Stems and leaves are hairless and the plant's base is woody. It grows on open, dry slopes. I photographed this one near Slate Mountain on the Trinity Divide. Look for them along the lower stretches of the trail to Duck Lakes in the Russians.

THREAD-LEAVED BEARDTONGUE, THREADLEAF PENSTEMON
Penstemon filiformis
Plantain family

5 irregular petals forming a tube

This species is highlighted by 10" - 20" flowering stalks arising from the woody rootstock surrounded by a thick basal cluster of narrow, thread-like leaves. The same leaves emerge along an equally thin flowering stalk, are opposite, entire, or sometimes finely toothed. The flower stalks are glandular and spread widely from the flowering stems. Flowers are deep bluish-purple and less than ½" long. It is endemic to the Klamath Mountains and found predominantly on serpentine soils where it prefers the edges of open forests or meadows. I have also found it growing around the periphery of sandy and rocky stream terraces where it seems to enjoy the company of buckbrush (*Ceanothus*). I photographed these along the Upper Trinity River in early June.

Note: This species, along with *P. azureus, P. heterophyllus,* and *P. roezlii* are part of a small group of beardtongues that have distinctive arrowhead-shaped anthers.

TORREY'S BLUE-EYED MARY
Collinsia torreyi var. *latifolia*
Plantain family

SISKIYOU BEARDTONGUE
Penstemon anguineus
Plantain family

AZURE PENSTEMON
Penstemon azureus
Plantain family

THREAD-LEAVED BEARDTONGUE
Penstemon filiformis
Plantain family

SMALL PENSTEMON, SHORT STALK PENSTEMON
Penstemon parvulus   5 irregular petals forming a tube
Plantain family

Even though the flowers of *Penstemon parvulus* are small, they stand out like neon lights on a dark night—even in the bright light of a noonday sun. The flower stalks are erect and without hairs or glands. The ¾" long, deep blue to pale violet flowers hug the tall, thin, stems, growing mostly to one side. The narrow gray-green leaves are mostly lanceolate but can be narrowly ovate and clasp the stem for over half the length of the flowering stalk. Several flowering stalks arise from a woody base which is where most of the leaves are congregated. I photographed these near Eagle Creek and the Upper Trinity River in early June where it was blooming in open, sandy and rocky stream terraces.

WHORLED PENSTEMON, SMALL FLOWERED PENSTEMON
Penstemon procerus var. *brachyanthus*   5 irregular petals forming a tube
Plantain family

This beautiful *Penstemon* blooms at mid-elevations in and around wet meadows and damp, open hillsides—most lakes in the high country are home to this species. The loosely crowded whorls of deep lavender to lilac colored flowers adorn the top half of strongly upright, hairless stems. They are common around Upper Albert Lake in the Russians, where I've found them blooming into September. I took this photograph at Log Lake in the Trinity Alps in July.

WHORLED PENSTEMON, PINCUSHION PENSTEMON
Penstemon procerus var. *formosus*   5 irregular petals forming a tube
Plantain family

This variety of *P. procerus* blooms at higher elevations, usually on exposed rocky outcrops and hillsides, above 6000'. The flowers are arranged in tight whorls along stalks that are shorter than those of var. *brachyanthus* and tend to be electric pink fading to light blue. I photographed these just below the ridgeline above Papoose Lake in late August. Other good places to see this species are on the rocky ridges above Caribou, Mirror, and Kalmia Lakes—all in the Trinity Alps.

ROEZL'S MOUNTAIN PENSTEMON, PURPLE PENSTEMON
Penstemon roezlii   5 irregular petals forming a tube
Plantain family

I found this little *Penstemon* blooming in profusion on Scott Mountain in late May and again just below Stonewall Pass (Trinity Alps) in late July. Color ranges from sky blue to deep purple. The flowers are short (½" to ¾" long) and crowded along one side of a tall, reddish stalk. The deep green leaves, are ½" long and lance shaped, attached alternately along the lower third of the flowering stalk, and arise from a central woody base. The plant prefers dry, rocky serpentine slopes and flats. This photograph was taken in serpentine soils near Stonewall Pass.

SMALL PENSTEMON, SHORT STALK PENSTEMON
Penstemon parvulus
Plantain family

WHORLED PENSTEMON
Penstemon procerus var. *brachyanthus*
Plantain family

WHORLED PENSTEMON, PINCUSHION PENSTEMON
Penstemon procerus var. *formosus*
Plantain family

ROEZL'S MOUNTAIN PENSTEMON
Penstemon roezlii
Plantain family

AMERICAN SPEEDWELL
Veronica americana
Plantain family

5 irregular petals forming a tube

I found and photographed these little beauties in late June while wandering around the Meadows below Lower Deadfall Lake on the Trinity Divide. There were several large populations blooming in and around water in the deep shade provided by stands of alder and willow. Individual plants were small—no more than 8" tall—and loaded with tiny blue flowers. The petals are streaked with deep magenta and white emanating from a green ovary at the center. Stamens are prominent and snow white. Leaves are deep green, oval, with toothed edges.

WATER SPEEDWELL
Veronica anagallis-aquatica
Plantain family

5 irregular petals forming a tube

This little naturalized *Veronica* is native to Europe but found widely around North and South America. In this area look for it along the banks of the Trinity River where it is quite common and often grows with its feet in the water. It also likes wet meadows. The plants are loosely branched and spreading. The pale lilac flowers have deep violet lines emanating from near the throat. The flowers are tiny, no more than ¼" in diameter. I found and photographed these in the Trinity River near Junction City in mid-August. I've also seen them along the lower stretches of the North Fork of the Trinity River.

COPELAND'S SPEEDWELL
Veronica copelandii
Plantain family

5 irregular petals forming a tube

This pretty little speedwell is endemic to the high Klamath Mountains of Siskiyou and Trinity Counties. Erect stems, rarely more than 6" tall, are topped with clusters of small, four-petaled flowers. Petals vary from rounded to wedge shaped, are of unequal size, with the broadest petal at the top and the most pointed at the bottom. They are light purple near the tips with a white patch at the center surrounded by a deep purple band. The two long stamens are a conspicuous feature, extending well beyond the petals. The stems are reddish holding opposite, oblong, pointed, sticky leaves. I photographed these in the upper reaches of Long Canyon in July. Another place to see them is in the basins above Kangaroo Lake on the Trinity Divide.

AMERICAN SPEEDWELL
Veronica americana
Plantain family

WATER SPEEDWELL
Veronica anagallis-aquatica
Plantain family

COPELAND'S SPEEDWELL
Veronica copelandii
Plantain family

GRAND HOUND'S TONGUE
Cynoglossum grande
Borage family
5 symmetrical petals forming a tube

Grand hound's tongue grows at lower elevations and is among the earliest wildflowers to bloom. The leaves, which look a lot like the tongues of hounds without all the drool, are large, broadest at the base, and stand strongly upright. Each plant has a single stout flowering stem that supports a mass of large, deep blue flowers with petal lobes radiating away from puckered white centers. Like Jessica's stickseed, the seeds of this one cling to anything—animal fur, socks, pants, and hairy legs. I photographed these along Rainier Road above Mule Creek and Highway 3 in mid-June.

WESTERN HOUND'S TONGUE
Cynoglossum occidentale
Borage family
5 symmetrical petals forming a tube

This hound's tongue is not as common or showy as its blue cousin. This is a tall, hairy, multistemmed plant bearing loose, terminal clusters of brownish purple flowers with yellow centers. Leaves taper to narrow bases. The fruits of western hound's tongue are distinctive nutlets, about ½" in diameter, covered with hooked barbs that stick to anything and everything. I photographed this bunch on Montgomery Ridge above Trinity Lake in June.

JESSICA'S STICKSEED, MEADOW STICKSEED
Hackelia micrantha
Borage family
5 symmetrical petals forming a tube

This is a common wildflower at mid-elevations in wet meadows, the banks of streams, and shorelines of lakes and ponds. The tiny, light blue flowers bloom in loose bunches scattered along tall stems that can reach 20" in height. When the seeds mature in late summer they stick to anything and everything—especially socks! I photographed these along the outlet stream to Doe Lake in August.

Note: the large toothed leaves in the background of this photograph are not those of Jessica's stickseed.

PURPLE MILKWEED
Asclepias cordifolia
Dogbane family
5 symmetrical petals forming a tube

Milkweed is a common sight along the edges of low elevation roads and highways throughout the area. The plants grow in large colonies, are tall (approaching 2′), and covered with large bunches of beautiful, hanging purple and white flowers. Corollas form a reflexed arch. The leaves are large and dark green. Break the stem and a milky, sticky latex appears. I photographed these along Highway 3 near Callahan.
Note: Butterflies love milkweed, it is an important food source for them

GRAND HOUND'S TONGUE
Cynoglossum grande
Borage family

WESTERN HOUND'S TONGUE
Cynoglossum occidentale
Borage family

JESSICA'S STICKSEED, MEADOW STICKSEED
Hackelia micrantha
Borage family

PURPLE MILKWEED
Asclepias cordifolia
Dogbane family

PURPLE MAT, MATTED YERBA SANTA
Eriodictyon lobbii
Borage family

5 symmetrical petals forming a tube

Purple mat prefers sandy, exposed, decomposed granitic soils. Plants are rangy with oblong leaves the same length as the flowering stalk. The deep purple, tubular flowers bloom along the upper third of the stalk which often is weighted down to the ground by flowers and leaves. The stalks, leaves, and sepals are hairy. I've found purple mat in two location. Once in July along the trail to Big Boulder Lake in the Trinities and the other along Forest Highway 24 on the Trinity Divide. It is also common on Mt. Shasta. The population along Forest Hwy 24 was huge, forming extensive mats along a 100 yard section of the road shoulder.

AMERICAN NIGHTSHADE, AMERICAN BLACK NIGHTSHADE, SMALL FLOWERED NIGHTSHADE, COMMON NIGHTSHADE, WHITE NIGHTSHADE
Solanum americanum
Nightshade family

5 symmetrical petals forming a tube

Almost without exception, every trip into the backcountry brings new surprises and this was one of them. I had found this little nightshade blooming along low elevation trails near Shasta Lake but never suspected I would find it well into the Trinity Alps. And yet, there it was halfway along the trail to Canyon Creek Lakes. It is considered a weed that usually inhabits disturbed places but this was not a disturbed setting. The plants occupied a wet shelf on a steep, exposed granite face. The plants at lower elevations are leggy but here they were more compact. The opposite leaves are egg shaped with wavy edges. The pale to dark lilac flowers have five petals, are about 1" in diameter, with green spots near the throat surrounding prominent, deep yellow pistils. Fruits are a large greenish berry. I shot this photograph above the Sinks along the Canyon Creek Trail in the Trinity Alps in late May.

BLUEHEAD GILIA, BLUE FIELD GILIA
Gilia capitata
Phlox family

5 symmetrical petals forming a tube

This delicate blue *Gilia* grows in troops on open, dry, rocky areas throughout the foothills in this area. The flowers bloom in compact clusters 1" to 1½" across at the tops of 1' to 2' stems. Leaves are ½" to 1½" long, deeply lobed, mostly basal, with a few scattered along the lower portion of the stem. I shot this photograph on Musser Hill along the Weaver Basin Trail system in May.

CALIFORNIA POLEMONIUM, CALIFORNIA JACOB'S LADDER
Polemonium californicum
Phlox family

5 symmetrical petals forming a tube

This is a deep shade loving wildflower, often growing in large colonies beneath the canopies of firs and pines at higher elevations. It is a low growing plant with stems covered in soft hairs. The leaves are hairy, lance-shaped to oval, and pinnately divided into multiple leaflets. The delicate, light blue to light lilac, bell-shaped flowers bloom in loose clusters along 4" stalks. They have prominent white stamens and a lemon yellow throat. Before the flowers open the backsides of the petals are a beautiful periwinkle blue. I photographed these on Mt. Ashland in Southern Oregon but I've also found it in Onion Meadows and around the upper reaches of Steveale Meadows in the Trinity Alps.

PURPLE MAT, MATTED YERBA SANTA
Eriodictyon lobbii
Borage family

BLUEHEAD GILIA, BLUE FIELD GILIA
Gilia capitata
Phlox family

CALIFORNIA POLEMONIUM
Polemonium californicum
Phlox family

WESTERN POLEMONIUM
Polemonium occidentale   5 symmetrical petals forming a tube
Phlox family

I found this pretty *Polemonium* blooming on a shaded, rocky slope just below Upper Albert Lake in the Russians. The periwinkle blue flower clusters caught my eye immediately, contrasted as they were against the granite rock. The same striking blue also colors the backsides of the petals. The petals fade from blue to creamy white and then a golden yellow and green at the throat. The stamens are prominent (as is the style) with fat little white anthers. The deep green leaves are long and pinnately divided with 15 or more slightly hairy leaflets. Plants are 12" to 14" tall.

SHORT JACOB'S LADDER, SKUNK-LEAVED POLEMONIUM
Polemonium pulcherrimum var. *pulcherrimum*   5 symmetrical petals forming a tube
Phlox family

This small *Polemonium* loves open, dry rocky, or sandy areas at high elevations. The pinnately divided leaves are linear, tough, and compact with small, egg shaped leaflets. Some folks think they smell skunkish but, while they do have a strong odor, I think it smells more like a chipmunk in need of a bath. The flowering stems are erect with several small (½" across) periwinkle blue to light lilac flowers in a loose cluster at the top. The color in the throat varies from yellow to deep orange. I photographed these on the ridge above Little Duck Lake in the Russian Wilderness and also above Upper Albert Lake in the Russians.

ALPINE BREECHES, ALPINE WATERLEAF, WOOLEN BREECHES
Hydrophyllum alpestre   5 symmetrical petals forming a tube
Borage family

Alpine waterleaf resembles California waterleaf (next page) except for its size and location—growing at mid to high elevations in open, sunny sites often at the edge of snow fields. Pale bluish-purple flowers bloom low to the ground (usually no more than 8" tall) in compact heads, tinged with light purple, with prominent stamens. The leaves are bright green, spreading, deeply cleft, and 5" to 6" long. A good place to find this little waterleaf is along the trail between Lion and Foster Lakes in the Trinity Alps and in the upper reaches of the Parker Divide.

WESTERN POLEMONIUM
Polemonium occidentale
Phlox family

SHORT JACOB'S LADDER, SKUNK-LEAVED POLEMONIUM
Polemonium pulcherrimum
var. *pulcherrimum*
Phlox family

ALPINE BREECHES
ALPINE WATERLEAF
Hydrophyllum alpestre
Waterleaf family

CALIFORNIA WATERLEAF, WESTERN WATERLEAF
Hydrophyllum occidentale   5 symmetrical petals forming a tube
Borage family

California waterleaf much resembles its alpine cousin except for size and location (see previous page). This one is much larger, often reaching 12" or more in height and, unlike the alpine version, prefers shaded, damp sites at lower elevations. The flowers bloom in heads that are not quite as compact as the alpine version with larger leaves, up to 10" long. Leaves spotted with light green gives the appearance of water spots—hence the name. I photographed these along the stream at Natural Bridge in Trinity County but have also found it along Big French Creek and the lower end of the East Fork of Stewart's Fork in the Trinity Alps.

SCOTT VALLEY PHACELIA
Phacelia greenei   5 symmetrical petals forming a tube
Borage family

This serpentine loving *Phacelia* is especially abundant on Scott Mountain, one of my favorite wildflower hot spots. The tiny blooms are ¼" in diameter and open in coiled bunches atop stems that reach 2" to 3" in height. Photographing them is difficult when trying to get the camera lens low enough to capture an image. I've had to dig holes to lower the camera enough without disturbing the plants. Unless you're attentive, you could walk over these tiny plants and never know it. I photographed these in late July on Scott Mountain.

SISKIYOU PHACELIA and PRINGLE'S PHACELIA
Phacelia leonis and *Phacelia pringlei*   5 symmetrical petals forming a tube
Borage family

These are two of the smallest and least obtrusive wildflowers I've ever photographed. They are so delicate that even breathing on them while making my exposures upset the entire shot. Compared to other *Phacelia* species, these leaves are narrower and more tapered, mostly basal, and slightly hairy. The flowers are 1/8" to 3/16" in diameter and mostly white to slightly bluish with the typically long stamens found on other *Phacelia* species. These two species are rare endemic to the serpentine soils found in the Klamath Ranges. The flowers of *Phacelia pringlei* are slightly larger than those of *P. leonis* but it can be difficult to differentiate between the two. I photographed these on Scott Mountain.

CALIFORNIA WATERLEAF, WESTERN WATERLEAF
Hydrophyllum occidentale
Borage family

SCOTT VALLEY PHACELIA
Phacelia greenei
Borage family

SISKIYOU PHACELIA
Phacelia leonis
Borage family

PRINGLE'S PHACELIA
Phacelia pringlei
Borage family

CALIFORNIA HAREBELL
Asyneuma prenanthoides
Bellflower family

5 petals joined into a bell

These diminutive little harebells are common at lower elevations where they bloom in scattered bunches along tall, stiff stems that can reach 24" tall. Each delicate blue flower has five petals with deep purple mid-veins that arch away from its center, where a long and conspicuous lilac colored style attaches to the top of the inferior ovary. I photographed these on the Bailey Cove Trail above Shasta Lake. I've also found them at low elevations along the Stewart's Fork and Long Canyon Trails in the Trinity Alps as well as along the Paynes Lake and Duck Lake trails in the Russians.

BLUEBELLS-OF-SCOTLAND
Campanula rotundifolia
Bellflower family

5 petals joined into a bell

Clusters of blue to light lilac, bell shaped flowers bloom in bunches along erect, hairless stems, 4" to 20" tall. The basal leaves are 3" long and narrow with smooth margins. The flower petals are pointed and flare slightly at the tips. Look for it in moist shaded areas at the edges of woods, on slopes, and in meadows. This is the same species found in Europe and through the northern latitudes of the world. Here in northern California we are at the southern edge of its range in North America. I photographed this one along the Fen Trail above Kangaroo Lake on the Trinity Divide in June.

WILKINS' HAREBELL
Campanula wilkinsiana
Bellflower family

5 petals joined into a bell

Wilkins' harebell is one of those rare wildflowers that, if you are attentive, you will find blooming in wet areas on serpentine soils in the Trinities and Marble Mountains. It can also be found growing in wet volcanic soils on Mt. Shasta—these are the only places on the entire planet where it exists. I've found it blooming next to melting snowbanks, the edges of streams, small snow-melt ponds, springs ,and seeps at higher elevations. The short flowering stems are erect, topped with a delicate lilac to purple bloom, petals that curve outward, and a protruding, purple style at the center. Several years ago I found a large population of snow white individuals in the serpentine above Lake Anna. I photographed these in Long Canyon in the Trinity Alps in mid-July.

CALIFORNIA HAREBELL
Asyneuma prenanthoides
Bellflower family

BLUEBELLS-OF-SCOTLAND
Campanula rotundifolia
Bellflower family

WILKINS' HAREBELL
Campanula wilkinsiana
Bellflower family

BACHELOR'S BUTTON, CORNFLOWER, GARDEN CORNFLOWER
Centaurea cyanus   Flowers in composite heads
Sunflower family

This is a naturalized European wildflower, considered a noxious weed in this neck of the woods. That aside, I don't know of anyone who would think the blooms aren't beautiful. The ones I found were growing alongside the Salmon River Highway just west of Callahan and there were so many it appeared an electric blue cloud was floating 18″ off the shoulder of the road. The multi-branched stems are tall, between 14″ and 30″, light green, and covered with hairs. The light green leaves are likewise coated with minute hairs and are mostly entire. I did find pale blue and some white flowers in this population, but mostly deep neon blue. The outer ray flowers flare away from the central axis into a deeply cleft fan shape and the entire flower head is about 2″ in diameter.

CHICORY
Cichorium intybus   Flowers in composite heads
Sunflower family

This common naturalized roadside flower has beautiful blue blooms that come early and persist late at lower elevations. The bright blue ray flowers (there are no disc flowers)—five-toothed at the tips—grow scattered along naked stems that reach 3′ in height. I grew up hearing these called bachelor buttons but have recently discovered that another naturalized flower, *Centaurea cyanus* (above) takes claim of that name. When I was a little kid, I often picked huge stemless wads of these to present to my mother who dutifully put them in water and kept them fresh until I was out of sight. I'll bet I'm not the only one who thought so highly of their mother. I photographed these along the road to Kangaroo Lake on the north end of the Trinity Divide.

Note: The roasted roots of chicory have a long history of use as a substitute for coffee or as a coffee flavoring. My grandmother actually liked the flavor of it better than coffee.

DIFFUSE DAISY, SPREADING FLEABANE
Erigeron divergens   Flowers in composite heads
Sunflower family

Daisies are renowned for their diversity and difficulty to identify. Alice Jones' *Flowers and Trees of the Trinity Alps* and Bill Ferlatte's *Flora of the Trinity Alps* both recorded locations in Big Flat and the Meadows around the Packer's Peak trailhead—which is where I found these. The flowers range in size from ¾″ to 1″ in diameter, are flat, with narrow pale white, blue or lavender ray flowers. The disc flowers are deep yellow to almost orange. The plants are 1′ tall, somewhat rangy, and slightly spreading. Narrow, grayish-green leaves about ½″ to 1″ in length are arrayed along the stems. I found these growing in abundance along Coffee Creek Road in a dry meadow in full sun—at the Packer's Peak Trailhead—in early June.

BACHELOR'S BUTTON
CORNFLOWER
GARDEN CORNFLOWER
Centaurea cyanus
Sunflower family

CHICORY
Cichorium intybus
Sunflower family

DIFFUSE DAISY
SPREADING FLEABANE
Erigeron divergens
Sunflower family

MT. LASSEN FLEABANE
Erigeron lassenianus
Sunflower family
Flowers in composite heads

This tiny daisy blooms in profusion in serpentine soil flats in the lower elevation. The flowers range in size from smaller than a little fingernail to a larger than a thumbnail and tend to grow in low mounds. The flowers open on long stalks that lie flat to the ground. Swift Creek and North Fork of Swift Creek areas are good places to find them. On one particular flat, where I photographed these, the population covered an area the size of a small house with delicate deep purple and blue fading to white flowers. I photographed these on a flat alongside the road to the Lake Eleanor Trailhead in the Trinity Alps.

CASCADE ASTER
Eucephalus ledophyllus var. *covillei*
Sunflower family
Flowers in composite heads

Cascade aster is easily recognized by the loose and haphazard formation of the blue to lavender ray flowers surrounding a small, compact head of yellow disc flowers. The flowering stems, each with a single flower head at the top of each branch, can be up to 2' tall. It tends to grow in scattered colonies but I have found it in thick, compact groups of 20 or more. I photographed these on the rocky slopes above Lower Russian Lake in the Russian Wilderness in September.

WESTERN MOUNTAIN ASTER
Symphyotrichum spathulatum
Sunflower family
Flowers in composite heads

This is an aster common to damp meadows, the shorelines of lakes, ponds, and streamsides throughout the high country. Flower heads bloom in loose clusters at the tops of erect and somewhat hairy stems. Basal leaves are 2" - 6" long and narrow. Leaves growing up the stems are smaller. The ray flowers are narrow and range in color from light lavender to deep purple and surround a dense cluster of yellow to brownish disc flowers. I photographed these in a wet meadow along the Pacific Crest Trail between Doe and Little Granite Lakes in August.

MT. LASSEN FLEABANE
Erigeron lassenianus
Sunflower family

CASCADE ASTER
Eucephalus ledophyllus var. *covillei*
Sunflower family

WESTERN MOUNTAIN ASTER
Symphyotrichum spathulatum
Sunflower family

ANDERSON'S TUNDRA ASTER, ANDERSON'S MOUNTAIN-CROWN
Oreostemma alpigenum var. *andersonii*
Sunflower family

Flowers in composite heads

In my book (literally and figuratively) this aster is the most beautiful and most vari-able of all the asters found in these mountains. Trying to identify it can drive some-one nuts—therefore I've included the three color variations I've encountered. Rang-ing from a beautiful powdery blue to a soft reddish-purple to snow white—they are all one in the same species. They can be found across a wide variety of habitats including wet and dry meadows, rocky slopes and flats, and the banks of snow melt streams. They range in height from 8″ to 24″. Look for grass-like leaves that are 6″ to 12″ long and ½″ wide. The flower heads occur individually at the tops of stems that are hairy near the tops. The ray flowers can be anywhere from ½″ to ¾″ long. The disc flowers are always yellow to orange. I photographed the blue form below the outlet of Smith Lake in late August, the purple variation in the meadows sur-rounding L Lake in late September and the white variation in the meadows behind Upper Caribou Lake in late August—all in the Trinity Alps. The white occurrences are rare. In addition to the Caribou population the only other place I've encountered it was on the slopes above Salmon Lake also in the Trinity Alps.

ANDERSON'S TUNDRA ASTER, ANDERSON'S MOUNTAIN-CROWN
Oreostemma alpigenum var. *andersonii*
Sunflower family

293

DEER BRUSH, WILD LILAC
Ceanothus integerrimus
Buckthorn family

5 symmetrical petals - ovary inferior

When most people think of *Ceanothus*, this is the one that comes to mind. Unlike the evergreen wedgeleaf and Lemmon's ceanothus, this is a deciduous shrub. It grows in huge thickets in open areas following fire or other disturbance, throughout the lower elevations in this area, and puts on magnificent displays of white, pinkish-lilac, or light blue flowers in pyramidal, clusters. Deer brush is a stiff shrub that often grows to 10' in height and is heavily branched. It is a favored over-wintering food for deer and host for deer ticks. If you want to see a beautiful display of wild lilac just drive Highway 299 over Oregon Mountain west of Weaverville. Following the huge wildfires between Junction City and Weaverville it has taken over the entire mountainside. I photographed these along Van Ness Road above Trinity Lake in May.

LEMMON'S CEANOTHUS
Ceanothus lemmonii
Buckthorn family

5 symmetrical petals - ovary inferior

This *Ceanothus* puts on a beautiful display of vibrant, deep blue flowers early in the season. It is a stiffly branched shrub that reaches 3' in height, with light gray-white bark. The tiny flowers bloom in tight rounded clusters about 2" in diameter. Leaves are small, alternately arranged, evergreen, oblong to almost round, tapered at the base, and finely gland-toothed. It is common throughout this region. I photographed this one along the road to the North Fork of Swift Creek Trailhead in late May.

YERBA SANTA, KNIT-BONE
Eriodictyon californicum
Borage family

5 symmetrical petals forming a tube

This is a leggy shrub that likes hot, dry, open areas and is one of the first to colonize an area after fires. The leaves are narrowly lance shaped, tough, leathery, toothed and, in the dead of summer, coated with a sticky, flammable, resin. It can form dense thickets with individual shrubs reaching 6' in height. The pink tinged white tubular flowers bloom in an irregular head at the tops of the branches. By late summer, depending on location, a majority of the shrubs have turned an unattractive brownish green with tall spikes of brown seed-heads. The common name "knit-bone" comes from old medicinal lore indicating that drinking tea made from the leaves would help broken bones heal. After suffering a shattered heel I was treated to a rather disagreeable drink at regular intervals until my cast was removed and I could hobble around again. I have no idea about its effectiveness but everything healed just fine and there have been no lasting consequences—except for having no desire to drink it again!

DEER BRUSH, WILD LILAC
Ceanothus integerrimus
Buckthorn family

LEMMON'S CEANOTHUS
Ceanothus lemmonii
Buckthorn family

YERBA SANTA, KNIT-BONE
Eriodictyon californicum
Borage family

MAHALA MAT
Ceanothus prostratus   5 symmetrical petals - ovary inferior
Buckthorn family

Mahala mat is common throughout these mountains in dry semi-exposed sites and likes road cuts where it forms dense, low growing mats 12" to 14" in height. The flowers are grouped in tight, sweet smelling clusters that are variable in color. They can range from a light violet (almost white) to deep blue with several shades in between. The leaves are small, stiff, and spiny. It's an attractive plant and I've known people who transplanted starts hoping for ground cover in their yards, but most attempts have been unsuccessful. A better bet would be to buy starts at a native plant nursery. I photographed the light violet version (top) alongside the road to the Granite Peak trailhead, the deep violet version (center) along the Scorpion Creek Road to Bonanza King, and the dark blue version (bottom) along the road to the Lake Eleanor Trailhead all in May. The side-bar photograph shows Mahala mat carpeting the edges of the Stony Ridge trail in the Trinity Alps.

MAHALA MAT
Ceanothus prostratus
Buckthorn family

three color variations

Green corn lily, arrowleaf ragwort and western yarrow decorate a granite outcrop above Middle Caribou Lake in the Trinity Alps Wilderness.

Green corn lily (*Veratrum viride*) blooming in September above Virginia Lake in the Trinity Alps Wilderness.

GREEN CORN LILY
Veratrum viride   3 or 6 petals
False-hellebore family

Green corn lilies are more common on the north slopes in the Trinity Alps and throughout the Russian Wilderness. They are widely interspersed with their more common, white-flowered cousin—the California corn lily (page 27). I photographed these on a shaded slope below Upper Albert Lake in the Russian Wilderness but I've also photographed them on the trail below South Fork Lakes, in wet meadows near Telephone Lake and in the Caribou Lakes Basin, all in the Trinity Alps.

CHECKER LILY
Fritillaria affinis   3 or 6 petals
Lily family

This little fritillary can be difficult to spot—plants are often scattered and the mottled yellow and reddish-brown petals blend nicely with the surroundings. Flowering stalks emerge from groups of long, narrow leaves. Each stalk can sport several flowers. The petal surface is dull from above—but lie down in the dirt and look up through the petals from beneath, back-lit by the sun and they appear brilliant yellow and red! This species is quite similar to spotted mountain bells, *Fritillaria atropurpurea*. I photographed these in Union Meadows in early June.

BROWNIE LADY'S SLIPPER, CLUSTERED LADY'S SLIPPER
Cypripedium fasciculatum   3 or 6 petals
Orchid family

This is a small and inconspicuous orchid. The plants blend nicely into the background of the forest floor and can be easily overlooked. The two large, parallel veined leaves are the most prominent feature and what I generally notice well before I see the flowers—which are often hidden beneath. The little reddish green or greenish red flowers bloom in clusters on a stalk rising from between the leaves. The entire plant is about 5" tall. Years ago, I was on the ground next to a popular trail, camera set up before me, taking photographs of a small bunch when a couple walked up and asked what I was doing. I felt it was important to show them these little blooms because they were growing in a heavily used area and one misstep would crush them. They were amazed that they had been visiting this place for years and had never seen them.

STREAM ORCHID, GIANT HELLEBORINE, CHATTERBOX
Epipactis gigantea   3 or 6 petals
Orchid family

As the name implies, this orchid favors wet places like springs, seeps, fens, and stream sides at mid-elevations. They are often found in large colonies and can range from a few inches to 3' in height. Flowers bloom in July and are borne in the leaf axils with three long, reddish-green sepals. The upper two petals are yellowish-green with prominent blood-red veins. The lower petals droop and extend outward with a deep yellow to white tongue that is lightly red-veined. Even though the plants are tall, they are still easily passed by because they blend in with the surrounding plants and grasses well. **Note**: I am always intrigued with common names and "chatterbox" is no exception. Research revealed that the lower "lip" (or, if you think the flower looks like a bird's beak, the lower beak) flutters up and down like a chatterbox when flies pollinate the flower. I photographed these along the Parks Creek Road on the west side of the Trinity Divide.

GREEN CORN LILY
Veratrum viride
False-hellebore family

CHECKER LILY
Fritillaria affinis
Lily family

BROWNIE LADY'S SLIPPER
Cypripedium fasciculatum
Orchid family

STREAM ORCHID, CHATTERBOX
Epipactis gigantea
Orchid family

SPARSE-FLOWERED BOG-ORCHID, GREEN REIN ORCHID
Platanthera sparsiflora   3 or 6 petals
Orchid family

This little green orchid often hides in plain sight—overshadowed by other plants in wet meadows, near seeps, springs, and stream banks. This is one of those delicate little "belly flowers" that rarely exceed 12" in height. My granddaughter claims the tiny blooms look like fish with their mouths open and observant hikers will likely agree. The left hand photograph was taken in a wet seep below Little Duck Lake in the Russians and the one at the right alongside a stream in Doe Flat the Trinity Alps.

LONG-TAILED WILD-GINGER
Asarum caudatum   3 or 6 petals
Pipevine family

Distinguished by the long tails on each sepal (there are no petals), this deep reddish-brown flower hides beneath a low canopy of bright green, heart-shaped leaves that do not exhibit the pale veins of Hartweg's wild-ginger (below). I photographed this one in Poison Canyon, alongside the trail to Lilypad Lake in late June, and have also found it along the Stewart's Fork Trail in the forested area above Morris Meadows. Alice Jones reports it from Boulder Creek in the Trinity Alps. It gets more common the farther west you go in Trinity County. It likes damp and deeply shaded sites.

HARTWEG'S WILD-GINGER
Asarum hartwegii   3 or 6 petals
Pipevine family

If you look closely at the sepals (there are no petals) you will see they are a deep brick red. The tails on the sepals are pronounced but not nearly as long as those of long-tailed wild-ginger described above. Leaves have distinct white venation notably lacking in *A. caudatum* (above). When I was a kid I would help my grandmother harvest a basketful of roots, which she would clean, cut into bite sized chunks, and boil lightly in a sugar solution. Once dried, they went in the candy dish on her table—delicious and spicy! She would also make ginger snaps using the candied roots. Our wild-ginger is not botanically related to the fresh or powdered ginger we buy at the grocery store, though the scent and flavor are similar. You will find them on deeply shaded forest floors. I photographed these along the Stewart's Fork Trail in the Trinity Alps in June.

SPARSE-FLOWERED BOG-ORCHID
Platanthera sparsiflora
Orchid family

LONG-TAILED WILD-GINGER
Asarum caudatum
Pipevine family

HARTWEG'S WILD-GINGER
Asarum hartwegii
Pipevine family

CALIFORNIA PIPEVINE
Aristolochia californica   3 or 6 petals
Pipevine family

Here's one that looks more like a little green duck out of water than a wildflower—but wildflower it is. This species is closely related to the Dutchman's pipe of eastern U.S. fame. It is among the earliest of bloomers in the lower elevations, often appearing in late January or early February in the Sacramento Valley and mid-March in Trinity County. The green and coppery red flowers open before the leaves begin to show and hang in thick masses on twisted, tough stems that climb into surrounding brush. The leaves and stems are fuzzy and bright green. I photographed these near Shasta Lake but look for them in more shaded sites at lower elevations along the Trinity River and other drainages.

ENGLISH PEAK GREENBRIER
Smilax jamesii   3 or 6 petals
Smilax family

This Klamath Mountain endemic is a climbing vine that prefers plenty of water and shade. You will find it in alder thickets along streams, springs, seeps, or other damp places. I've found it in abundance along the Stewart's Fork, Bowerman Meadows, and Poison Canyon Trails in the Trinity Alps. It climbs on herbaceous stems to heights of 8' or 9'. Leaves are large and heart-shaped with three to five main veins converging at the leaf base. The tiny and delicate flowers have petals and sepals that are indistinguishable from each other and called tepals. Tepals bloom in umbels along the length of the vine. The flowers are so delicate that I found them difficult to photograph. Just breathing on the flowers or the slightest movement made them scatter and fall to the ground. Pea-sized fruits develop in bunches ripens in late summer to deep black. I photographed the flowers along the Stewart's Fork Trail in mid-June and the fruit in late August.

Note: Another species, *Smilax californica*, is also common in this area. The two are similar, but can be distinguished by the fact that the stems of *S. californica* are spiny while *S. jamesii* has smooth stems.

Bowerman Meadows in the Trinity Alps: Just above where the Long Canyon and Bowerman Meadows trails split (Long Canyon right - Bowerman Mdws left) there is a creek crossing at East Fork of Stewart's Fork. Here, the trail stair-steps through four distinct meadows—ending at the steep rocky cliff face marking the ascent to Lake Anna. The lower (1st), middle (2nd) and 3rd meadows are separated by boggy, alder filled patches, rich with flowering plants like English Peak greenbrier, Fendler's meadow rue, Salmon Mountains wake robin and White flowered bog orchid. The flat, open upper meadow (4th) is home to a field of Macloskey's violets, Long stalked clover and Water plantain buttercups. These meadows and surrounding alder thickets are popular hangouts for bears so, if you visit, keep your eyes open and your food safely hung!

CALIFORNIA PIPEVINE
Aristolochia californica
Pipevine family

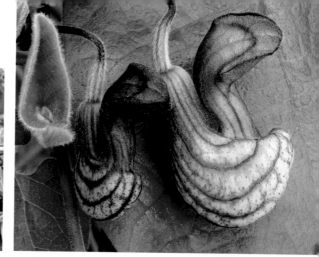

ENGLISH PEAK GREENBRIER
Smilax jamesii
Smilax family

Bowerman Meadows in the Trinity Alps

Heterotrophs frequent mixed conifers forests, like those surrounding Morris Meadows in the Trinity Alps Wilderness.

Striped coralroot
Coralloriza striata

PHANTOM ORCHID
Cephalanthera austiniae
Orchid family

3 or 6 petals

Phantom orchids are not only gorgeous but they are also predictable—growing in the same place year after year. The creamy white plants grow to 10" in the deep shade of mixed conifer forests at lower elevations in the mountains. The stems, sepals, and petals are all white except for a small patch of deep yellow orange on the lower lip. Some people confuse these with ghost plants but the two are easily distinguished. Flowers of the ghost plant lack the yellow patch on the lower petal, hang downward like bells and the petals are arranged regularly around the superior ovary, while those of the phantom orchid face outward and upward with irregular flower parts attached at the tops of inferior ovaries. Because of their tendency for inhabiting deep shaded forest, it is fairly easy to pass them by. I photographed these above the Long Canyon Trail in late June.

FRINGED PINESAP
Pleuricospora fimbriolata
Heath family

5 symmetrical petals - ovary superior

Years ago I photographed this plant near Josephine Lake in the Russians and years later I ran into it again, this time on the trail to Duck Lakes. My grandkids actually found them blooming beneath a dense canopy of white fir and weeping spruce saplings in late August. The plants below Josephine Lake were typical for this species, about 6" tall with pinkish-white stems and red, scale-like clasping leaves. The flowers are distributed around the top of the stems and point outward and upward. The Duck Lakes examples were ground huggers, the stems buried in duff with all of the flowers arrayed evenly around the tops of the stems, pointing outward and upward. In both cases the flowers were creamy white, bell shaped, and flared at the tips.

GHOST PLANT, INDIAN PIPE
Monotropa uniflora
Heath family

5 symmetrical petals - ovary superior

I prefer ghost plant to Indian pipe because, in this mountainous region, they are harder to find than ghosts in the closet! I've seen it twice in 50 years—once near Slate Mountain on the Trinity Divide and once at Lipstick Lake in the Russian Wilderness. Alice Jones found it along Boulder Creek in the Trinity Alps. When fresh, these gregarious plants have bell-shaped, translucent white flowers tinged with pink. The stalks are likewise translucent white and 6" to 10" tall. Plants begin to develop black spots as they age until, eventually, the entire plant turns black and withers. They prefer deep duff in conifer forests. I photographed these in Redwoods National Park in early July. If you do happen to find one, take a photograph, record the location, and let a Forest Service botanist know. Your data would be greatly appreciated!

PHANTOM ORCHID
Cephalanthera austiniae
Orchid family

FRINGED PINESAP
Pleuricospora fimbriolata
Heath family

GHOST PLANT, INDIAN PIPE
Monotropa uniflora
Heath family

PINEDROPS
Pterospora andromedea
Heath family

5 symmetrical petals - ovary superior

This is a giant among mycotrophs, often reaching heights of five feet. It is common in the understory of mixed conifer forests at mid to upper elevations throughout this area and, because of its size, easily recognized. The stalks are stout, reddish brown, and leafless. Masses of deep orange-yellow bell-shaped flowers nod downward from the ends of short red stems on the upper fourth of the plant. The entire plant is covered with sticky, short hairs. Even after the flowers have faded, the stalks and dry seed pods are still evident, sometimes lasting into the next flowering season. I photographed these along the Swift Creek Trail in the Trinity Alps.

CANCER ROOT, CLUSTERED BROOMRAPE
Orobanche fasciculata
Broomrape family

5 irregular petals forming a tube

Following a large wildfire near Shasta Lake, cancer root emerged during the blooming season in huge clusters. It Is a mystery to me why someone would choose to name such a beautiful little flower as they did. Maybe it's because they suck the life out of their hosts! At any rate, I find them delightful and enjoy the deep reddish brown, erect, hairy stems that support a single, tubular mustard yellow flower. Even though they are small, they are hard to miss. I photographed these along the road to the Lake Eleanor and Shimmy Lake Trailhead in the Trinity Alps in mid-May.

NAKED BROOMRAPE
Orobanche uniflora
Broomrape family

5 irregular petals forming a tube

These exquisite members of the broom-rape family are often difficult to find. Those that I've been fortunate enough to photograph have been small (2" to 3" in height) and hidden within the surroundings. The reddish-brown stems are erect, supporting a single deep bluish-purple flower with an orange-yellow throat with lighter yellow extending toward the lower petal. I found it blooming in a colony of *Sedum* in mid-August at Papoose Lake and along Canyon Creek it was growing with a mix of *Sedum* and saxifrage. On Scott Mountain I found solitary blooms in the open. I photographed the large group along Canyon Creek in mid-April and the small inset on exposed serpentine on Scott Mountain in July.

PINEDROPS
Pterospora andromedea
Heath family

CANCER ROOT, CLUSTERED BROOMRAPE
Orobanche fasciculata
Broomrape family

NAKED BROOMRAPE
Orobanche uniflora
Broomrape family

SPOTTED CORALROOT
Corallorhiza maculata
Orchid family

3 or 6 petals

Spotted coralroot is a common trailside mycotroph found throughout the area covered by this book. This one is distinguished by its overall deep reddish-brown coloration. The sepals are dark reddish-brown around the edges and yellowish brown near the center with dark striations running the length. The lateral petals are much the same as the sepals. The broad lip is snow white with deep maroon spots and ruffled tips. The prominent column, a deep buttery yellow with small maroon spots, consists of a fused style and stamens and curves upward and outward from the throat. I understand that lemon yellow plants, lacking the reddish pigment, are not uncommon. The plants tend to grow in large clusters in deep shade under conifers. I have photographed these on the Long Canyon Trail in the Trinity Alps and lower down along Swift Creek just below Highway 3 in early July.

STRIPED CORALROOT
Corallorhiza striata
Orchid family

3 or 6 petals

This is a beautiful coralroot that is sometimes hard to find. The species prefers shaded, damp sites with knee deep forest litter. The first time I encountered it was during a heavy snowstorm in late May as I was hiking from Emerald Lake back to Morris Meadows with niece and nephew in tow. Photographing it at the time was questionable so, several years later, when this guide began to take shape, I went on the hunt for it again. I returned to the same area and found several plants scattered in tangled masses of downed branches and other woody debris. The dark reddish brown stems grow to 10" tall and host several candy-striped flowers along the upper half. The lower lip is deep maroon while the sepals and lateral petals are lighter with deep maroon stripes. The column is a vibrant buttery yellow. This photograph was taken above Morris Meadows on the trail to Emerald Lake in early June.

WESTERN CORALROOT, MERTENS' CORALROOT
Corallorhiza mertensiana
Orchid family

3 or 6 petals

Like some of the other coral roots, this one has a reddish pink stem and stands 10" to 14" tall. The orchid flowers are scattered alternately along the stem and face outward. The lateral petals are maroon and yellow with small maroon spots at the tips. The reddish sepals are narrow and elongated. The lower lip is much broader, whitish rimmed, with deep lavender. A prominent yellow column curves upwards and out over the throat. Lemon yellow variations are not uncommon but I profess to having found them only once. They were entirely yellow except for the lower lip which was snow white. I photographed them alongside the Stewart's Fork Trail in mid-August. I photographed the bunch on the left along the trail just below Doe Lake in September—which is fairly late for coral roots.

SPOTTED CORALROOT
Corallorhiza maculata
Orchid family

STRIPED CORALROOT
Corallorhiza striata
Orchid family

WESTERN CORALROOT, MERTENS' CORALROOT
Corallorhiza mertensiana
Orchid family

SUGARSTICK, CANDYSTICK
Allotropa virgata
Heath family

5 symetrical petals ovary superior

Here is a strikingly beautiful mycotroph found commonly throughout the area on granitic soils. The tall (up to 15") red and white vertically striped stalks are, at first, wrapped with white bracts that furl outward revealing small, bowl shaped white flowers with a mass of short dark stamens. Typically, they grow in clusters One of the nicest populations I've ever seen was at Eaton Lake in the Russians in early July. They are also quite common in the Sugar, Duck, and French Creek drainages. This photograph, however, was taken at Crater Lake in south-central Oregon.

SNOW PLANT
Sarcodes sanguinea
Heath family

5 symetrical petals ovary superior

This is definitely the flashiest of all the mycotrophs and, because of the size and brilliant red color, are hard to miss. The robust plants reach 12" in height and achieve deep red throughout because of the numerous red flowers. They bloom in large, extended colonies. At one time in California (back in the 1950s and 60s), I remember hearing that these plants were protected and that there was a $500 fine for picking them but I am uncertain if that was even true (I was 10 at the time). They are actually quite common at mid elevations. I photographed these along the trail to Stoddard Lake in early July. Look for them around Eaton Lake in the Russians where my grand-kids spotted them blooming on a decomposed granite flat way above the opposite shoreline more than 300 yards away.

GNOME PLANT
Hemitomes congestum
Heath family

5 symetrical petals ovary superior

It's hard to miss this one if it is within eye-shot of a trail because of the vibrant pink to white blooms. It first appears as a small, rounded mound of almost yellowish-salmon pink flowers on the forest floor in deep litter. As the flowers open they exhibit a translucent pink vibrancy. Individual plants are generally 3" - 6" in diameter. The name gnome plant is entirely fitting because of the size and the shaded locations where it is found. It's easy to identify because it does not look at all like any of the other mycotrophs.

The first time I ever laid eyes on these was next to a spring of ice cold water along the trail to Eaton Lake in the Russians (one of those springs where you get eaten alive by mosquitoes if you stop to take photographs!). For successive years after, I would look in the same place but I never found it there again. It was years later, while exploring for mushrooms and lichens in Patrick's Point State Park on the North coast that I came across another population. Later, my grandson and I stumbled onto a colony growing along the Boulder Creek Trail just above Boulder Creek in the Trinity Alps. That was in late August and is where I took this photograph.

SUGARSTICK, CANDYSTICK
Allotropa virgata
Heath family

SNOW PLANT
Sarcodes sanguinea
Heath family

GNOME PLANT
Hemitomes congestum
Heath family

CALIFORNIA GROUND-CONE

Kopsiopsis strobilacea
Broomrape family

5 irregular petals forming a tube

Spend time in a patch of manzanita or around a grove of madrones and chances are good you will find California ground-cones. At first glance, they appear to be pine cones lying about. Young ground-cones are somewhat fleshy and pliable and have gorgeous purple flowers. As they age, they dry out and turn brown and brittle. At lower elevations the 'cones' can be quite large (9″ tall). At higher elevations, say along the trail to Duck Lake or around Eaton Lake in the Russians, where I photographed the brownish-purple one, they rarely exceed 5″ or 6″ in height. The yellow variation, which I photographed on the ridge between Josephine and Horseshoe Lakes in the Russians was, likewise, only about 6″ tall. Look closely for them in May in the foothills or in July higher up.

A colony of California ground-cones found in association with madrone along Canyon Creek in the Trinity Alps. This is a prime example of a parasitic plant which was a small part of a large population spread out over an eighth of an acre.

CALIFORNIA GROUND-CONE
Kopsiopsis strobilacea
Broomrape family

DWARF MISTLETOE
Arceuthobium spp.
Mistletoe family

No obvious petals

There are approximately twelve taxa of dwarf mistletoe (*Arceuthobium* spp.) found commonly on conifers like true fir (*Abies* spp.), incense-cedar (*Calocedrus decurrens*), pine (*Pinus* spp.), Douglas-fir (*Pseudostuga menziesii*), and juniper (*Juniperus* spp.) in the Klamath Mountains. These are parasitic in nature, tapping into the vascular system of the tree and draining nutrients and water. Late in the season, if you lightly pinch the fruit between your fingers they explode with a popping noise that kids and inquisitive adults find fascinating. They are often called exploding booger plants because the seed coats are sticky and, once ejected, fly and stick to a new host tree. The photograph at left was taken near Lewiston and the photograph on the right below Bear Gap at the lower end of Morris Meadows in the Trinity Alps.

OAK MISTLETOE, AMERICAN MISTLETOE
Phoradendron leucarpum subsp. *tomentosum*
Mistletoe family

No obvious petals

This is a hemi-parasitic plant commonly found growing in oak trees and occasionally manzanitas throughout the area. As a hemi-parasite, they derive some energy from photosynthesis and the rest they take from their host. *Phorodendron* is characterized by large, stiff, gray green to olive-green branches with numerously paired, oval, stiff, coarse leaves. Mistletoe probes the host tree for nutrients and eventually leads to the decay of the branches it has attached itself to. The plants are dioecious, producing either male or female flowers in long clusters. Female flowers yield pink to salmon colored berries. A similar species, *Phoradendron juniperinum*, is found on conifers across the region. I photographed these with the berries where they had fallen beneath black oaks above Lewiston Lake in early May, The small photograph was taken in the foothills above Redding.

Note: Dioecious means "two houses" in Greek. Male and female plants are separate and any one plant will produce only male or female flowers.

DWARF MISTLETOE
Arceuthobium spp.
Mistletoe family

OAK MISTLETOE
Phoradendron leucarpum subsp. *tomentosum*
Mistletoe family

INDEX TO COMMON NAMES: Most accepted name in **bold** type

INDEX TO SCIENTIFIC NAMES

PLANT FAMILY NAMES REPRESENTED IN THIS GUIDE: Common versus scientific

Barberry family - *Berberidaceae*
Bellflower family - *Campanulaceae*
Bittersweet family - *Celastraceae*
Blazing star or Loasa family - *Loasaceae*
Bog asphodel family - *Nartheciaceae*
Borage family - *Boraginaceae*
Brodiaea family - *Themidaceae*
Broomrape family - *Orobanchaceae*
Buckthorn family - *Rhamnaceae*
Buckwheat family - *Polygonaceae*
Butcher's broom family - *Ruscaceae*
Buttercup family - *Ranunculaceae*
Carrot family - *Apiaceae*
Century plant family - *Agavaceae*
Dogbane family - *Apocynaceae*
Dogwood family - *Cornaceae*
Evening primrose family - *Onagraceae*
False-asphodel family - *Tofieldiaceae*
False-hellebore family - *Melanthiaceae*
Figwort family - *Scrophulariaceae*
Flax family - *Linaceae*
Gentian family - *Gentianaceae*
Ginseng family - *Araliaceae*
Gooseberry family - *Grossulariaceae*
Gourd family - *Cucurbitaceae*
Grass-of-Parnassus family - *Parnassiaceae*
Heath family - *Ericaceae*
Honeysuckle family - *Caprifoliaceae*
Horsetail family - *Equisetaceae*
Hydrangea family - *Hydrangeaceae*
Iris family - *Iridaceae*
Lily family - *Liliaceae*
Lopseed family - *Verbenaceae*
Madder family - *Rubiaceae*
Mallow family - *Malvaceae*
Maple family - *Aceraceae*
Milkwort family - *Polycalaceae*
Miner's lettuce family - *Montiaceae*

Mint family - *Lamiaceae*
Mistletoe family - *Viscaceae*
Morning glory family - *Convolvulaceae*
Muskroot family - *Adoxaceae*
Mustard family - *Brassicaceae*
Myrsine family - *Myrcinaceae*
Nightshade family - *Solanaceae*
Olive family - *Oleaceae*
Onion family - *Alliaceae*
Orchid family - *Orchidaceae*
Pea family - *Fabaceae*
Peony family - *Paeoniaceae*
Phlox family - *Polemoniaceae*
Pink family - *Caryophyllaceae*
Pipevine family - *Aristolochiaceae*
Pitcher plant family - *Sarraceniaceae*
Plantain family - *Plantaginaceae*
Poppy family - *Papaveraceae*
Primrose family - *Primulaceae*
Rock-rose family - *Cistaceae*
Rose family - *Rosaceae*
Saxifrage family - *Saxifragaceae*
Sedge family - *Cyperaceae*
Silktassel family - *Garryaceae*
Smilax family - *Smilacaceae*
Soapberry family - *Sapindaceae*
St. John's Wort family - *Clusiaceae*
Stonecrop family - *Crassulaceae*
Storax family - *Styracaceae*
Sumac family - *Anacardiaceae*
Sunflower family - *Asteraceae*
Sweet shrub family - *Calycanthaceae*
Twin flower family - *Linnaeaceae*
Valerian family - *Valerianaceae*
Violet family - *Violaceae*
Waterleaf family - *Hydrophyllaceae*
Water plantain family - *Alismataceae*

Literature cited:

A Flora of the Trinity Alps of Northern California
Wiliam J. Fermate
University of California Press, 1974

Flowers and Trees of the Trinity Alps
Alice Jones,
published by the Trinity County Historical Society,1986

Keys for Identification of Wild Flowers, Ferns, Trees, Shrubs and Woody Vines of Northern California
Vesta Holt
Mayfield Publishing Company, Palo Alto, Ca., 1964

Selected Rare Plants of Northern California
Gary Nakamura & Julie Kierstead Nelson
University of California, 2001

The Jepson Manual - Vascular Plants of California, second edition
Bruce G. Baldwin, Douglas Goldwin, David J.Keil, and others, editors
University of California Press, 2012

Wicked Plants - The weed that killed Lincoln's Mother & other botanical atrocities
Amy Stewart
Algonquin Books of Chapel Hill, 2009

Wildflowers of the Pacific Northwest
Mark Turner & Phyllis Gustafson
Timber Press Field Guide, 2006

Mountain Wildflowers of Canada
Julia W. Henshaw
Toroto, W. Briggs, 1903

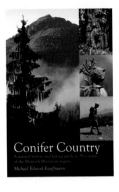

Notes:

Contributors

Ken DeCamp was born to parents who took him on his first back-
packing trip when he was 4 months old into Glacier National Park.
Since that time he has logged thousands of trail miles in the Pacific
Northwest, Alaska, the Carolinas, Georgia, Pakistan, Australia, and Switzerland. He has been drawing and photographing wildflowers for over
40 years and it is from this collection of images that this book became
a reality. Though he has travelled widely, he has always considered
the mountains of northern California his home and has, for 60 years,
explored their most hard to reach places. He retired from the USDA
Forest Service in 2008 after a 38 year career in Fire, Land Manage-
ment Planning, and Public Affairs. He lives with his wife Pam in Shasta Lake where they spend
time with their family and their only pet, a cardboard dog named "Flat fido," gifted by a friend
who thought that, someday, they might need serious protection from something. Ken is also
an avid backpacker, trail runner, and mountain biker.

Julie Kierstead Nelson has been a working botanist since 1976,
doing rare plant surveys and conservation work in Oregon and Cali-
fornia. She has a B.S. in botany from Oregon State University and an
M.S. in biology from Northern Arizona University. She worked for the
Berry Botanic Garden in Portland as conservation director, developing
a seed bank for rare & endangered plants of the Pacific Northwest and
helped get a state endangered species act passed in Oregon. Since
1989 she has had the good fortune to serve as Forest Botanist for the
Shasta-Trinity National Forest in northwestern California, where she is
ideally situated to promote plant exploration in the Klamath Ranges and southern Cascades.
This is not her first venture into the field of publishing having served as co-author and technical
editor for the University of California Agriculture & Natural Resources publication *Illustrated
Field Guide to Selected Rare Plants of Northern California* published in 2001.

Julie Knorr retired as a botanist after a 33 year career with the
U.S.D.A. Forest Service on the Klamath National Forest. She grew up
in Colorado where she gained a lifelong love of the mountains from
her biologist parents. In 1978, after receiving a B.S. in botany from
University of California at Davis, she started work on the Klamath N.F.
During her career as a botanist, she worked primarily in the areas
of rare plant protection, vascular plant and lichen monitoring, habitat
restoration, and environmental interpretation. Post retirement, she has
continued to do volunteer and contract surveys for the Klamath Na-
tional Forest, primarily in the Marble Mountain, Russian, and Trinity Alps Wilderness areas. She
lives along the Scott River with her partner, Marsha, in the shadows of the Marble Mountain
Wilderness Area in Siskiyou County, California. She now spends much of her time viewing the
world from a bicycle.